net benefit

By the same author:

*Guaranteed Electronic Markets: the backbone of
a 21st century economy*

There is a web site dedicated to *Guaranteed Electronic Markets* where
readers may wish to comment on this book: www.gems.org.uk

net benefit

Guaranteed Electronic Markets: the ultimate potential of online trade

wingham rowan

First published 1999 by
MACMILLAN PRESS LTD
Houndmills, Basingstoke, Hampshire RG21 6XS
and London
Companies and representatives
throughout the world

ISBN 0–333–76009–3 hardcover

A catalogue record for this book is available
from the British Library.

This book is printed on paper suitable for recycling and
made from fully managed and sustained forest sources.

10 9 8 7 6 5 4 3 2 1
08 07 06 05 04 03 02 01 00 99

Editing and origination by
Aardvark Editorial, Mendham, Suffolk

Printed and bound in Great Britain
at The Bath Press, Avon

contents

....

section two

....

A new democratic capitalism: the impact of public electronic markets   55

conclusion

appendix one

appendix two

What trading revolution? Electronic commerce for the perplexed

In 1997 it was still possible to dismiss the Internet as a harmless hobby: now it has become the backbone for what is widely described as a 'new economy'. This is a world in which holiday flights, for instance, can be booked by calling up a travel agent or airline Internet site then selecting a departure, typing in a credit card number and address for delivery of tickets. The information is sent instantly from the shopper's computer down phone lines to the seller's machine which can be on the other side of the world. Flowers, clothes, wine, toys plus countless other goods and services can likewise be browsed, then bought, by visiting suppliers' sites on the Internet's World Wide Web. This shopless shopping offers several advantages over a visit to the high street. It is more convenient and allows access to a wider range of suppliers. More significantly it can be much cheaper: retailers no longer have to fund high-street premises or significant numbers of staff. Increasingly, online customers are expecting to see this reflected in lower prices. British insurance company Eagle Star, for example, offers its premiums at an effective 25 per cent discount to shoppers at its web site.[1]

The new dynamics of Internet trading have caused turmoil in some business sectors. Amazon Books has been mentioned in reverential tones at almost every e-commerce convention of the past two years. This start-up operation in Seattle, which sells only through the Net, offers titles at up to 40 per cent off high-street prices. It now claims with justification to be 'earth's biggest bookstore' and has left comfortably established book retailers scrabbling to build a comparable operation online. Similarly, Auto-by-Tel offers 'pain relief for car buyers' through the Web. Anyone typing in details of their dream vehicle will be contacted soon afterwards by a local dealer who has that model in stock and will confirm an immediate non-negotiable price. Web-based car buying services now account for 15 per cent of auto sales in the US, the figure will be 50 per cent by the year 2000 according to one research firm.[2] Some of the new players emerging on the Net come from industries unrelated to the service they offer. Peapod for example is a home grocery delivery service with order-taking online. It is a software company whose expertise is in automated processes; they have simply found suppliers for the groceries.

Predictably, perhaps, the US leads the world in consumer electronic commerce. But the new marketplace is global in its reach and can undercut national suppliers. A New York delicatessen that set up an order-taking web site was surprised to find an initial customer was in Tokyo. When staff queried his order for $50 of food that would cost him $100 to be delivered they were assured the same ingredients would cost $300 to purchase locally.[3] Alongside this price advantage are unique tools that can attract shoppers from around the world. The Amazon online bookstore, for instance, features software that can advise a browser of new titles he is likely to enjoy: it registers his tastes at each successive purchase and compares what he has already bought with similar lists from other shoppers. This 'relationship technology' that allows automated sales pitches is an area of frenetic development activity at present. More advanced still is the facility, offered by several major parcel companies, whereby a package can be tracked through their delivery chain from departure to delivery by keying in a unique code number at their web site. As their staff scan barcodes on each parcel the information from their vehicles on the road is beamed by satellite to a central computer, which constantly updates the site. Worryingly for many Net sellers, software called 'intelligent agents' is becoming increasingly sophisticated. This can be used by someone seeking perhaps a copy of The Beatles' *Hard Day's Night* CD to call up all the online music stores and compare prices before displaying the cheapest in seconds.

Despite having been the spine of the world's financial markets for decades, electronic trade is in its infancy. The next big step is likely to come from a trend towards 'pervasive computing': computers so intuitive to use and accessible that they become almost inescapable. Already some portable phones can connect to the Internet and shop. NCR Corporation have revealed a serious commitment to developing a microwave oven that allows banking activities, such as account queries, to be carried out from the kitchen.[4] The crucial development, however, is likely to be interactive television. With an estimated 90 million personal computers in the world but 900 million TV sets, it is clearly a technology with which nearly everyone is comfortable. Cheap, enticing, efficient shopping with the remote control is expected to have enormous impact. Around the world, governments are having to grapple with issues of regulation and tax collection in a new marketplace which crosses national borders and allows sellers to migrate to favourable regimes without losing any of their presence for customers.

The significance of this trading revolution is not in what has happened so far but what is to come. Without so far making a cent in profits Amazon Books has been valued by the stock market in billions of dollars. Its potential lies in having established a commanding lead that will reap its full worth when we are all shopping online. Already Wal-Mart, the world's biggest retailer, has ordained that their new stores must be convertible to housing units in anticipation of a time when they no longer need costly bricks and mortar across the country.[5] Even companies who ignore the potential of online trade are unlikely to escape its effects. Car dealerships in the US, for instance, are predicted to shrink from 22 000 today to 10 000 in the near future, as services like Auto-by-Tel mentioned earlier erode margins and allow dealers using the system to reach far more customers. Analysts talk of the Auto-by-Tel effect sweeping across 'industry after industry'.[6] The rapidity of change can be bewildering: no one knows quite where the trading revolution is heading. That is where this book hopes to make a contribution.

Notes

1. Building sites for sales, *Information Week*, 10–23 December 1997, p. 95.
2. JB Power quoted by Kevin Turnbull, Chief Executive of Auto-by-Tel, speaking at Non-Shop Shopping: dealing with the real issues, conference, London, 17 September 1998.
3. The Digital Earthquake, Stop the Technology Madness, *Daily Telegraph/Sun Microsystems*, 1998, p. 15.

4. Surfing for your supper, *Future Shopping*, October 1998, p. 3.
5. *The Grocer*, 6 September 1997. Quoted at Non-Shop Shopping: dealing with the real issues, conference, London, 17 September 1998 by Helen Bridgett, Marketing Manager, Tesco Direct.
6. The quote comes from Matt Eriksen of Boston Consulting Group quoted in Evan I. Schwartz, How Middlemen can Come Out on Top, *Business Week*, 9 February 1998, electronic edition.

Acknowledgements

Many people have contributed to this project, not all of whom would wish to be named.

Particular thanks for help with research are due to:

Adrian Duffield, Mikael Estvall, Peter Jaco, Tracy Muirhead and Peter V. Thomas, Reuters Transactional Products, London; Alan Sayers, British Shops and Stores Association; Brad Trask and Walt Reiker, McDonald's Hamburgers, Chicago; Cheryl Artim, International Liaison, Auto-by-Tel, US; Chris Sundt, security consultant, ICL solutions, UK; Colin Brown, Consumers' Association, UK; Francis Aldhouse, Deputy Registrar, Office of the Data Protection Registrar, UK; Julie Ros, editor, *FX Week*, UK; Keith Collins, London Pride Waste Action Partnership, UK; Michael Linton, Landsman Community Services Ltd, Canada; Professor Adrian Wood, University of Sussex, UK; Ray Eglington and Peter Heath, UK representatives, SABRE; Rupert Hodges, British Retail Consortium; Sam Eaton PRO and Paul Dale, Senior Service Creator, British Interactive Broadcasting; Sigurd Hogsbro, Head of IT, London Financial Futures Exchange; Stuart Norris, Association Cambiste Internationale – The International Financial Markets Association; Tammy Lindsay, Time Warner Cable, US; Tina Kane, Electronic Broking Services, London

The following have contributed valuable encouragement, criticism or advice:

Adam Singer, Chairman, Flextech, UK; Alison Gray, *The Scotsman*, UK; Arjay Choudry, Head of New Media, United News & Media, UK; Ashley Faull, Director of Programmes, Telewest, UK; Bill O'Neil, Editor, *Guardian Online*, UK; Bruno Giussani, *New York Times*; Charles Cohen, Managing Director, Thought Interactive Internet Services, London; Charles Handy, author, UK; Colin Lloyd, Chief Executive, Direct Marketing Association, UK; Cotton Ward, *.net*, UK; Dave Birch, Hyperion Payment Systems, UK; David Gold, PA Consulting, London; David Pringle, *Information Strategy*, London ; David Wilcox, Communities On-line, UK; Deborah Jenkins, Common Purpose, UK; Dee Hock, Founder, President and CEO Emeritus, Visa International; Dianne Nelmes, Granada Television, UK; Don Tapscott, Alliance for Converging Technologies, US, author of *The Digital Economy and Digital Blueprint*; Dr Roger Till, Chairman, Electronic Commerce Association, UK; Dr Jay M. Tenenbaum, founder, CommerceNet, US; Dr Michael Chamberlain, Managing Director, Transactions, Informed Sources, UK; Dr Rafael Guzman Llorente, University of California at Santa Cruz; Duncan Lewis, then CEO Granada Media Group, UK; Ed Mayo, Director, The New Economics Foundation, London; Edward Bonnington, Chairman, Greenland Interactive, UK; Emmett Power, Editor in chief, Electronic Commerce Briefing, UK; Esther Dyson, President, Edventure Holdings,

US; Eva Pascoe, *Independent*, UK; Evan Davis, Economics Correspondent, *Newsnight*, BBC TV; Frances Cairncross, *The Economist*, London; Frank Wainwright, Editor, *DM Business*, UK; Gail Rebuck, Chief Executive, Random House Publishing, UK; Gavin Howe, President and CEO, Reed Elsevier Technology Group, Cambridge, US; Glenda Cooper, *Independent*, UK; Heather Stark, Senior Consultant, Ovum Technology Consultancy, UK; Ian Hughes, Chairman, The Direct Marketing Association New Media Council, UK; Ira Magaziner, electronic commerce advisor to The President, US; Jason Finch, Port 80 Internet Consultancy, UK; Jock Gill, Penfield-Gill consultants, US; John Elkington, Chairman, Sustainability Ltd, author of *Cannibals with Forks;* John Harvey Jones, author, UK; John Seely-Brown, Head of Xerox Palo Alto Research Centre, California, US; Jon Epstein, ResultsRUs Data Services, UK; Keith Ferguson and Shirley Williams, NatWest Electronic Markets, London; Khalil Barsoum, Chairman and Chief Executive, IBM UK; Lester Thurow, Professor, Massachusetts Institute of Technology, US; Lord Hollick, Chairman, United News & Media, UK; Mark Radcliffe, Gray Cary Ware & Freidenrich, Palo Alto, US; Martin Bartle, PRO, The Direct Marketing Association, UK; Mary McAnally, Managing Director, Meridian Television, UK; Melanie Howard, co-founder, The Future Foundation, London; Mike Flood Page, Commissioning Editor, Information Technology programmes, BBC TV, UK; Monika Kosmahl Aring and Rebecca Bischoff, Education Development Centre Inc., Massachusetts, US; Neal Rimay-Mvranyi, The Database Group, UK; Nicholas Booth, Times Interface, *News International*, UK; Nicholas Negroponte, Massachusetts Institute of Technology, US, author of *Being Digital*; Paul O'Reilly, MD, Invaco software, UK; Peter Grimsdale, Channel 4 Television, UK; Professor Tony Davies, Director, British Telecom Electronic Commerce Innovation Centre, University of Wales, UK; Ray Hammond, author of *Digital Business*; Robb Wilmott, Robb Wilmott Associates, Palo Alto, US; Rosabeth Moss Kanter, Professor of Business Administration, Harvard Business School, US; Steve Johnston, Director of Development, Interactive Media in Retailing Group, Europe; Steven Rutt, Isobel Munday and Louise Crawford, Macmillan Press, UK; Sugra Zaman, Watson, Little Literary Agents, London; Thomas Blum, Product Planning & New Product Development, Consumers Union, US; Tim Jackson, founder Quixell, UK; Tony Davison, Head of Futures, IBM UK; Victor Keegan, Economics Correspondent, *Guardian*, UK; Violet Berlin, Presenter and Toby Murcott, Producer, *Soundbyte*, BBC World Service, UK

The potential of Guaranteed Electronic Markets was first recognized by the non-aligned London think-tank Demos. Particular thanks are due to:

Geoff Mulgan, George Lawson, Debbie Porter, Lindsay Nash, Ian Christie, Richard Warner, Perri 6, Tom Bentley, Helen Perry.

Thanks also to Dr Mike Fitchett for resourceful support over the years of this project.

The final frontier for electronic trade

A new technology can be slow to reveal its full potential. Rail, for instance, revolutionised the coal industry many years before their promise of mass public transport and universal postage was fulfilled. The history of broadcasting likewise reveals a pioneering phase when the new invention was perceived primarily for its usefulness to existing organisations: it finally allowed shipping companies to communicate with their fleets at sea. The radical concept of a home entertainment industry took two decades to emerge. More recently, hardware that enabled computers to communicate with each other was seen by its developers as an important contribution to US defence systems. Only when the World Wide Web was launched a quarter of a century later did the full potency of their work become discernible. Now we are witnessing the emergence of new trading technology. This book suggests that electronic commerce, even though it is overturning retailing and business practices around the world, is still only in a relatively insignificant pioneering phase, akin to mine railways or early ship-to-shore radios. There is an, as yet, unanticipated impact that will go much further in reshaping societies, largely for the good. To explore this lurking potential it is necessary to divide online purchasing into two distinct strands. The first is sales channels, in which specific retailers, manufacturers or service companies offer their output. The second is interactive marketplaces, in which anyone can sell.

The first strand of online commerce, sales channels, has its roots in a chance meeting between two Mr Smiths on a 1953 flight from Los Angeles to New York. IBM representative R. Blair Smith found himself seated next to the President of American Airlines C. R. Smith and, making the most of a captive prospect, began persuading the aviation magnate to automate his company's seat booking procedures. A conversation continued between the two companies until in 1959 consumer electronic trade, on any significant scale, was born with the launch of American's SABRE reservations system. At first travel agents seeking a reservation used their telephone to speak to a clerk in the computer room, who would confirm availability and fares. Then terminals were moved out to retail premises so agents could interrogate the database and make bookings online. As other suppliers saw the advantages of such a facility SABRE allowed additional airlines, hotel chains and car hire companies on to their computer. By the 1990s it was so profitable that American's CEO reputedly let it be known that if he had to choose between selling SABRE or selling the airline he would 'let the planes go'. Based on core computers in a vast high-security cavern deep beneath Oklahoma's Tulsa airport, SABRE is now the world's largest online order-taking system, processing thousands of messages from around the globe every second. Along with competing systems set up by other big airlines in the 1970s, the Tulsa goldmine defined electronic trade as a gateway to inventory, set up to offer customers increasing convenience and sophistication of choice. Online consumerism in the 1980s and 90s has been overwhelmingly driven by the same model. The French Minitel, Time Warner's Full Service Network and virtual malls were in turn overhauled by more focused operators including stellar performers of Internet trade such as Amazon Books, Cisco components and Dell Computer. All are channels to market operated by or on behalf of specific sellers. It is for the benefit of companies like this that a new generation of software for 'relationship marketing' to individual online customers is being developed. Interactive television, which simplifies remote shopping with on-screen versions of well-known high-street stores, will further advance this form of electronic trade.

Open markets: a second tier of electronic trade

It is online sales channels that have attracted most of the coverage of electronic commerce, but the true potency of the new trading technology rests in its secondary strand: open online marketplaces. One undercutting sales channel, like Amazon Books, can re-orientate a retail sector but a computerised marketplace available to any seller can rewrite the rules of trade. Developments in global money markets over the last decade demonstrate the difference. World-wide currency deregulation in the 1980s created trading opportunities for finance houses which their floors full of brokers using telephones and e-mail-based 'conversational' online purchasing facilities were ill equipped to exploit: continued moves towards online trading were inevitable. These could have taken the form of each bank setting up an interactive selling site enabling purchasing dealers to shop around among vendors they trusted in search of the best deal for their needs of the moment. Instead, in 1988, financial information supplier Reuters took a hotel room at the annual gathering of currency dealers in Hawaii to demonstrate a prototype for something they called the 2000–2 matching service. At its heart would be a computer on Long Island accessible by any dealer whose employers subscribed and on which they could list ever-changing requirements for funds they wished to buy or offers of currency they needed to sell. The central computer would instantly match a buyer with the best value supplier for their needs of the time, underpin each trade by checking the credit status of the two parties and issue a confirming contract.

Launched four years later, the new trading forum was received with some disdain. 'At first it was junior traders who were assigned to the electronic services, their colleagues called them the Gameboys', recalls the editor of a foreign exchange newsletter.[1] This distancing eventually gave way to enthusiastic embrace, particularly among smaller banks who were now able to trade directly in the market instead of having to constantly use a larger, more trusted institution as a costly intermediary. Market entry costs dropped to near zero: any company with the required funds can trade on 2000–2 without need of existing business relationships, awareness raising or means of order taking. This, coupled with gossamer-thin transaction costs, has kept the electronic currency markets ever widening. As new players join, prices increase in competitiveness, so trading became more attractive, swelling market turnover, which creates new opportunities and a wider spectrum of deal sizes that entice further resources into the system: a classic virtuous circle for the participants. It is this creation of a coordinated market for the benefit of financial institutions that underlies the billions of dollars of 'hot money' now ricocheting around the world.

There are Internet sites that appear to operate open marketplaces for the public: Auto-by-Tel[2] for pre-owned cars is one example, e-bay[3] for general goods and OnSale.com[4] majoring in computer supplies are others. Verification of sellers is a constant problem for their managements. Each has had to make a choice: to restrict providers to those who can be vouchsafed in some way, Auto-by-Tel, for instance, will only sell used cars from their affiliated dealers not ordinary motorists, or to allow all sources of supply and then find some way of enforcing honesty. Anyone buying a second-hand soldier doll at the e-bay site, for example, is not only charged up to 5 per cent commission for being matched with the seller, but also asked to e-mail a final analysis of that person's integrity for display to anyone else contemplating trading with him. It is a time-consuming and fallible mechanism: National Consumers League statistics in 1998 found online public auctions as a sector were home to a variety of enduring scams.[5] Databases that pair buyers and sellers are obviously valued by Net users who have taken the time to understand how their risks can be minimized. Indeed, e-bay, the leading net auction provider, is a a rarity: an Internet-based company that is already profitable. But such services fall far short of the trading environment that currency dealers can take for granted: a truly secure market, fully informed, preserving confidentially, with automatic deal enforcement and minute transaction charges. Reuters' task was made easy because financial institutions are so highly regulated. On the Internet there are no immediate solutions to problems associated with unknown sellers, hence the continuing rise of reassuringly branded online sales channels.

Secure electronic marketplaces open to any seller?

If the mechanisms that underpin electronic currency markets could be adapted from transfer of digital millions to more tangible goods and services, online markets that were completely secure, convenient and available to any seller would be realisable for almost anything. Imagine further that such marketplaces were universally accessible through the Internet or interactive television. That is the breathtaking potential of the new trading technology. Take, as one example, a hypothetical marketplace in car hire, running on one central computer, within which Hertz or Avis were as welcome to offer vehicles as a local garage with only three autos available or even an individual motorist who did not need his car for a weekend. Someone requiring transport for a day would input their location and desired standard of vehicle to be matched with the cheapest, closest option available, regardless of supplier. These as yet unrealised marketplaces have been christened Guaranteed Electronic Markets: their complex underlying procedures, that would make sure each deal was as safe as any presented to a foreign exchange dealer, are outlined in section one of this book. In the case of car hire, for instance, the central computer would need to satisfy itself that any vehicle being hired was provenly roadworthy, that the hirer could easily be made to pay for any damage or late return and it was only displayed to people who met requirements pre-selected by the owner (a long record of safely returned hired vehicles in the past perhaps). This would take a level of programming and support from state agencies (who need a way to assure the central computer that a putative hirer has a valid driving licence, for instance) that would be considerably more sophisticated than anything envisioned for interactive television or public Internet services at present. Demand for car hire simply does not warrant that level of investment. But auto rentals could be only one sector among thousands offered from a core computer which had developed the basic software and liaison required to underpin truly reliable open electronic markets in every area of legal trade. As the money markets have shown, making such a facility available should lead to sharply reduced costs of selling, which widens each market and attracts new resources, and which in turn should increase the 'granularity' of deals on offer. In such a market, for example, it may be possible to hire cars for a period of one hour and, because the vehicles on offer were no longer clustered at company depots but more evenly dispersed, there would be more likelihood of one being available close to any enquirer. This can sound improbably utopian (for everyone except the big car hire corporations of course) but as later chapters will show, money and resources behave very differently in genuinely open electronic markets.

To be truly useful this potential car hire forum would need to be flanked by additional markets running on the same core computer. Delivery would be one, allowing anyone who wished to trade as a car transfer driver to be verified and then price themselves competitively into work, with each assignment contracted and enforced by the computer. Insurance would be another, again not on the basis of a link to a favoured company but an automatic match with whoever offered the lowest price of the moment for the exact requirements of that hire. Once this technology was working it could be extended to marketplaces that scarcely exist at present. Motorbike hire? Child's tricycle hire? It would be up to individuals and companies whether they wished to sell in these virgin sectors but, like currency dealers, they would be able to call up data showing the extent of demand at any time.

Guaranteed Electronic Markets could trade goods with the same protection as services. Books provide a convenient example. An Internet user accessing Amazon's site at present can buy the latest John Grisham novel for 30 per cent less than the price a high-street book-seller with far greater overheads is likely to charge. But in a Guaranteed Electronic Market a purchaser might be matched with someone nearby who had just finished that novel and was willing to sell it second hand for 50 per cent off the published price. Assuming a flourishing market in local deliveries it could be at his door in less time at lower cost than anything despatched from Amazon's warehouse for carriage by the postal service. A local market in door-to-door hire of popular titles might even emerge from enterprising individuals around the country. Like every other deal on the putative system, such transactions would fully protect the property of the seller while ensuring adequate redress against anyone defaulting on a transaction. In time, marketplaces like this might trade contracts for periods of employment, training, groceries, household services, raw materials for industry and so on. Each sector should lower prices and constantly widen the range of suppliers by abolishing market entry costs and providing full informa-tion on levels of demand. As it gained momentum, a system offering these markets should demolish many economic realities currently taken for granted: oligopoly suppliers, market distortions and lack of price information for example. In their place an atomized economy of count-less individual traders and ever-changing suppliers should emerge.

Could electronic commerce ever deliver this theoretical potential?

On current trends the kind of trading just outlined looks set to remain conjectural for some time. In the early days of electronic commerce it was widely assumed that online trade would inevitably graduate to an ultra efficient marketplace and unleash countless suppliers. That is now questioned: certainly new trading software is offering benefits to small outfits but, as section three will show, it offers hyper advantage to large corporations. The trading revolution is not the information revolution. Big players are understandably developing the new infrastructure to increase their corporate profitability; there is no equivalent of the shared incentive to grow a new medium that powered the World Wide Web's growth. Additionally, a simple, wide-open online marketplace would require coordination of software standards well beyond the comparative simplicity of web site construction. Issues to be resolved would include payment systems, authentication of traders, deposit taking, protection of privacy, connections between disparate market-places (making a purchase then selecting delivery from an open pool of carriers for instance), bonding of sellers and dispute resolution. Emer-gence of common standards in these areas is likely to be protracted, not least because pioneers now have to invest so heavily to create the programming, after which coming second is not an acceptable outcome. Years of 'browser wars' give some taste of the possible road ahead. Since inception the Web needed a consistent software platform for those who wanted to set up sites and those who wished to access them. What emerged was Netscape and Microsoft warring to own crucial tech-nology, incompatible programming deliberately developed and outsider's attempts to promote an emerging standard, Java, obfuscated through proprietary modifications.[6] Yet this winnowing process does not necessarily deliver the best technology: many attribute Internet Explorer's ascendancy in the browser wars to marketing advantage rather than incontrovertible superiority.

Aside from the struggle for standards, a justifiable fear of commoditi-sation is likely to stop the Internet moving towards a series of truly open marketplaces. Consumer finance companies, for instance, are migrating to the Net and investing in 'relationship management' software. But the real bonus an online economy could bring to their customers would be if it allowed individuals to access one big pool of all the cash currently available for consumer lending in the way foreign exchange dealers trade direct in the market, not with a retailer who has only a small proportion of overall merchandise on offer. Within such a pool a borrower would be likely to find a loan of exactly the size and duration required at a fiercely competitive rate. But, were one massive effectively underpinned consumer loans market to be set up, the financial companies would become redundant. They have to cripple the potential of the new marketplace to retain a place in it.

Entrepreneurial capitalism, it is argued, should ensure that if the finance industry will not pool its resources for the benefit of clients, it is sidelined by a new competitor who, assuming standards issues have been resolved, sets up software in which lenders and borrowers meet each other for secure transactions with charges representing little over the cost of running such a straightforward service. Who might do this? Computing companies certainly have the technological might required, but each of the hundreds of finance company Internet sites at present requires a server computer, probably bought from IBM, Sun or Compaq, then software developed by specialists such as Baan, SAP or Oracle with regular upgrades from the same companies' consultants. None of these companies has any incentive to promote truly open markets akin to the Reuters 2000–2 that runs, very efficiently, on one machine with no need for expensive relationship technology. Unsurprisingly, they unite to promote electronic commerce as a fragmented mass of individual sales channels.[7]

Establishing pure online markets with all the attendant liaison to make them completely trustworthy would be expensive and unpredictable. Might someone like Rupert Murdoch nevertheless scent profitable possibility in making the full capabilities of electronic markets universally available? Were he to decide to do so, his problems would be twofold. First, the very precise laws required to underpin such an operation are not in place and would be difficult to envisage in a globalizing economy. How, for instance, could the putative marketplace operator conclusively avoid being a counterpart in disputed deals? It would need the legal status of say a telephone company, which is deemed not liable for the conversations its customers conduct. That principle could not be extended lightly to a profusion of Internet marketplaces. Second, the neonate Murdoch service would require expensive advertising to rise above the babel of often hyperbolic customer propositions from competing marketplaces. It might then be difficult to maintain momentum towards critical mass because start-up operators could also offer buyer–seller matching with the same features but charging much lower commission. There are, for instance, hundreds of forums which trade second-hand personal computers online, all with their own formulae for 'adding value' and individual charging structures, ranging through various kinds of auction to straight sales or exchanges. No software can compare like with like in this mass of uncoordinated marketplaces. Together they certainly offer a more convenient way of shopping compared to phoning or physically visiting a range of outlets but do not make the major market-widening advantages, currently enjoyed by global money dealers, available to all. In the fast-mutating online world Rupert Murdoch will not make his money from long-term commitment to realizing the deep social benefits of electronic trade. Safer returns are available from setting up a fully featured trading environment using interactive television then selling exclusive use to big retailers. It is the same model adopted by companies like AOL/Netscape which concentrate traffic towards 'portal' sites where prefential retail display can be sold for millions of dollars. Foreign currency dealers could attest to the likely desire among ordinary people for a new pure marketplace. The febrile electronic commerce industry is unlikely to be able to provide it for the foreseeable future.

Government's role as initiator of new technology

History shows a way these hindrances have previously been bypassed and the full promise of an infant technology made real. It is, however, a possibility completely at odds with current thinking in the computing establishment. Study of the last 200 years shows how frequently politicians have transiently involved themselves in emerging technology, not as regulators but as initiators. In a latter-day version of this scenario a government could decide it wanted one simple, fully protected, electronic markets system for its population, perhaps funded by flat rate commission on each deal and built by private enterprise. These Guaranteed Electronic Markets could centralize technologies such as bonding, verification and payment transfer for low-cost use by franchisees running thousands of markets as diverse as household services, transport and accommodation. Certain privileges that only government can bestow could be outlined in legislation that shapes a clear business opportunity for whoever funds the system. These benefits might include: direct legal protection of contracts between buyers and sellers on the system, courts willing to accept disputes forwarded by the software so accusations of unfair trade can be automatically resolved, a right to mesh the system with licensing authorities and other state bodies (without compromising its independence) and a prominent channel on the country's interactive televisions alongside major broadcasters.

There would be commitments to be extracted from the operators of these markets to reflect the scale of opportunity inherent in being sole beneficiaries of these government-awarded rights. They might, for example, have to pay for a network of dedicated terminals in public places so that even those with no connection at home could enter the new markets. Once these terms were decided, competing consortia would bid to build and run the nation's Guaranteed Electronic Markets system using whatever technology standards were practicable at the time. Selection between them need not involve politicians picking winners. It could be as simple as each group specifying, in a sealed bid, the flat rate percentage on each deal they proposed charging if awarded the contract, with the lowest commitment winning.

This would be a nation-by-nation initiative, rather than a global scheme. It would not involve restraining existing electronic commerce in any way: a country's Guaranteed Electronic Markets (GEMs) system would exist alongside the multiplicity of sales channels and Internet buyer–seller matching services. It simply provides an alternative for those who wish to trade in a wide, more convenient, marketplace. The legislative process described is not always popular but it is common and it can work. When Margaret Thatcher wanted a Channel tunnel built, for instance, she pragmatically sidelined her aversion to government-initiated schemes to ensure a successful consortium which, although having to compete with ferry, hovercraft and airline services, was granted an officially enforced monopoly on tunnels between England and France until the end of the year 2020. Anyone else seeking to burrow a competing route, however well funded, will be stopped because protecting one operator was the only realistic way to find the large investment required for a long-term project without taxpayers absorbing any risk.

Parliamentary initiative to enable new technology swiftly to reach its full potential was a conspicuous feature of Britain's economic supremacy during the technological chaos of the Industrial Revolution. The birth of public water supply, in particular, forms a useful analogy with the kind of act that might eventually realise a GEMs service anywhere in the world. Until the 1850s hundreds of water companies were exploiting early pumping and piping technology to supply well-off homes in their locality. Dozens of incompatible pipe networks were spun across the new cities by branded suppliers who delivered marked variations in quality and pricing. A typical company piped water to customers for two hours or less on alternate days with the product then needing to be filtered and boiled before consumption. In 1842 a report looked into appalling public health problems of the time and mooted the notion of a mass water system to run alongside existing companies, growing to offer an affordable 24-hour, immediately drinkable, supply to anyone who wished to plumb in to the new network.[8] Many people found the idea so ambitious as to be inconceivable.

Owners of the water companies at first dismissed, then vehemently opposed, mass supply, which would commoditize their carefully nurtured customer relationships. They ensured a vigorous campaign labelling the idea of an officially instigated water service as unaccept-able centralizing of power by politicians.[9] Nevertheless, and despite a parliamentary commitment to *laissez-faire* at the time,[10] the 1848 Public Health Act initiated such a service. It did not banish existing suppliers. Records from 1867 show London having nine water companies along-side the municipal pipes, for instance.[11] But the posited mass system was awarded advantages that would have been of little use to small operators: primarily, access to new large-scale sources of supply.[12] These new resources brought the cost of domestic water down by a claimed 30 to 50 per cent.[13] Coming in the age of Municipal Socialism it was largely local government money that inaugurated the new network but, at a different time, investment could as easily have originated in the private sector. The Act's significance was the focus and momentum it created by outlining and facilitating a bold vision for water that went way beyond industry aspirations or market demand. The masses were not clamouring for 24-hour water: still relying on communal bore holes and delivery carts, they had little conception such a facility could exist. By making the leap of faith as to a new technology's ultimate capability the UK government ensured a low overhead service and created a potentially profitable mass market harnessing the economies of scale.

Would it have eventually happened without parliament? More companies would almost certainly have entered the market for water provision in later decades, lowering costs and extending reach. The Byzantine tangle of piping would eventually, through expensive attrition, have been whittled down to a small handful of dominant providers. This cartel would probably then have set common standards for pipe sizes, junctions and valves and begun discussing intake and outfall siting. But the unique efficiencies of a system planned from the start for mass use would have been missing. Piping expertise soon travelled around the world. It is worth comparing provision in London 60 years after the act with nearby Paris, which had to rely on market forces alone: a 1911 study found 96 per cent of the British capital's households were connected to a water supply against only 17.5 per cent in Paris.[14]

The role of government as initiator can be seen in most of the infrastructure considered essential to modern life. Table 1 shows how governments in just two countries, the US and Britain, have been crucial in supplementing a pioneering phase of genuinely useful technology with a vision for its maximized public usefulness. A notable exception on this chart is the Internet for which there was never an Act to create focused commercial opportunity. There did not need to be: the US government directly paid out cold war tax dollars to build a computer communication backbone. This funding, starting in 1965 with the Advanced Research Projects Agency and eventually through the National Science Foundation, did not end until 1995.

Competition between governments: a coming force in electronic trade?

It is the contention of this book that universal access to reliable electronic markets will become as essential to a healthy society in the networked computer age as was provision of quality water to industrializing cities. Further, the only decisive way to ensure its realization would be for government to craft a combination of opportunity and obligations which amounts to a viable business opportunity for private enterprise. Electronic markets, however, would be a considerably more sensitive public utility than facilities like water supply. A centralized system would forever have the potential for misuse of user data or skewing of markets to favour predetermined outcomes. It would be unacceptable for such a system to be run or even supervised by government; instead control would be in the hands of a web of companies

Table 1   The role of government in the US and UK in turning new technology into public infrastructure

TECHNOLOGY	PIONEERING PHASE	GOVERNMENT ACTION
Public gas supply	Experimental intermittent supply to factories and workshops.	**1817:** (US) Baltimore facilitates first gas lighting in streets. **1820:** (UK) Public Utility Act launched a uniform gas supply in Manchester then the rest of Britain.
Public water supply	Regional water enterprises, differing in standards, reliability and level of service.	**1848:** (UK) Public Health Act made water supply the responsibility of regional government. **1895:** (US) Metropolitan Water District of Massachusetts – the first regional supply system.
Mass postage service	Ad hoc stagecoach services.	**1839:** (UK) Penny Postage Act. **1847:** (US) Use of stamps legally recognised.
Public railroad system	Assorted mine and factory railways.	**1840s:** (UK) Various Railway Acts. **1850s:** (US) Federal Land Grants financed construction in return for cheap carriage of government goods.
Telephone	Experimental local systems.	**1880:** (UK) Court ruling bought co-ordinated planning of a telephone system under jurisdiction of the Post Office. **1921:** (US) Graham-Willis Act exempted phone companies from antitrust laws.
Public electricity supply	Sporadic service to factories using differing voltages and AC/DC.	**1882:** (UK) Board of Trade starts licensing companies to provide regional domestic supply. **1920:** (US) Federal Power Commission created. It encouraged building of transmission lines on public domain.
Road system for the motor car era	Countless local track-laying initiatives.	**1909:** (UK) National Road Board. **1916:** (US) First Federal Highways Act.
Radio transmissions	Ham radio, point to point communications, manufacturers' output.	**1927:** (US) Radio Act creates FRC for station licensing. **1927:** (UK) BBC Charter.
Television transmissions	Manufacturer's experiments, unlicensed test stations.	**1936:** (UK) BBC Charter extended to TV. **1941:** (US) FCC authorised first commercial TV station.
The Internet	Experimental computer bulletin boards.	**1960s:** US Defence Dept funding. **1970s/80s/90s:** US Education Dept funding.

making up a winning consortium and more importantly their franchisees operating thousands of individual market sectors. Additionally,
inspection regimes exceeding that of any existing utility and designed to
nullify this damaging potential will be detailed in later chapters. The
most important guarantee such a system should give users is constant
proof that if ever they lost faith in the core computer's security or
integrity they could immediately close their account and in doing so
irrevocably destroy all personal data.

Within the short lifespan of electronic commerce, so far parliaments
have been largely content to act as unimaginative backstays: promising
regulation, or, more often, the absence of regulatory restrictions, to
keep new sales channels competitive. But politicians are of course
themselves subject to competitive pressure and have much to gain from
offering their electorates unique benefits. A Guaranteed Electronic
Markets system would cost the originating country's taxpayers nothing
to build and no citizen would be coerced into using it. If properly
executed and widely taken up, however, it could open up new vistas of
work and consumption opportunities for users. It should bring new
resources into the economy because market entry costs and the chances
of a deal going sour have withered. However, the possibility of public
electronic markets poses enormous threats as well as opportunities for
politicians. Their danger lies in a temptation to launch compromised
markets, aiming to shield existing industries or power bases from the
brutal efficiencies of such a reliable marketplace. Protective forays into
computer trading by the London Stock Exchange (LSE) demonstrate
the perils that could one day be faced by entire countries. As Europe's
overwhelmingly dominant exchange, the LSE moved tardily to electronic trading in 1993 with their TAURUS system. This enshrined
labourious, but politically sensitive, settlement procedures in the new
process, which then collapsed under the resulting complexities. A
second system similarly protected the LSE's legacy of market-making
procedures from the brunt of electronic market forces. Meanwhile,
Frankfurt's less historically encumbered stock market had moved unre-
servedly to a simple open electronic marketplace, attracting an ever
increasing proportion of trade. Eventually out-traded by the German
exchange, London was compelled by its senior customers to merge with
Frankfurt and trade on their software.[15] Any country attempting to
constrain their embryonic public markets would be likely to find them-

selves similarly overtaken by other nations who learned from that mistake. Significantly, it could be Second World countries, where opposition would be less formidable, who would be first to launch Guaranteed Electronic Markets systems. If those public markets were incorruptible they could remove many of the factors that can often make such nations financially unstable. Like the Frankfurt bourse they may then start dramatically catching up with previously implacable international rivals.

Net Benefit aims to introduce all aspects of this emerging potential for electronic trading technology. Section one, overleaf, demonstrates how a Guaranteed Electronic Markets (GEMs) system might enact a variety of transactions. Section two explores the impact such a system might have in the country of operation, including the effects of a possible official online parallel economy to include those with little hard cash in the new way of trading. In section three the steps necessary to launch a GEMs service are discussed, as well as the probable opposition to such a move and its possible tactics. The fourth section asks how businesses might adapt to a world of genuinely open electronic markets for all. Finally, Appendix one outlines the five principles of Guaranteed Electronic Markets that define a system in which every aspect of operation is genuinely guaranteed for the good of all users and Appendix two offers a tentative business model for any consortium looking to build a first GEMs system.

The effects of online consumerism and business-to-business purchasing are now inescapable. If its ultimate potential is ignored by governments, the rewards of this trading revolution are likely to accrue progressively to those with dominant seller sites: firms that are employing decreasing numbers of people. Yet, as following chapters will show, this technology, with a nudge from politicians, offers an answer to many pressing contemporary problems: economic inefficiency, social exclusion, crime and national determination in the global age. The downside, if significant numbers started using public market systems, would be felt by many organizations that form the backbone of today's economy who could lose their previously unquestioned status as economic activity widens. The battle over whether electronic trade should be left to reinforce concentrations of economic power, or moulded to drive a newly inclusive, atomized, economy of widening participants, could be one of the defining political issues of the next decade.

Notes

1. Julie Ros, Executive Editor of *FX Week Newsletter*, published by Waters Information Services. Interview with the author 28 August 1998.
2. www.autobytel.com
3. www.ebay.com
4. www.onsale.com
5. Evan I. Schwartz, At Online Auctions, Good and Raw, Deals, *New York Times*, March 5 1998 – electronic edition.
6. Susan B. Garland, Sun takes the stand, *Business Week*, 26 October 1998, p. 49.
7. Proving the exception to the rule, Microsoft does run matching services including Expedia for travel and Carpoint for cars. They are heavily restricted on the seller side.
8. *Report of the Sanitary Condition of the Labouring Population of Gt Britain*, written by three Poor Law Commissioners assisted by Edwin Chadwick, Secretary of the Commission. Its eventual recommendations were so radical the former had their names taken off the cover and Chadwick alone is credited with recognising water supply as an essential utility (M. W. Flinn, *New Introduction to the Report*, University of Edinburgh Press, 1965, p. 46).
9. S. E. Finer, *The Life and Times of Sir Edwin Chadwick*, London, Methuen, 1952, p. 320.
10. In 1846, for instance, the protectionist Corn Laws had finally been repealed.
11. *Encyclopaedia Britannica*.
12. In 1850, for example, the new system was allowed to develop wells at Farnham and Hindhead to supply London 30 miles away. Smaller water enterprises were still drawing from the River Thames, an inhibitor for the private market because it was then the capital's main sewer. (S.E. Finer, *The Life and Times of Sir Edwin Chadwick*, London, Methuen, 1952, p. 394).
13. Ibid. p. 394.
14. Jean-Pierre Goubert, *The Conquest of Water: the Advent of Health in the Industrial Age*, Princeton University Press, 1986, p. 196.
15. Melanie Bien, Traders Force the Rate of Exchange, *The European*, 13–19 July 1998, pp. 8–10.

The ultimate potential of e-trade: how open public markets might work

In 1993, after nearly three decades of networked computing, the Internet consisted of 800 unrelated networks with a mass of incompatible operating systems and programming languages.[1] A group of particle physicists in Switzerland constructed an additional network based on what they called the http protocol and designed to allow them to easily exchange documents. Unofficially they christened it The Web. It was this creation of one very simple way of reliably accessing data or adding new pages of information in a maelstrom of options that turned the combination of computers and telephone lines from an academic accessory to a social force. Within a few years, users opting for the http protocol far outnumbered those using any of the established networks. This chapter assumes a GEMs system has achieved something similar for the more complex requirements of secure online trading: offering a single convenient entry into an enormously varied marketplace in which anyone can sell anything instantly. There would be no controlling authority acting as gateway to the new markets, only automated procedures to ensure each deal was safe. I have further assumed that dependable public markets were initiated by a government, motivated either by political expediency or egalitarian conviction, who enshrined two crucial principles in the enabling Act. First, the putative system is confined to providing only the services that can be most efficiently delivered by a public markets service. The consortium running GEMs is not allowed to leverage that pole position, through technological domination or contact with customers, into a commanding lead in further areas. Their profits come only from continuing investment in neutral, confidential, relentlessly inspected public markets. Second, that there is no social engineering attached to the project: no attempt to manipulate markets or arrive at a planned outcome. The only aim is finding a best possible match for each buyer's enquiry across every area of trade that is legal in the country of operation. Consequences of such a system, not least as outlined in later pages of this book, can only be speculative.

Any citizen in the country of operation could open an account then buy or sell in the new marketplace, which would be available through the Internet or interactive television sets. They would need to prove identity and banking arrangements, at a Post Office perhaps, where they would receive a PIN generated on the counter clerk's GEMs terminal. On first logging in, the system would ask for a link to their bank account enabling it to add and subtract funds as they trade. Alternatively they could use a smart card. Such a system would start modestly and grow as new sectors were added. The following scenarios, however, demonstrate the operation of a mature, widely used system.

Demonstration: booking overnight accommodation in a GEM

It is half past six on a Friday evening. A couple looking for a weekend on the coast have turned to the GEMs system to find somewhere to spend tonight. After the customers have entered their PIN (personal identification number) and navigated to the 'overnight accommodation' marketplace, an initial screen asks 'do you want to rent a room or do you wish to sell accommodation?' One click tells GEMs they are buyers rather than potential providers: they are then asked for detailed requirements. On completion their screen might look like this:

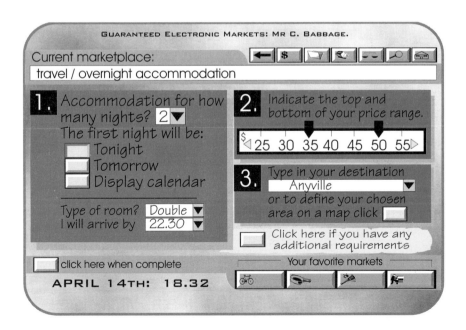

It has taken seven clicks to tell the central computer they seek a room in nearby Anyville for tonight costing $35–50 and they will be arriving by half past ten. Immediately GEMs displays a map of accommodation it has still available that most closely matches their demands.

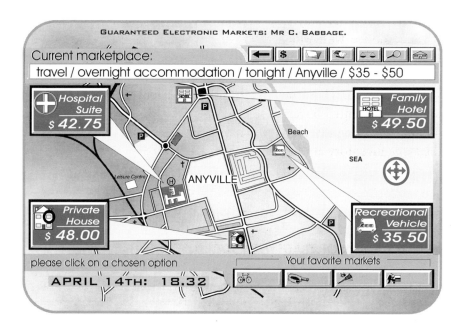

Market entry

Any individual or organization can sell in this market which will offer a room in a branded chain hotel as readily as accommodation with a householder letting out a spare bed. It is up to the purchaser to decide which they favour. Market entry is an automated process with no charges levied by GEMs: anyone with a room to sell simply completes three tasks. First, they must prove their accommodation complies with any relevant legislation. They might, for instance, need to acquire a fire safety certificate for which the Fire Officer would give them a GEMs compatible PIN (Box 1.1). Then they need to transfer a specified sum of money that will be held as a bond from which compensation can be paid if they default on any deal. This would not be as arduous a requirement as it may seem: interest accumulated on the bond is paid into the room owner's account, anyone having problems raising the cash could turn to a GEM for insurance. Their supplier could then have their commission automatically extracted from each transaction. Finally the market entrant will be asked to input a pricing formula. This can be as simple as a flat nightly rate or it can change according to the day of the week, time of year, length of stay, the arrival and departure times of guests, advance notice with which a booking is received, occupancy level at time of sale and so on. The formula can also be set to attract particular customers; those who can prove to GEMs that they are *bona fide* students maybe. These details are used to calculate a price for each individual potential buyer. Hotels letting dozens of rooms may want to link their existing reservations computers to GEMs so both are trading the same inventory at identical prices.

Box 1.1

VERIFICATION OF TRADERS BY STATE AGENCIES

This would probably be achieved through encryption algorithms. In the case of fire certificates National Fire Service Headquarters would be given a PIN which they use to identify Senior Fire Officers to the system. Each of them is then allocated an algorithm by GEMs. When they certify a premises as safe they type the address into a GEMs terminal, it is fed through their algorithm and the 4 letters returned are the owner's proof to be typed into a GEMs market entry page. The key principle is that GEMs does not centrally store assessments of any individual's fitness to trade: the only information it holds on a user is that he has chosen to input, with proof where required. Fire stations could charge for this service just as they currently charge for a paper certificate in most countries.

This instant access to the market should make many new resources available. The offer of accommodation in a hospital, for instance, might be the result of cancelled operations tomorrow and an administrator releasing the patient rooms as bed and breakfast for that one night. He has nothing to lose, if there are no takers at his minimum price the hospital has suffered no costs for market entry, its sum in bond being transferred back in full in the morning. The recreational vehicle option may seem implausible but again the owner who has an expensive asset parked on his drive has nothing to lose by putting it in the market occasionally on the terms of his choice.

It is the private house that appeals to the couple seeking a place to stay. They click for a details page on that option.

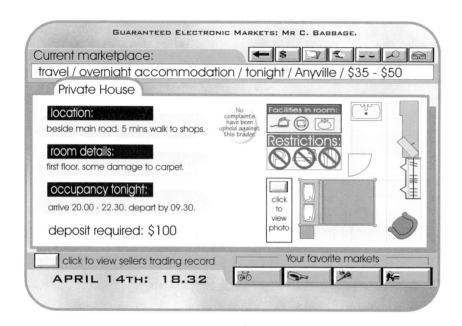

This information was input by the owner. It is no place for hyperbole, the details given become part of a binding contract with any buyer. Some sellers would opt to provide only the most basic information, others could click through GEMs' detailed questions for overnight accommodation market entry, including sections on availability to the disabled, views, historical significance of their building and so on. There may be potential buyers for whom one of these headings is a key selection criterion. Sellers who want to offer still more enticing detail can use a friendly interface to assemble a floorplan of the room or have a photograph of the building scanned and sent to GEMs. The symbols in this details page show the facilities available in the room: a kettle, television and sink, and the restrictions imposed on hirers: no parking on the premises, no smoking and no eating in the room. Again, this becomes part of the contract.

GEMs' ability to compile a trading record for each user is essential to faith in the marketplace. The system can monitor a buyer or seller's number of trades and any complaints upheld against them. No user has to release this personal information to potential trading partners but those that do not might be judged to have something to hide. The owner of the room in Anyville, still anonymous to browsers, has chosen to make her record across multiple categories available to potential buyers. One click reveals a background of unimpeachable reliability throughout a range of GEMs market sectors.

Satisfied that they are dealing with a solid individual, the couple click for a contract with which to book tonight's stay.

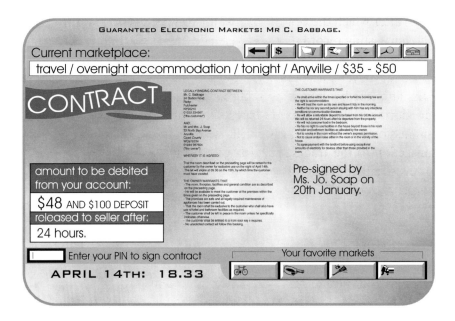

Written by GEMs lawyers, this is the system's standard contract for overnight hire of a room at the $50 or less price point. The core text is immutable, specifying legal minimums for this particular trade but sellers can remove additional clauses, one stipulating towels will be provided perhaps. Or they can add their own: a demand for 'complete silence after 23.00', for instance. Any such changes show up in red. Without these eye-catching amendments a buyer knows they are dealing with the typical agreement, one that does not favour the seller as is the case in owned sales channels but is designed only to facilitate the market. As experienced GEMs users the couple do not bother to read the contract, they know it will be firm but fair on both sides. One standard stipulation is 'no unsolicited approaches', the seller cannot use this transaction as a launchpad for relationship marketing unless a buyer clicks to remove the clause.

The room owner pre-signed this contract when laying out her terms of trade, the couple now sign their side by re-entering his GEMs PIN. The system now reveals the address of their place of residence tonight and offers a map. Simultaneously a booking information page is sent to the room owner, she can use this to confirm details when the couple arrive on her doorstep. A copy of the contract is sent to each side's files and GEMs retains its own version for a month in case of legal comebacks, after which the centrally held copy is wiped. The system does not keep any lasting record of a user's specific transactions.

As the contract is signed the agreed sum, plus a deposit, are taken out of the buyer's account and held in escrow by the system until 24 hours after the booking is over. If the system does not hear from either side during that period it will release the fee, minus GEMs' own commission, to the seller, return the deposit and add another successful transaction to the trading records of both parties. During this period, however, either buyer or seller may freeze the cash by instigating a complaint about the other.

Complaints procedures

Safe electronic trade rests on dependable and prompt resolution of complaints between buyers and sellers with sanctions applied against offenders and compensation for victims. GEMs would address this need with an automated three-stage process once a completed transaction in any one of its markets was disputed. It would be demanding but that commitment to fairness should minimize the times it was called upon by deterring defaulters. The deals complained about could range from the supply of hundreds of thousands of dollars worth of ingredients for industry to lowly domestic breakages. Each transaction in every market would be bonded with funds held by the system for a safety period after completion. Let us assume as an example that the room owner in Anyville finds the couple have broken her kettle during their stay. She would call up her archived copy of the contract and click a box marked 'I wish to complain about the room occupier'. As a first stage, all the money involved in the transaction, the fee, deposit and supplier's bond would be frozen. The room owner is now invited to type in her account of the problem and click on the amount of compensation she believes is her entitlement, under the published scale of fines for this market. As a second stage, that resulting page is sent electronically to her former guests and GEMs asks if they accept culpability for the problem as outlined. If they do so, restitutive payment is deducted from their frozen deposit, transferred to the owner and the matter is closed. If they resist, the software asks for their version of events, the amount of any fine they would accept and seeks agreement from the other side. If agreement is not reached, the complaint is finally forwarded to arbitration.

Every GEMs sector would be backed up by a relevant adjudication authority, either an existing organization or a panel brought into being by system staff when they launch a particular market. In both cases judgements are financed by the bond/deposit mechanism and buying or selling in that marketplace are conditional on accepting the results. The overnight accommodation market might be overseen by tourist development bodies, for instance: any unresolved issues are electronically forwarded to their panel which reads the accounts of both sides. It can also speak to those involved by phone and, more usefully, ask to see their GEMs trading records, if available. Should the couple have a track record of complaints against them by diverse landlords, or if they choose not to release their record to the panel, their credibility would be diminished and they would be more likely to find the cost of the kettle and adjudication coming out of their bond. Particularly serious allegations would be forwarded to the courts.

Persistently misbehaving sellers or buyers would be automatically barred from a given market after a certain proportion of upheld complaints. Likewise, wilful complainants would be purged from GEMs trading after a specified number of groundless grievances. This is the same principle by which bad drivers are banned from the roads: no one has an incontestable right to use GEMs, they do so only as long as they obey the rules that make the market safe for everyone else. No trader would be immune from this relentless drive for a quality marketplace. If a big name hotel in one city was accruing too many upheld complaints and failing to live up to the standards laid out in GEMs' contract for luxury accommodation it would be mechanically ejected from that level of the market for a predetermined period, as would any caravan owner who failed to live up to the less extensive demands at the budget end of the accommodation sector. No member of GEMs staff makes judgements about who is in or out of the markets: it would be an automatic process, based on ground rules available to all.

2

Growing the new markets

Market overviews

Finding a room in Anyville that most comprehensively matched the buyers' requirements from the widest possible pool, then putting together a deal that could be promptly enforced would have taken seconds. Market entry would be equally effortless and made all the more enticing by GEMs' market overview capability. Available to any user in any sector, these screens could bring data interrogation to an entire population as they constantly collate market information that can be displayed according to a user's individual preferences. A householder in Anyville with a spare room, for instance, might call up this screen before deciding whether to start offering bed and breakfast.

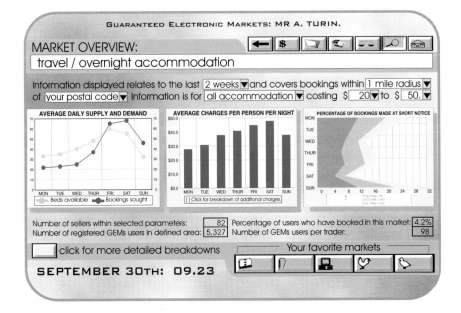

This screen shows there is unmet demand at weekends with predictably high prices being charged. The householder may now want to check levels of supply already available for next weekend and, if they remain low, perhaps take five minutes to go through GEMs' step-by-step market entry process for bed and breakfast. The parameters defining information displayed in a market overview can be changed continuously. However, if an enquiry focuses on too narrow a segment of the market, no data will be shown. A rigid commitment to user privacy prohibits display of information that may be used to deduce the income or sales patterns of any one user, corporate or individual. Only market overviews drawing on multiple anonymous sellers can be compiled.

A market in everything

GEMs would trade goods with as much thoroughness as services. A seller in the men's shirt market, for instance, would answer basic questions about size, style, sleeve length, colour (selected from an on-screen palette) and quantities available, which would then become details pages for each variant on offer. Additionally sellers could have illustrations of the garment being modelled, or a life-size patch of the material scanned for display to putative purchasers. It does not matter if the seller has a warehouse full of clothes to shift or one second-hand calico garment: as long as they set a price and describe the condition truthfully their goods will be offered to interested buyers. A contract between the two ensures that any inconsistency between what is described and the item received will, ultimately, be referred to trading standards officers for judgement. Shirt sellers would also have to specify how promptly and securely they will despatch goods. Will they manufacture the garment specified in 10 minutes and then access the 'rush deliveries' GEM for the best deal on same day transit? Or do they only check their nearest GEMs terminal once a fortnight and then send anything sold by second-class mail? Either way, if a buyer can prove non-arrival within the promised time, compensation from stored bonds awaits them. Cautious customers may want to check and only deal with a supplier, whether an individual clearing his wardrobe or an international designer label whose trading record demonstrated that they have much to lose from any lapse in integrity.

Standardised goods – refrigerators, roof tiles or bulldozers, for instance – would have their details held in GEMs archives. A seller need only input a product number for a picture and full specifications to immediately appear on their details page.

It would take several years of evolutionary development, but a mature GEMs system could eventually provide the levels of service just described across thousands of sectors. This would not take the form of one uniform market structure into which diverse trading requirements are shoehorned: instead each sector is run by a GEMs franchisee, one person handling the market for aircraft components for instance, another motivated to grow trade in a GEM for fresh vegetables. Both would develop the adjudication procedures and levels of bonding required to ensure users had unquestioning faith in the market. Additionally, each franchisee would look continuously at how a centrally provided range of electronic trade tools might make their area of responsibility more attractive to likely buyers or sellers. Anyone shopping for a second-hand car in GEMs, for example, might find a range of sellers had clicked to enable a 'purchased hold' option. This could allow potential purchasers, on payment of a fee determined by each owner, to have the vehicle taken out of the market for, say, a week until they had time for a test drive. In the plumbers' market the supply side could be offered a geographical component in their pricing formula: towards the end of each day they might choose to automatically lower charges for jobs that brought them ever nearer home. A GEMs for carpets might allow prospective purchasers to assemble a floorplan by entering room measurements on a grid. Using details input over similar squares by sellers, the core computer then demonstrates whether a proffered carpet of shape A can be made to fit room B and, if so, exactly how the new owner should proceed with dissection. Because GEMs is an all-sellers-welcome marketplace, it should steadily build the turnover that amortizes the costs of ever-increasing sophistication in its service.

3 The system's relationship with users

Λ GEMs system would have multiple responsibilities to its users. Crucially, it must prove that it does not abuse its position by compiling information about any company or individual's activities, apart from an optional generalized trading record. Unlike the Balkanized world of uncoordinated electronic commerce channels, users can be sure there is no data capture at any stage in the buying process. Instead, GEMs offers a user questionnaire which asks for ever-changing individual preferences in all sorts of markets. The couple seeking a weekend away, for instance, might have both clicked that they prefer a vegetarian cooked breakfast option in the overnight accommodation section of their questionnaire and GEMs would make that a search priority in ranking their options for any particular location. Persuading users to be completely at ease with GEMs, however, would take more than peerlessly detailed software. Non-binary aspects of system stewardship must be equally reassuring. To this end GEMs should operate by the principles of Guaranteed Electronic Markets (listed in Appendix one). These mandate neutral markets, distance from government or any particular seller and the right of a user to leave the system and have all their details expunged at any time. This would be enforced by transparency of operation (Box 3.1). The likelihood of being found out notwithstanding, a GEMs consortium would have no incentive to invade users' privacy. Restricted by statute to running passive electronic markets, the system has no application for individual information. The greatest business risk faced by operators would be analogous to a run on a bank: users lose faith in the system and exit *en masse*. It should be commercial logic more than regulatory threat that keeps the public markets system acting according to its published aims.

Box 3.1

TRANSPARENCY OF OPERATION

The operating consortium's commercial secrecy would be a secondary consideration to open publication of GEMs' core programming. Anyone technically competent could devise their own ways of checking that this code did not allow sensitive information to be compiled, nor markets skewed. They could then devise endless ways of confirming that the programming as published matched that actually running on the central machine. Testing would be random and never-ending, not at the hands of a potentially corruptible national body which would inevitably have links to politicians. Groups from across the geographical and ideological spectrum would be paid to visit the country of operation and pursue the inspection regime of their choice. Would this openness be a boon to hackers? GEMs' central computer would not allow remote access to restructure the core code by anyone, there is no authorization to fraudulently replicate. Users should be able to read the core programming at home should they wish but otherwise have only very low level access to the system from remote terminals. You cannot hack into a bank's computer from a cashpoint however much you know about its core programming because access is physically not possible. GEMs could follow the same protocol with security at the central control room to rival that in a missile command bunker.

Unlike existing e-trade channels, GEMs would want to go largely unregistered in its users' consciousness. Its combination of unobtrusiveness and universality would probably be a key appeal. The system would do everything possible to avoid imposing its own values on the trading process: government defines which goods and services can be legally traded, multiple sellers determine the breadth of each market and relevant outside organizations operating adjudication panels shape the acceptable behaviour in each sector. GEMs' software should aim to be like the equipment involved in a telephone call, having no character that impinges on the process it facilitates. Other companies have mastered this transparency in similar areas already. De La Rue, for example, print banknotes for over 150 countries but, despite a pivotal role in those economies, impose no values, beyond an objective commitment to quality, on any of them. Even the most persistent monetarist would not think of lobbying De La Rue to print fewer notes for a client economy; it is understood that the company implements decisions made elsewhere. Certainly GEMs' operators would have to make constant editorial decisions about which organizations to involve in markets, how to present options to users and the system's navigation paths. But those decisions, uniquely among online services, would be focused on reducing GEMs and its enforcement procedures to a commoditized service. The system should be no more than a timeless trading platform on which others build a vibrant marketplace of the moment.

4 Demonstration: connected transactions – hiring a van and driver in GEMs

A key advantage that public markets would have over piecemeal e-commerce networks is the way in which diverse marketplaces could interlock. A deal can be constructed that fits together something bought in market A, from a wide pool of informed sellers, with goods or services purchased in the same conditions from market B. Imagine, as an example, a plastic moulding company in a small town that just before 7.00 p.m. on a weekday has received a rush order for a van-load of their wheeled bins required 250 miles away by 9.00 a.m. the following morning. The company's van and driver are elsewhere, vehicle hire depots that may still be open are far away and the trusted driver hire agencies with local presence have all closed for the night.

For a harassed factory owner the solution might be found in a GEM for *vehicles/hire/vans/immediate*. By clicking through on-screen diagrams and questions he specifies overnight hire of a box van capable of at least 1000 kg payload and $10m^3$ capacity. (GEMs could offer illustrations showing vehicle size relative to an adult figure to help illustrate these characteristics.) He is shown a map of his surroundings flagged with suitable vehicles and their prices for his assignment. He browses details pages before selecting a Ford belonging to an electrical goods company 4 miles away. They have chosen to put their vehicle in the market until 10.00 p.m. (when their security guard goes home) on nights when it is not required for their own deliveries. A glance at the relevant GEMs market overview showed high prices being paid for such hires, meriting the increase in cover required for all drivers, input against a PIN issued over the phone by their insurer. Since they already sell their electrical products in GEMs, the firm had no problem topping up their interest-paying bond with the system for this extra liability (Box 4.1). To protect their property, they specified additionally that only someone with at least 100 complaint-free vehicle hirings on their trading record could be eligible as a buyer. GEMs checked that the factory owner cleared this hurdle before allowing him to see the vehicle as an option. This kind of restriction on buyers, available to any seller in any GEM, should be an important factor in coaxing cautious providers to make their resources available. It encourages buyers to act responsibly because a creditable trading record then allows them to shop in a wider market, where they can expect more competitive prices.

Box 4.1

THE GEMS INSURANCE MARKET

GEMs' requirement for insurance to underpin every deal can seem intimidating. If trading on the system requires that much effort might not sellers simply go elsewhere? But insurance itself could be traded in a GEM so the most competitive cover for a very precise liability and period could be constructed instantly. Had the company letting out their van chosen to go down this route they simply would have clicked on 'find my bonding' in the market entry screen and it would have been put in place at once. Sellers of insurance could link their pricing to market overview information so that, when there is clear demand for van hires, for instance, they might opt to offer commission-based cover.

Back at the wheeled bin company the factory manager signs his half of the contract. His account is debited for price and deposit, both to be held by GEMs, this time for 72 hours to allow sufficient time for symptoms of any mechanical damage inflicted during the hire to emerge. A booking confirmation screen is sent to the supplier, it includes an eight-letter codeword, selected by the van owner and revealed to tonight's hirer after the contract has been signed. Without it the security guard would not hand over his set of keys.

Although constructed in seconds this deal would provide full back-up for both sides. If the Ford were not available for collection when promised, for instance, the hirer would tell GEMs. The system then automatically accesses the defaulting owner's bond to rent an equivalent or better vehicle and engage a driver to deliver it to the hirer. Next time the van's owner logs in he would then be asked whether he admitted culpability and reminded that, if so, he must top up his bond before trading again. If the owner denied that his vehicle was unavailable, the system would relay a message to the hirer and ask him to click on a resolution that it can administer if both parties agree: perhaps splitting costs of the replacement vehicle equally if the problem was misunderstanding on both sides. If the hirer maintained that the fault was wholly with the owner and the owner disagreed, GEMs would freeze the required sums to finance adjudication, probably in a small claims court, and then instantly forward the contract plus allegations and responses in the complaints page, to court officers.

A new world of work

After signing his contract for van hire the mouldings company manager is asked 'do you require a driver for this hire?' Clicking on 'yes' would tell the central computer he needs someone immediately for a journey and return that should end by 5.00 a.m. The system would then need to know how much he is willing to pay.

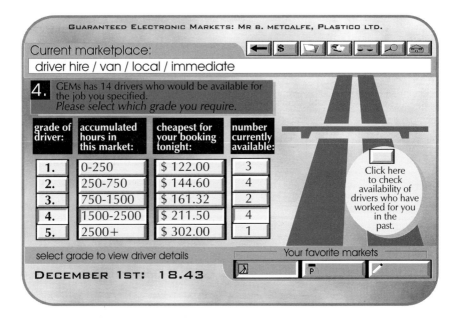

Anyone wanting to sell their services as a van driver in GEMs would have to input proof of a driving licence, renewable with a fresh PIN every

6 months as additional security to show they have not been banned from the roads in that time. Then they pinpoint their home location and specify the hours they will work, while GEMs enforces any legal restrictions on their individual timetable of availability. Finally, the aspiring driver is asked to input a pricing formula. This could be a crude hourly rate or a sophisticated set of percentages by which that basic fee is to be increased or reduced depending on, for example, length of booking, with how much notice of it was given, time of day, destination, even type of vehicle to be driven and whether the driver is allowed to smoke at the wheel. Cancellation fees could also be specified and would be relentlessly enforced. Additionally, workers could drop their prices for employers for whom they have enjoyed working and discretely raise them for less acceptable clients. GEMs computes their price for each incoming assignment from this information, which can be changed daily, perhaps in the light of intelligence from the appropriate market overview page.

GEMs would grade drivers, automatically promoting them through its ranks as the hours they have been booked mount, assuming that the number of complaints upheld against them is low. As they move up the grades, workers can charge more for their services while remaining competitive. For the mouldings company, tonight's delivery is critical enough to merit a grade 4 driver, of whom four are available. One click reveals their details sheets, cheapest first.

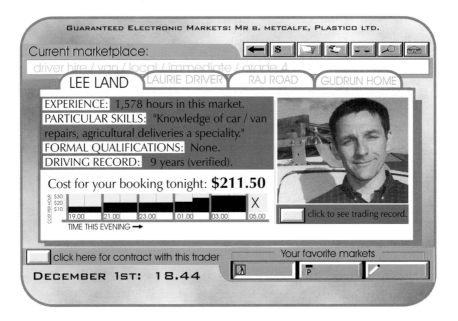

Clicking for the first driver's trading record would reveal what was already obvious: he has many hundreds of hours and dozens of satisfied customers behind him, with a negligible number of upheld complaints. Without this resumé he would not be trading in grade 4. His enviable career is a precious asset, he would be highly unlikely to endanger it with a cavalier attitude towards tonight's assignment. Once more a contract is offered, the mouldings company's transport department PIN is entered and the driver is hired. His first job will be to pick up the van, confirming that it is roadworthy in the process.

Several miles away the driver, who has told GEMs he will be at home and available for short-notice bookings all evening, is automatically paged and told to check his GEMs terminal. Once there he sees details of his night's work, including a suggested timetable calculated by GEMs based on legally permitted maximum driving periods and its ability to time the journey between two postal codes.

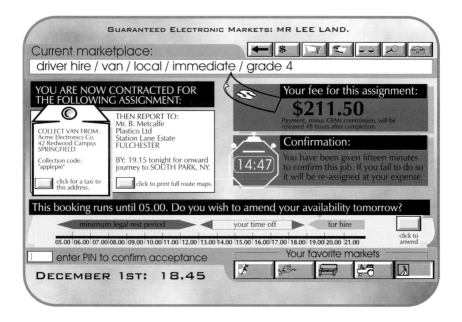

This driver would be charging a premium to be available at such short notice. He is now given only 15 minutes to enter his PIN signifying that he is on his way. Should that not happen, GEMs will re-assign the job and compensate the employer from the driver's bond. Once he has signed, GEMs might ask if he wants to book a taxi to the pick-up point: one click would then bring the nearest available, best value cab to his door with the destination already displayed on the driver's dashboard panel and the fare transferred automatically into escrow. Assuming the journey passes without incident, payment would go across to the taxi man the following evening. Before the van driver leaves home, however, GEMs is looking ahead to his next booking and asking if he wants to adjust tomorrow's availability in the light of tonight's income and hours on the road.

5

Contractual
chains

Although taking less than a minute, the process for hiring a van and engaging someone to drive it just described would be unnecessarily arduous. It would be far quicker to access a GEMs template for 'van and driver hire' which could calculate the combined costs and arrival times of multiple options for van and driver, then allow the chosen package to be bought with one PIN entry, both payments going into escrow separately so any link in the chain can become the subject of a complaint. GEMs could memorize its users regularly used settings. If a company makes regular deliveries from their factory to a customer depot utilizing drivers of the same grade, it should take less than half a dozen clicks to have fully a qualified worker and vehicle ready for a long journey at the factory gate in 20 minutes. Both would have come from a widening, competitive, informed marketplace and be contracted for exactly the company's requirements at that moment.

A firm that had used this facility for occasional out of hours emergencies when their own delivery fleet was overtaxed might begin to see advantages in arranging the ebb and flow of daily transport arrangements through GEMs instead of relying on a dedicated fleet and employees. Staff drivers, too, may decide they could have a better life if self-employed and selling their services in GEMs to a pool of buyers, accumulating a trading record while using market overviews to price themselves into desired opportunities. Further potential of this new way of working will be examined in later chapters.

More complex packages

The van and driver scenario demonstrates a basic, two link, contractual chain: GEMs could construct a far more complex series of commitments. Preparing a funeral could be one example. A 'When Someone Dies' template would examine the availability and pricing of a sequence of provenly competent local traders in the funeral business who were selling their time on the system, then assemble a timetable and overall price for a buyer's particular needs. Once contracted, each individual is then responsible for vouchsafing the work of their immediate predecessor in the chain. So, a qualified mortuary assistant collects the deceased and delivers them to a chapel of rest that has availability for sale in GEMs, later a freelance undertaker lays out the body and confirms to GEMs he has completed his tasks in the period he had originally offered. When the embalmer arrives at the chapel of rest inputting her PIN signature not only attests that her job is done but also that she found the body ready for her ministrations. If not, she would instigate a complaint procedure: if the dispute was not immediately resolved GEMs would use the undertaker's bond to hire a replacement, extend the timetable if necessary and compensate the buyer. Later judgement by a funeral trades body would rule on whether the undertaker or the embalmer was in the wrong and bonds would be rearranged accordingly. It is a complex process with multiple layers of protection built in, but as ever with GEMs, it would be presented to each user in a very simple display of their best options at the time.

Only traders who could prove insurance cover sufficient to reconstruct the whole chain, should they default, would be offered in a template. Insurers are likely to demand a credible track record of bookings before providing such cover, so templates will naturally assemble their components from middle to high grade traders. Families who wish to use less-experienced, cheaper providers would be able to bypass this template and make individual bookings, but they would be responsible for ensuring that each stage was completed satisfactorily. Equally, they could choose to buy all their needs from one full-service funeral company. GEMs has no bias for or against particular kinds of business; it is interested only in the best value for each individual enquiry. However, it is unlikely that a company constructing off-the-peg funeral deals from a small number of employees and facilities, then adding their own overheads and mark-up, could match the prices constructed by GEMs from its pool of informed, infinitely flexible individuals in a personalized chain.

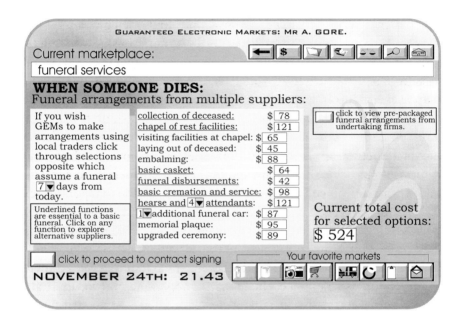

Would grieving relatives be in the frame of mind to want to turn to their interactive television and then point and click to make a loved one's final arrangements? When the telephone first appeared it was widely derided as a device for 'nattering shop-girls'. Now of course it is used unquestioningly for even the most important arrangements. The device's sheer usefulness has made it emotionally and culturally neutral. If GEMs could match that reliability and convenience, it could lead to a population pointing and clicking their way to a far wider range of goods and services than is currently envisaged. Its appeal is, not least, that customers will be hiring providers who are decentralized, working for themselves, and each treasuring a trading record of continuing good faith, even among clients who may not be a ready source of repeat business.

Other GEMs templates might include screens that construct entire journeys, from availability offered by train, long-haul bus and taxi companies, to move a GEMs user from one precise postal code to another at the times of their choice. A separate codeword printed or copied on to a piece of paper would constitute a prepaid ticket for each segment. Should the first leg, say on a train, be delayed beyond the 20 minutes specified in the contract and as a result the traveller misses his coach connection, then the train company's bond is used to finance automatically re-booked legs of bus and taxi travel and, of course, to fund nominal compensation to all passengers. In industry a manufacturer with spare capacity on their bottling line could hire it out in GEMs, specifying which of their staff were required to make it operational. GEMs would then parcel up the line's availability with their staff's individual pricing formulae and raw materials as specified, thus enabling another drinks maker to investigate availability and costs for his excess production requirements. GEMs could enable holidaymakers to construct their own package from flights, rooms, transfers and representatives' services. Like inclusive funeral arrangements, complete package tours could still be offered in this market, of course, and when they fitted a user's requirements they would be put forward as an option, but they would be a blunt way for providers to trade in such a sophisticated marketplace. Instead, tour companies might enter a details sheet and pricing formula for each room in a hotel or each seat and level of service on a flight. No longer need mass market tourists be charged the same for a room overlooking the bins as for a panoramic view just because none of the dozens of tour company sales channels warrants the detailed programming for more precise marketing.

chapter

6

Easy access
to capital

A public markets system would allow users to lend and borrow money without incurring the overheads of a financial institution, or the fragmenting of the marketplace for capital under multiple sales channels. The GEM for loans would be an anomaly within the system, the only market in which one user could be in danger of defaulting on another. Elsewhere, contracts cannot be signed unless funds are available to go into escrow. GEMs' commitment to guaranteed trading precludes the uncertainties of debt chains or potentially defaulting creditors. Users without reserve funds of their own would need to turn to the loans market, where lenders decide the level of risk they are willing to assume. Once again the matching between suppliers and purchasers is of fine 'granularity': a typical transaction might involve lending $100 for a week.

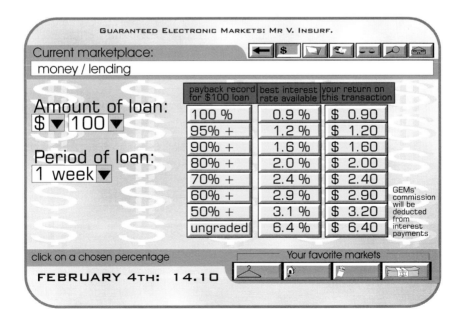

Here, the lender is being asked to select the grade of borrower with whom he is willing to sign a contract for the loan of his $100. GEMs would compile a borrower's payback record on past loans. Someone who regularly needs $100 or more to tide them over the last week of the month, and just as reliably transfers the money plus interest back on time, will start to build a payback record for that sum in the 95 per cent plus range. This enables them to access ever cheaper money, reaching a point where the continued value of their rating outweighs any short-term gains from non-fulfilment of an individual loan. Cash providers with an appetite for risk can opt for higher-return, lower-grade, borrowers who are still climbing this ladder, but are then more likely to find themselves pursuing their claim through the courts at payback time. Details of the borrower would be revealed by GEMs once a contract is signed. It may often be that one user is borrowing large sums and entering into qualified agreements simultaneously with dozens of lenders, or that the $100 is split between five users each needing $20 and backed by the selected credit rating. Matches do not have to be one to one.

Borrowers with a 100 per cent grading qualify for 'automatic rescheduling' and have clicked for that option. If there is not $100 plus interest in their account on the day for payback GEMs will automatically take out an ungraded loan in their name to pay off the debt. They would have longer to pay off the new liability, but at much higher interest, and their credit rating will be scaled down thereafter. Alternatively, one user can be underwritten by another, an indulgent parent perhaps. In that case, the borrower would attain instant 100 per cent status because GEMs has been authorised to deduct any unpaid accounts from the parental bond.

There is no human input to the process of setting interest rates. Instead the computer assesses demand and supply for each grade of borrower from second to second and calculates the ever-changing figure that will generate maximum turnover. Alternatively, a borrower, for example, can specify the rate they will pay and see if they obtain a match but they are likely then to be either beached below the day's trading range or paying over the market rate to a lucky seller. This forum, as accessible to major institutions with millions to lend as to thrifty 6-year-olds with their weekly allowance to invest, would obviously be influenced by the country's official exchange rate and global demand for its currency. But its spread between lending and borrowing rates, representing only GEMs' tiny commission, should undercut anything available in the outside economy. Additionally, users should find significant liquidity, responsiveness and equilibrating market overview information.

A flexible money market

Much of the time GEMs users were harnessing the system's capital markets they might not be aware they are so doing. The couple signing a contract for overnight accommodation earlier in this section, for instance, had to put down a $100 deposit. It may have been that those funds were not available in their account, so GEMs borrowed the sum automatically for 48 hours on an 'automatic rescheduling' basis building the interest into the room cost it constructed for them. The sum would then be returned, without any involvement on the users' part, two days later. Similarly suppliers who cannot wait for money owed to come out of escrow can click to try selling their unpaid debts in the loans market. If they can attach a solid trading record with no previous freezing of payments they should be able to receive immediately 98 per cent or more of the money due. Days later GEMs would transfer the funds leaving escrow to the debt purchaser. 'Autotrade' functions could further feed the cash pool; for instance a user telling GEMs that every time her bank account exceeded $300 credit the surplus was to be instantly invested in $50 blocks for two weeks as long as the interest rate is 2 per cent or more. The less well off might instruct GEMs to assemble an automatic overdraft at the best rate for which they qualified, once their resources dipped below a certain level. Pressure in the market-place should quickly limit any drift towards excessive debt because their trading record would indicate such a degree of risk that only the highest rate money would remain available.

This beguiling process for 'vanilla' loans would be the bedrock of a financial exchange which might cautiously develop a range of instruments for users. In time the system might be able to parcel serial loans together into seamless debt for house purchasing. Authorized lawyers would hold deeds as collateral for non-payment. Templates for futures contracts in which one party constructs the deal of their choice, backed up by a contract, and awaits any takers could be offered. So too could long-term funding agreements, enabling pensions to be accumulated according to an individual's requirements. Financial services companies would, as ever, be welcome to trade in the GEMs money market and, initially at least, could find a niche acting as 100 per cent borrowers then lending back at a higher rate to unproven users lower down the credit rating ladder. However, as swelling numbers of ordinary borrowers attained the proven solidity that ensures eligibility for the 100 per cent 'automatic rescheduling' option, and with confidence in the market building, as bad debtors were mechanically evicted, the financial companies would probably find their overheads, and comparative inefficiency, made them uncompetitive. GEMs should de-brand the flow of money, turning capital into the atomized commodity that a truly inclusive digital economy requires.

7 Would populations start to use a GEMs system?

Public electronic markets would be particularly vulnerable to the law of network externalities: the more who use the system, the more valuable the service to each of them becomes. Starting with only a handful of sectors and growing to the scale of operation outlined in this section, GEMs' need for secure trades in an open market would demand its users follow procedures that are going to be unfamiliar to most and daunting to some. A cultural leap would be needed to take computer issued codewords from their currently rarefied status in, for instance, ticketless business travel to routine use between neighbours hiring each other's lawnmowers. Likewise, we are so used to entering into unstated webs of contractual protection, and shrugging off their periodic failures, that signing a written contract for transactions as small as buying a second-hand music CD then engaging a teenager to cycle round and deliver it could seem frighteningly formal.

New infrastructure always imposes unfamiliar requirements on users: early adopters of the telephone struggled to attach a string of digits to each acquaintance. Cashpoint machines required widespread use of PINs. This unprecedented need for users to hold a number in their memory did nothing to stop take up of cash cards far exceeding original projections. In the case of GEMs, would the inconveniences of registration and adjustment to alien procedures be offset by the benefits from the fledgling system? Anyone shopping in GEMs could escape the cacophony of promotional offers, loyalty schemes, spurious discounts, relationship marketing, loss leaders and bundled merchandise through which we must currently pursue value for our needs. New efficiencies in online technology presage a sharp increase in this blizzard of information which shopping software will be able to penetrate only partially.[2] In contrast, the GEMs buyer compares like with like, gets the best deal available at once and then knows it will be ruthlessly enforced. More appealing still, he escapes the costs inherent in sellers making themselves heard in an uncoordinated marketplace. Gone too is the expense of fraudulent traders, levied on prices generally in the non-GEMs trading environment but paid by a defaulting buyer or seller's bonds or deposits within the system. The sophistication of matching offers with users' enquiries in a growing any-seller-welcome marketplace should better that of any one company's sales channel or squeezed buyer–seller matching service. Facilities such as buyer's clubs (Box 7.1) would bring unique benefits to users. With this elaborate programming, masked behind friendly interfaces focusing in intuitive steps on a user's specific enquiry, buyers would be unlikely to scythe their way through competing sellers' claims in search of the outside marketplace's best deal.

Box 7.1

GEMS' BUYERS' CLUBS

Guaranteed Electronic Markets would work very much on the principle of buyer 'pull' rather than provider 'push'. The infrastructure for purchasing is passive, not set up to favour the seller's objectives as is the case in sales channels. One way this can be exploited is for geographically close purchasers of a particular commodity to be banded together by the system for bulk buys. Everyone on a particular housing estate who regularly bought Marlboro cigarettes, for instance, might be asked if they wished to join with other smokers of that brand. The system might then buy 1000 packs with pooled funds and engage someone locally to act as a point of delivery and disperse the smokes according to a printable list. Every link in the chain would be completely bonded, the deliverer could disappear with the cigarettes but as he would have had to put more than their value into bond there would be little point. More complex buyer's clubs for groceries in neighbourhoods, stationery between businesses or over-the-counter drugs for the long-term ill could be available to anyone willing to sacrifice immediate realization of the order for likely cost savings from combined purchases.

Could distrust of such a large, potentially all-knowing, central computer be an inhibitor? The world aviation industry was founded on a concept once considered unthinkable by many: hundreds of thousands of people hurtling through the air in converging tubes of thin metal, flammable fuel sloshing around on either side of them. Customers have been largely persuaded to set aside fears about the technology because everyone working for an airline is imbued with a commitment to safety procedures that becomes ingrained. The public electronic markets industry likewise would have to grow alongside unending efforts to maintain and assert its probity.

Individual market sectors could be slow to take off and might require experimentation until the right balance was found between over-easy entry and costly verification procedures that deter even the most desirable sellers. Take a highly sensitive marketplace such as childcare, for instance, in which there could be deep scepticism about an automated market. Would even a provider who had attained grade 5 or 6 in GEMs' child-minding be sufficiently trusted? To attain that level they might have had to pass examination by both police and a local government panel every 6 months of, say, a 10-year career. If that was still not sufficient, further vetting requirements would be added by the franchisee. Would personal endorsement by the child's school, at candidate's expense obviously, be sufficient? Or proof of bookings with friends of the family who had been entered as acceptable referees? Proven acceptance by a well-established agency? Or perhaps a system of mutual imprimatur whereby, say, five local baby-sitters agree to be bound by shared responsibility: if one of them is found guilty of unprofessional behaviour they all lose their bonds? Maybe a free visit to meet the parent in advance arranged by the system would tempt the ultra-cautious buyer? GEMs will always allow users to enter the lower rungs of its markets easily, in this case perhaps as mother's helpers who only work with children while a parent stays in the house. Providers can then begin to climb a ladder of increasingly profitable verification that could see top-level customers paying enormous sums because so few suppliers clear the hurdles they have demanded.

Public electronic markets have been seen by some as a potentially useful service for downscale consumers while more valuable deals could be expected to remain in less utilitarian, branded channels. It is a dangerous assumption to make, which mirrors early predictions for the phone system and cash machines. In the first case, Bell's device was seen as something for people who could not afford messenger boys: in the second, banks widely saw ATMs as a facility for the kind of customers who withdrew small amounts and were probably intimidated by a human teller. It is usefulness to users generally, not an emotional hierarchy of business, that drives long-term take up of new technology. A system that can allow van drivers to structure a career on their own terms could easily do the same for management accountants. Attractiveness to those seeking overnight accommodation suggests a similar appeal to buyers of 6-month leases on office blocks. In each case there would be a GEMs franchisee, who understood the needs of that specific market, shaping the service.

Would sellers enter such a competitive marketplace?

Sellers on GEMs would probably be self-selecting. Anyone offering genuine value and able to deliver what they promise has little to fear in this new sales regime. If company strengths are more in marketing than manufacture, with hefty margins reaped from the advantages gained, boardroom strategists need to be sure the brand will continue to merit a premium in a wider marketplace. Once GEMs were established, however, any seller choosing to exclude the system from their channels to market would be vulnerable to an upstart competitor, the GEMs-friendly newcomer having all the facilities of interlocking electronic markets with which to launch a business. Once a GEM for selling portable office buildings was written, for example, if no-one started to sell in it and if the market overview showed customers looking but not finding, an opportunist might decide to begin fabrication. He could use GEMs to find raw materials, production line capacity, workers, haulage and then, if he remains alone in the market, add a substantial mark-up to his costs. An additional danger, assuming selective distribution is not legally protected in the country of operation, is that manufacturers who baulk at the system find unwanted middlemen selling their output in the public markets. A century ago, Edison predicted that one day every going concern would have its own electricity generating division within the organization. That vision soon gave way to the efficiencies of a secure mutual supplier. There may yet come a day when competitive pressure will push companies away from the costs of maintaining and updating their own sales servers, security systems, payment mechanisms and back office functions, in favour of one independent mechanised market.

Cost of transactions has yet to emerge fully as a competitive edge in Internet buyer–seller matching services. The efficiencies of online-pairing are so far ahead of any comparable function in the world of physical commerce that services like the e-bay auction site can easily offer value with up to a 5 per cent take. However, the GEMs model could be planned from the start as a business driven by currently inconceivable volume. That was the rationale behind an equally radical development in Britain in 1839: nationwide flat-rate postage. Before that date, mail was carried using a combination of local and national stage-coach services, with charges paid by the recipient of each letter according to distance travelled and weight of missive. Outside *ad hoc* local cheap postage schemes a typical letter delivered across London cost 4 pence and a one sheet communication between the capital and Scotland around 16 pence. The campaign for a flat rate of just one penny, paid by the sender, for an envelope of less than half an ounce (14 grams) between any two points in the country was considered laughably naïve. The then Secretary of the Post Office described the plan as 'a most preposterous one, utterly unsupported by facts and resting entirely on assumption'.[3] It was an understandable assessment in the market conditions of the time, given that few people could read or write and fewer still knew anyone outside their locality. Once realised, however, penny postage fully justified all the unsupported assumptions underlying its business model. It sparked an explosion of literacy as workers began to move away from home knowing they could now keep in touch. It took only 14 years for the new mass service to become more profitable than all the old postage schemes combined, a short time indeed given the relatively slow pace of Victorian business cycles.[4] It is possible that what could appear an absurdly cheap GEMs commission rate could induce individuals and firms to trade in ways that can scarcely be imagined until e-trade is truly commoditized: an eventual system might deduct as little as 0.25 per cent of each deal.

GEMs would have their limitations, of course. As a dumb utility, restricted by law to core functions and with no exploitable customer knowledge, the central computer could not advise users which new books they might enjoy, or pass them to an online consultant to help shape hazy requirements, nor send e-mail to remind husbands when it is time to buy their partners birthday flowers. (There would of course be nothing to stop GEMs users subscribing to any number of companies that provided these facilities.) Similar objections about low levels of service were made by opponents of penny postage. They pointed out that in the patchwork postage market a sender could in effect tell the deliverer 'if the recipient of my letter is not in, you'll find her at her friend's house with blue curtains further down the street or try the shop next door'. Replacing this customer-friendly flexibility with tightly timetabled operatives who would simply shove mail through a hole in the door, which householders would have to cut for the purpose, appeared retrograde to many.[5] But they had failed to appreciate the extent to which populations were ready to move beyond a confusing, often irritating and cost-heavy process into an environment where sending a letter was an untaxing mundanity. For postage in the 1840s, perhaps, read buying and selling in the 2000s?

Notes to section one

1. *The Glory of the Geeks*, Channel 4 Television, (UK) 3 October 1998, Programme 3 of 3.
2. Powerful retailers, for example, are learning how to block automated enquiries by coding price displays in ways that software cannot read or bundling goods so true prices cannot be ascertained. (Shopbots – Friend or Foe? *Information Strategy*, July/August 1998, p. 42.)
3. Douglas N. Muir, *Postal Reform and The Penny Black: a New Appreciation*, The National Postal Museum, 1990, p. 50.
4. Ibid. p. 181.
5. Colin G. Hey, *Rowland Hill: Genius and Benefactor*, Quiller Press, 1989, p. 69.

A new democratic capitalism: the impact of public electronic markets

8 The effect of GEMs on business: a decline in big institutions

It was a surreal morning, even for hardened financial journalists. On Easter Monday 1998, Wall Street opinion formers were invited to the opulent Hilton banquet room at Manhattan's Waldorf-Astoria to be told that Nations Bank was merging with BankAmerica to form the largest bank in the US. 'Bigger is indeed better' a beaming head of Nations Bank told the press conference.[1] Two hours later the financial commentators trooped back to the same building's Empire banquet hall to learn that First Chicago and Banc One had followed suit, creating the continent's fifth largest bank. Both mergers were explained in terms of advantages of size in a globalizing economy and economies of scale: BankAmerica and Nations Bank announced plans to shed between 5000 and 8000 jobs within two years of fusing. The creation of megabanks represents one part of a long historical trend in business: the need to be big. Factories and centralized distribution facilities in the Industrial Revolution spawned big business. Craft-based worker alliances then metamorphosed into big union power as an essential counterweight. When the weaknesses of those antagonistic forces were painfully revealed in the depression years, big government emerged to provide a safety net.

The trend towards 'bigness' is being accelerated in surprising industries as we move to an online economy. An oil company's optimum size is obviously large; it requires hugely expensive installations and worldwide operations, but there are no comparable physical factors in the drive towards big accountancy. The big eight companies did not become the big six, en route to becoming the big four or fewer, to maximize their usage of desks, telephones and chairs. They are melding not least because a crucial currency in the online uncoordinated market is 'mindshare'. By being big you offer the reassurance of a widely recognized brand name. The possibility of becoming a 'one stop shop' for global-izing clients can then be staked on this, widening the range of services to include, for instance, consultancy within your all-important brand values. Under this philosophy, once humble banks are expanding into big finance offering, for instance, stockbroking and insurance services to exploit the flexibility that comes with their size. There is an argument often raised about the Internet asserting that it creates 'a level playing field' in which small players can easily challenge the big boys. In reality, establishing an upstart brand to entice customers away from entrenched and – when they get it right – massively efficient corporations on any appreciable scale is so costly that few will attempt it. Consumers do not use the Net to constantly shop around for new suppliers to meet their every need. They prefer a simple life. Industries based on human resources, which might have been thrown open to diversified players by the digital economy, are evolving into the kind of battle between titans reminiscent of the motor industry, with its need for participants to possess a gargantuan asset base. It is hard to see how customers benefit, except in the sense that it helps them navigate an otherwise bewildering marketplace. There is little evidence it brings lower prices. In 1998, for example, The Federal Reserve reported US banks' net interest margin between lending rates and borrowing costs had widened from around 3.5 per cent in the mid 1970s to 4.3 per cent, despite waves of mergers in that time.[2] 'As these banks get bigger, they'll get more confident that they can get away with [increased] fees, because they'll have such a large captive customer base' commented a spokesman for the US Public Research Group.[3] It was a point not explicitly raised in either presenta-tion at the Waldorf-Astoria.

The pursuit of bigness has had its critics of course. A former economic adviser to the British National Coal Board, E.F. Schumacher published *Small is Beautiful: A Study of Economics as if People Mattered* in 1973. In it he suggested smaller units of work and production could be both more productive and more rewarding for participants than large unified organizations. His message was not without its detractors. During subsequent tours of the USA, Schumacher was provided with police protection because of threats, deemed serious, from 'pro-busi-ness' groups.[4] But even those who supported his analysis and sought to apply it to the developed world came up against an unarguable reality: in the uncoordinated marketplace capital can usually be more effectively accessed and exploited by a large firm than by small traders. As money continues to acquire a newly aggressive mobility from digital transmission and the imperatives of big finance, human considerations are in many cases receding even further.

A Guaranteed Electronic Markets system would reverse this situation, making small units not only more humane but, crucially, more economically efficient than large corporations. Banking is not a useful example: GEMs could render banks, big or small, largely irrelevant in the core area of straightforward lending. Instead, consider as an illustration the market for long-distance bus travel in the UK. It is a sector dominated by large providers, notably the Stagecoach group. Dominance in routes, numbers of drivers employed and vehicles owned bodes well for their future in the uncoordinated online marketplace. With high brand name recognition and corresponding 'mindshare' their Internet or interactive television page will be a logical first stop for anyone wanting to travel from say Cardiff to Liverpool. As Stagecoach takes in details of individuals' travel requirements and pricing sensitivities it can start to make them personalized offers while building an increasingly sophisticated database of patterns in demand. This likely growth in business will be combined with enhanced efficiencies in driver rostering and vehicle utilisation across the organization. As long as adequate standards of service are maintained, the sheer size of Stagecoach creates an escalating barrier to entry for competitors.

Now consider a typical coach operator that might trade in a public electronic markets system. Three qualified drivers in Cardiff could band together and, given easy access to capital by GEMs' loans market, lease a 52-seater which they take in turns to drive on a self-employed basis. Each buys bus station slots and sells seats in GEMs, perhaps using market overview information to see which routes out of their hometown are likely to offer the best returns. On a typical day one of them might depart from Cardiff at 6.00 a.m. on a run to Liverpool, returning 8 hours later for the second man to operate a late afternoon service to Holyhead, returning in time for driver number three to operate his overnight journey to London. They do not need the resources of a big organization for flexibility. If one of them is ill one day he can hire his replacement in the appropriate GEM. If a problem with the vehicle makes a journey impossible, they can turn to the bus hire marketplace. Were only ten seats to be sold on one of their departures they might hire a minibus that provides the levels of comfort stipulated in that contract and rent out their own vehicle for those eight hours. Because they are trading on a GEMs contract with money in bond as potential compensation, they do not need a brand name to reassure potential customers (Box 8.1).

Box 8.1

CUMULATIVE CONTRACTS

GEMs could aggregate contracts of purchasers in case of supplier default. This would provide a level of customer assurance well beyond anything offered by a brand name. If a self-employed bus driver, for instance, operates a service that is late departing or with a vehicle in unacceptable condition a number of passengers are likely to call up their contracts for that journey and initiate a complaint. If the driver accepts culpability, or is found in fault after arbitration by the panel for long-distance bus travel, all the passengers automatically have an amount in compensation transferred from his bond to their accounts. The underlying principle is that the driver is held personally responsible to each passenger.

In this environment Stagecoach would be disadvantaged. They are obviously free to list their departures and sell seats in the GEMs travel market but their prices will carry marketing, scheduling and central office overheads for which smaller operators have no need. Nor are their centralized decision-making processes likely to rival local busmen who can respond to immediate market conditions with new routes, times and prices, on a weekly basis if they wish. This eclipse of Stagecoach would not be a temporary phenomenon awaiting the emergence of a new big player but a lasting consequence of a diversified marketplace. However successful the three drivers in Cardiff were to be, they would find it hard to build an extended empire of owned vehicles and employed drivers in this new era. There would be no market advantages to being big, just additional costs. Instead of aspiring to size they might look to market diversification for more profitable opportunities: trading up to a more luxurious bus perhaps, or starting to offer week-long tours of North Wales.

Would large scale manufacturers retain the current benefits of their size? The advantages of bulk buying of ingredients or components are likely to be minimized in a truly efficient, more fluid marketplace. Additionally, the market for distribution would now be both decentralized and probably more active, so the benefits of a fleet of vehicles and warehousing agreements disappear. GEMs would be driven largely by consumer pull. A buyer's club on the system seeking, perhaps, 500 1 kg boxes of cornflakes with no brand specified would have delivery costs automatically factored in, when shopping for the best deal. That is inevitably going to favour more dispersed manufacture: the advantages centralized companies enjoyed in the producer push model of grocery distribution would have evaporated. The quality levels required for cornflakes would be contained in a cumulative contract with all purchasers, any maker who cleared those levels would no longer need bigness to create consumer awareness: buyers would find him regardless (Box 8.2).

Box 8.2

SETTING MINIMUM STANDARDS FOR GEMS TRADES

A criticism sometimes made of GEMs is that they would hand control of market standards over to the operating consortium who could then make or break sellers with their stipulations. It is true that GEMs' franchisees would need to establish quality levels in their sectors: someone would have to decide for instance what is the legal definition of a cornflake, otherwise all sorts of cereal by-products could be marketed as cornflakes. Setting those definitions would obviously rest on existing consumer law where available. Where there are no existing statutes and customers have previously relied on brand name trust for a fair deal, GEMs will have to originate a definition. This would be crafted not with an eye to positioning GEMs as an arbiter of food standards but simply to grow that market. What paragraph of legalese will define a cornflake acceptable to shoppers but not so daunting to manufacturers that no seller will want to comply with the definition? Shoppers of course need not spare a thought for this complex contractual small print. They could take it for granted that GEMs will satisfy their basic expectation of a cornflake as much as could Kellogg's or Nabisco. The system could not, however, guarantee the distinctive taste of a known brand. Although there will be shoppers who will trade down in this wider marketplace, it should not signal a death knell for distinctive and well-marketed products that could, of course, also be sold on the system if the makers wished.

This economic model, based on ever-changing, easy-to-enter markets would move a country closer to the vision of thinkers like Adam Smith and Friedrich von Hayek who defined capitalism. By making the buyer truly sovereign it should promote flexibility and bring increasing resources to market. In 1776 Smith himself wrote 'people of the same trade seldom meet together, even for merriment and diversion, but the conversation ends in a conspiracy against the public, or in some contrivance to raise prices'.[5] Public electronic markets would do much to end an era where a key aim of so many enterprises has been to achieve the scale necessary to manipulate their market. As huge opposing forces give way to competition among millions of individual protagonists trading in a near perfect market competitiveness, stability and efficiency should all increase. It is the 'snowballing' effect of this trend, sweeping through sector after sector, that can make the truly atomized, post-GEMs economy so difficult to envisage from our current perspective.

chapter

9 GEMs and employment: the rise of portfolio working

A database enigmatically named Monster Board is currently the Internet's most popular means of finding work.[6] Its twin pools of job seekers and job openings are diluted by dozens of rival marketplaces; nevertheless, it is indisputably useful, attracting nearly two million visitors a month. But the service it performs – matching employers and candidates – is becoming an anachronism. The world is drifting inexorably towards fragmented employment, with individuals shouldering the costs and time required to find work and then juggling any competing requirements. An online facility for putting the two sides together in this ever-splintering marketplace would have to be far more exacting than any existing job matching service. PeopleBank, the UK Internet employment matching service offers probably the most sophisticated programming for matching employers and potential workers but, even so, does not foresee a future trading in short-term work contracts as a low-cost automated service.[7] 'I couldn't see us getting into temporary work placements unless it was with the involvement of a major agency', says Bill Shipton, MD of PeopleBank, 'the administration and vetting would be too complex'.[8] Guaranteed Electronic Markets could of course crack this problem and embrace the new reality of work, offering increased stability for an evolving workforce. Fifty years ago it was firms who largely absorbed the risks and cycles of business, shielding employees from the ravages of each downturn. In today's marketplace, profitability frequently survives a slowdown in demand: it is the workforce who immediately suffer the consequences. Individuals seeking a flow of customers for their services, rather than the erstwhile security of life on a single payroll, is the way of the future.

GEMs would trade periods of work like any other commodity, using the mechanisms already illustrated to enforce each deal. A window

cleaner could be hired for 15 minutes with only a few more clicks
required to engage an experienced management consultant for two
weeks. Both individuals would have to prove any qualifications necessary for that market and be able to display their past trading record,
with identifying details removed, to prospective hirers. Each could use a
pricing formula to prioritize the opportunities they sought. Payment
would be through the system, allowing everyone involved to enjoy accu-
rate diary keeping, accounting and issuing of contracts. With end-to-end
automation of the drudgery of finding work, the need for one main
employer, or even a specialized profession, would disappear for many.
British management theorist, Charles Handy, pioneered the concept of
'portfolio working' in which individuals construct a customized range of
part-time jobs that together build a discernible career path. With
GEMs, that attractive option, already easily available to a $150 000-a-
year high flier, would come within reach of a blue-collar worker
surviving on a tenth of those earnings. For example: a typical week's
diary for a 25-year-old male working sometimes as a window cleaner but
also as a car mechanic and general cleaner might look like this.

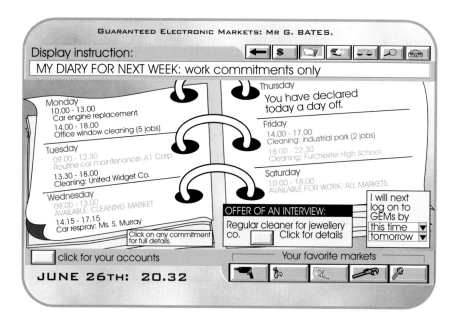

Every GEMs user would be offered a diary from which blocks of time can be sold. A business version, trading assignments for a musical instrument repair company maybe, would be far more complex than the illustration above. The bookings in black on this diary are confirmed, automatically accepted by GEMs because they fall within the user's availability and pricing as currently defined. Periods of work in grey are offers still available for which he qualifies but which require approval because the hours or compensation are outside his formula. The cleaning work on Friday for instance is being offered by an educational establishment that regularly needs three operatives for an evening at the end of each week. Instead of taking on permanent staff, they have a pool of ten local cleaners who understand the building and are regularly given work. GEMs offers contracts from the school in randomized order to all ten: the first three to sign, or automatically accept, are rostered. More hierarchically minded employers could choose to rate their approved workers. GEMs would then offer jobs to the most favoured first, descending down the list if they are not available. The offer of an interview at the bottom of his screen demonstrates how GEMs might replace the hunt through classified adverts for its users seeking new openings. A local jewellers could be looking for someone to join its roster of cleaners and has told GEMs to contact individuals with more than 1000 hours experience in that market, living within a

---

Box 9.1

GETTING PRE-GEMS ACCOMPLISHMENTS RECOGNIZED BY THE SYSTEM

A public markets system could very simply capture a true record of a user's past bookings. However, there would have to be a transition period in the early days of the system, when people who had perhaps been office cleaning for years wanted to sell their time on the system but understandably did not feel comfortable about joining in a starter grade. The solution owes more to the 'old world' of imperfect judgments than the new order on GEMs. It would involve traders paying the adjudication panel for that market to review their resumé, references and maybe tax statements or bank accounts and to assign a grade that would have been achieved had the bookings been through GEMs. These awards, which could never match the concrete standards demanded by the system, might be flagged to potential buyers: GEMs bookings in black, for instance, calculated previous bookings in grey.

mile of their depot. They specified five applicants be interviewed for the post at times compatible to both diaries. If the system does not get five qualified interview acceptances within a mile after two days it has been authorized to extend the range to two miles and so on until the desired number of pre-screened locals are scheduled for a meeting in the manager's office (Box 9.1).

Anyone hiring themselves out in this way would have to bear occasional costs that might previously have been carried by an agency or employer. If the worker above were to fall ill and be unable to fulfil his commitment to visit an individual's garage and change his engine on Monday morning, for example, he would call up that contract and click 'I can no longer complete this obligation'. GEMs would re-assign the task to the next available trader who most closely matched the car owner's original requirements, trading up the grades rather than down for customer peace of mind. Additional costs would be met from the defaulting worker's bond. Corporate employers, too, would have to be compensated with a potentially higher grade operative to replace an ill contractor. It would be an unusual convention for workers to pay for the cost of their replacement in cases where they were not at fault but a reliable automated market can only work if each trader carries total responsibility for every commitment into which they enter. Users who feared illness would of course be able to insure against costs of their replacement. They could certainly console themselves by comparing the flexibility and low overheads of GEMs trading against overhead ridden agency work or staff employment.

Widespread portfolio working would realize a holy grail of international competitiveness: a fully adaptable and responsive workforce. In a world of monolithic employers this has to be achieved largely by weakening employee protection. With momentum in a public markets system the workers would have as much to gain from new-found pliancy as their former masters. Fresh opportunities can be painlessly sought, for instance. The window cleaner/mechanic/school cleaner might actually dream of life as a ski instructor. Equipped with PIN evidence of the required qualification and an increased bond he can start to price himself into occasional work for individuals seeking basic instruction at nearby slopes. He might chose to make his trading record of reliability in current markets available to prospective customers knowing that new on-piste bookings will similarly mount up allowing him to climb an additional set of grades. He would have every reason to diversify like this rather than spend a life majoring in window cleaning. The top grade in a household services market would probably be attained after 5000 hours of bookings. It is hard to envisage a home-owner so punctilious as to pay a further premium for a window cleaner with, say, 10000 hours of window cleaning behind them. The trader with 5000 hours would have every incentive to parlay them into new and more lucrative markets.

Of course there is no reason why an individual's work diary should not be blocked out to one employer. GEMs would be equally helpful to seekers of long-term posts. An experienced production line controller, for instance, might release her trading record into the GEM for senior factory personnel and set a salary formula that would make her attractive to manufacturers in areas which she wished to live. As soon as a potential match with a prospective employer was found the system would schedule an interview at a time when both had specified availability in their diary. Even if offered a five year contract the production controller may ask that GEMs remain an intermediary in their agreement. By signing the system's contract for factory personnel rather than the company's document she would be assured of an impartial framework that was in use across the country. By utilizing her diary on the system for rostering she would be assured that all conditions in her contract about hours of work, periods of leave, even levels of support staff on duty during her shifts were adhered to. GEMs would not allow managers to roster her beyond the levels allowed in that initial agreement. Payment would be calculated according to the contract, independently of management, then transferred to her account. The employer could not trade in GEMs without a bond, part of which could be frozen awaiting outside adjudication if she had a dispute about conditions or remuneration.

If the manufacturer planned to be a reliable employer they would have much to gain from hiring and then rostering all staff on GEMs. Automatically compiled trading records in a mature system would be more reliable than potential candidates' resumés for instance: a US study has found that a third of job applicants lie about their backgrounds.[9] It is a problem that the uncoordinated market in Internet job matching simply moves online. 'I don't see how we could ever get into verifying [career resumés] and make it financially viable', says People-Bank's Shipton. In return for GEMs' infinitesimal commission on salaries, however, employers would be certain they were hiring the level of experience and previous employer satisfaction claimed. As part of a government's package to enable GEMs, education authorities could provide PINs to accompany individual exam grades, perhaps for an additional fee. Subjective achievements, samples of past work by an advertising copywriter for instance, could be loaded on to an individual's details page to be bound into any contract they sign. Any lack of veracity is then a legal offence with no confusion possible about which work the employee had claimed to have created.

Employers would also be relieved of the need to administer payroll, holiday scheduling or sickness cover. Audit costs should disappear: their tamper-proof accounts on the system would show who had been paid what and when. A factory handling human resources this way, for instance, might decide to replace centrally imposed duty rotas with market-based rostering, in which workers actively trade their daily willingness to work. Approved members of staff could each set a pricing formula and GEMs would buy their time to construct the cheapest possible timetables of cover, based on required grades of staffing. White and blue-collar workers could then increase their rates for unpopular periods while charging less for more convivial shifts. Anyone tempted to form a cartel with their colleagues and push up prices may need to be reminded how easily a GEMs-empowered manager could increase his pool of available employees and how attractive those positions would look if market overview screens are showing generous rates being paid.

Employers already geared towards part-time workers would have every incentive to trade likewise. A teenage burger flipper, once authenticated with a PIN from his local McDonalds or Burger King might input availability to them alongside his willingness to serve in half a dozen other markets. GEMs then follows his pricing formula to construct a diary of commitments that might lead to increasing amounts of time spent, perhaps, in storeroom work for local warehouses, rather than in ketchup application. Why should the burger boss choose to hire his front-line staff this way instead of tying them to rigidly timetabled weeks that suit his average business flows? First, he gains flexibility: by training then approving a larger pool of workers he can change his requirements from day to day without the delay in feeding new workers into his system or the awkwardness of disengaging them during temporary downturns. Wages also become more competitive among a thick market of licensed employees in which any absenteeism is sorted out by the defaulter. No longer need the manager fear epidemics of calling in sick on unexpectedly fine weekends, for example. Each of the sun seekers would automatically finance their own replacement from his pool of employees. Second, he gains a motivated workforce. The individuals who report for duty are there because burger assembly is the best available job for them that day in a wide-open market of multiple opportunities, not because their dreams of stumbling across something better in the uncoordinated marketplace have yet to be fulfilled.

It would be up to government how ruthless this market for work was allowed to become. Can employers in sought-after sectors drop rates to the minimum needed to maintain a required level of workers? Are individuals with qualifications in scarce supply permitted to resign and seek better-paid jobs week after week? Or are minimum wage levels and contract completion enshrined in law to dampen swings in the market? These are political decisions, outside the remit of GEMs which neutrally enforces any legal restrictions. There would, however, be some factors unique to Guaranteed Markets which need to be decided: how punitive the system is on traders who accumulate complaints, for instance. If a carpet layer trading in grade five of that market has a complaint against him upheld after 4000 hours of flawless assignments, does that sit permanently on his trading record, a handicap for years to come, or does it become spent at some point? The answer stems not from ideology but from the GEMs' consortium's overweening need to earn back its huge investment in building the system. In other words: what balance does a franchisee need to strike between unquestioning faith in his market by buyers and the need to remain attractive to sellers if market turnover is to be maximized? It may be that the carpet fitter is automatically given a chance to have the complaint expunged if he will agree to having 500 hours wiped from his record, thereby dropping a grade. Even while cursing the professional panel that found him in the wrong after a publicly accountable adjudication process, he might find solace in the fact that the response of GEMs itself is fully automated. The scale of sanctions for particular offences in any market could be published openly: unlike employers or agencies the system can not be ageist, racist, homophobic, religiously prejudiced or misogynist. It is simply programmed to grow the market. There would, however, be discrimination between professions and grades, recognizing the differing seriousness of unprofessional behavior. An entry level hairdresser who inadvertently applied too much perming fluid to one of her GEMs clients would be treated more leniently on the system's scale of sanctions than a grade five childminder judged to have left her charge alone in the house.

A new market in local services

To be fully useful to its clients GEMs would need to create new categories of employment. Individuals who deliver goods traded on the system around their area are one example. Anyone hiring a child's paddling pool on a sunny afternoon maybe, or a video game console for a rainy weekend or a scientific calculator to finish a college assignment could well find the best possible deal came from a nearby household. They could choose to collect the item but would be more likely to click for 'include delivery in price'. GEMs would not of course employ people to do these deliveries, or decide who provides the service. The consortium simply sees that a 'local deliveries' market is written with all the back-up of any other Guaranteed Electronic Market. Individual traders can then define their area, rates for different journey lengths and particular times of day. The competitiveness of this pricing formula would determine how much they work. For small goods, some of the work might go to teenagers with a carry rack behind their bicycle saddle: higher levels of the market would demand proof of a driving licence and currently insured vehicle. Anyone who was providing this service may choose to sell additionally in other local markets such as taxi journeys. Given the short notice with which most bookings would arrive, they may eventually opt for a simplified GEMs terminal on their vehicle dashboard; using this they could constantly vary their prices, increasing them perhaps on days when market overview showed a paucity of competitors willing to trade. They could also allow GEMs to price them into a logical pattern of trips. If they have won a trip from town A to town B, for example, they could then automatically undercut all other players for a fare or delivery from B back to A. All their obligations would be displayed in a diary broken down minute by minute using GEMs' estimates of their journey times. They could obviously override their automatic diary at any point. Full-time traders in this market may chose to paint their vehicle with the name of their area in a bid to persuade GEMs shoppers to tell their user questionnaire which individual was to be their first choice for all neighbourhood delivery jobs. As these localized traders criss-crossed their patch they could become a vital component in an intangible community spirit, unlike the effect of fleets of vans from UPS, FedEx or TNT delivering from remote depots.

Another market would provide for 'holders': individuals who look after goods for their neighbours. Someone renting out a vacuum cleaner for the 99 per cent of the time it had previously idled in the cupboard under the stairs, for instance, may not want to have to keep track of a GEMs diary of commitments and be constantly answering the door to their new-found customers. They might deposit the machine, together with any other household assets for which market overview screens were showing local demand, with a nearby pensioner who undertook to remain at home and handle the mechanics of letting. GEMs would insert hirings for the cleaner in his diary and construct a contractual chain for each booking that automatically deducted his stipulated percentage. A combination of 'holders' and deliverers could solve the problems that dog home delivery in the uncoordinated online market-place. While someone currently ordering a parcel of clothes from an Internet site usually needs to be in for their arrival, GEMs would effortlessly route delivery to a nearby holder who signs for acceptance. The purchaser could then click 'deliver now' when she arrived home. Anyone entering the 'holder' market with a capacious freezer could cash in on grocery deliveries, perhaps breaking up loads bought by a neighbourhood buyers' club. Once again, all stages in the contractual chain would be bonded, individually competitive and subject to prompt arbitration in case of dispute.

The rise of sole traders

In the 1940s in the USSR Joseph Stalin turned a blind eye to limited decollectivisation of agriculture, allowing transfer of land from large state enterprises to individual holdings. Painfully, a generation of Soviet planners then had to adjust to the reality that small farms produced more food for less expenditure. Furthermore, not that it mattered to anyone in Moscow, the newly empowered farmers were much happier working for themselves. In an uncoordinated capitalist marketplace the big is beautiful mantra makes sense as much as it did for Kremlin strategists determined to build the USSR into a global competitor. A sprawling 4000 hectare farm in East Anglia or Kansas today merits the biggest, most cost-effective machinery or can allow one hand to tend thousands of animals and permit bulk purchase and delivery of feeds. GEMs could change this rarely questioned principle, not through penalties on the large operators or any Stalinistic switch in government policy, but by opening the marketplace while dramatically reducing the risk and overheads of trading.

A farmer with 50 hectares might own one tractor which he hires out 80 per cent of the time, but only to those with at least 75 complaint-free agricultural equipment rentals on their record. At the same time he could hire in implements for the precise times required. GEMs market overviews will show if local farms are having to hire, say, a muck-spreader from miles away with each hire involving high transport costs. That would represent an opportunity for any local contractor purchasing their own model, possibly in the GEMs market for second-hand agricultural machinery, perhaps with a GEMs facilitated loan. Anyone who wanted to join a GEMs buyers' club for feed or fertiliser could enjoy the benefits of bulk buying with one farmer being paid by the group to break up the load and deliver the required amounts to each member. Staff would be available according to precise demand in the kind of market described for van drivers earlier. Livestock could be sold within precise time periods: a farmer with good quality pasture might, for example, use GEMs to automatically buy cattle between 9 months and 1 year old, inputting a formula that maintained his herd at 30 beasts through automatic buying and selling as they aged. One motivated individual, with full local market information to hand and comprehensive trading ability only a few keystrokes away, is likely to get more out of a patch of land than a remote manager averaging cultivation methods across one monocultured strip. He would also be able to contribute to a more varied market. In Britain for instance the demand for organic produce is not matched by supply, 70 to 80 per cent has to be imported.[10] A nimble small farmer could check the prices being paid in his locality and shift to this kind of output knowing GEMs would ensure customers find him, can trust him and could have delivery speedily arranged without intermediaries, before the expiration of shelf life. As the advantages of large farms were progressively nullified their owners should find the newly realized value of small plots reflected in prices they could charge in the GEM for farmland.

It is hard to think of a service industry on which a public markets system might not have similar shattering impact. Instead of turning to a breakdown organisation's easily recalled phone number or web site when her car will not start, a motorist away from home accessing the GEM for immediate car repairs would be likely to find a local high-grade repairer was cheaper and could guarantee to be at her side faster. A manufacturer seeking round-the-clock security for a new plant could turn to a GEMs template that would ensure all the individuals involved had cleared comprehensive vetting: no company need be involved. High street bookmakers might find themselves losing out to individuals offering their own odds on a race in the GEMs betting market. The system would ensure they had sufficient funds in bond to pay out on any stake accepted: in case of dispute between punter and bet taker all moneys would be frozen until resolution. Even companies with assets that are genuinely most efficient when large could find the fringe 'value added' parts of their operations under threat. The telecom companies, for instance, are unlikely to be challenged by very small providers selling in GEMs. But their legions of installers and repairmen, who currently rely on, say, Australia Telecom or Bell Canada for work, might go free-lance and hire themselves out to a mix of individual householders, companies with telephone problems and their former employers. Would these fragmented traders miss the social aspects of a workplace? If so, they could turn to GEMs to find others who wanted to jointly rent office space. Six self-employed data entry clerks for example might hire convenient accommodation and if they enjoyed each other's company deepen their relationship by accepting joint liability on GEMs, then trading as a group able to tackle large assignments. Like shocked Polit-buro members in 1945, many senior managers could find this loss of centralization inconceivable. The likely extent of opposition to public electronic markets will be examined later in this book.

Starting work in public electronic markets

A youngster wanting to start work through GEMs might be shepherded on to the system by her school. Senior teachers would be able to issue a

PIN that proved their endorsement of a student to enter selected low-level markets as a provider. Pet walking might be one such sector. Once endorsed, a 13-year-old uses her PIN to shop for bonding from an insurer, perhaps on a pay-per-booking basis. Then, with a blank trading record, she must price herself into work. There would be little incentive for teachers to endorse unsuitable pupils. Once a proportion of their protégées became the subject of upheld complaints, that educator's ratification would be downgraded by GEMs' software, hurting the chance of their more meritorious scholars obtaining insurance cover.

Having opened a bank account, proven their identity at a Post Office and obtained an initial GEMs PIN, a teenager would find entering the markets for work as easy as any other user. The following example assumes another 13-year-old, trading with the blessing of his school, perhaps with a nominated teacher offering guidance on his embryonic career, which would be automatically confined to legally allowable hours for his age group. He has no clear idea of what he wants to do, relying instead on GEMs to reveal where there is likely to be demand for his services locally. His first step would be calling up the 'work for under 16s' template and choosing a sector.

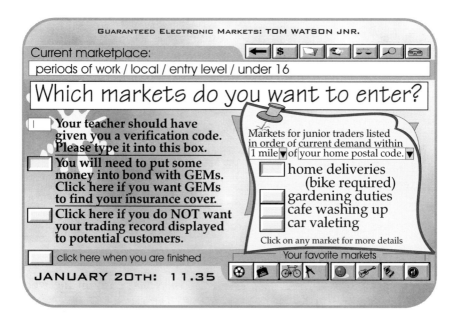

GUARANTEED ELECTRONIC MARKETS: TOM WATSON JNR.

Current marketplace:

periods of work / local / entry level / under 16

Which markets do you want to enter?

Your teacher should have given you a verification code. Please type it into this box.

You will need to put some money into bond with GEMs. Click here if you want GEMs to find your insurance cover.

Click here if you do NOT want your trading record displayed to potential customers.

click here when you are finished

Markets for junior traders listed in order of current demand within 1 mile ▼ of your home postal code. ▼

home deliveries (bike required)
gardening duties
cafe washing up
car valeting

Click on any market for more details

Your favorite markets

JANUARY 20TH: 11.35

He is not being shown available jobs here. It is unlikely there would be any for someone his age. Instead GEMs is telling him in which of the markets he is legally entitled to enter he could earn the highest rates per hour locally at the moment. He could chose any combination of them, or try to price himself into an already saturated sector not on the list. GEMs' helpfulness is not to be mistaken for control of users. Assuming he opts for delivery work he is then asked to construct a pricing formula starting by stipulating which hours he wants to be available for jobs. This is done by sliding a pricing bar up and down within each hour that he is allowed to work next week. GEMs assists by underlaying last week's market overview information about average earnings around his home postal code at those times in this market. He can go above that level for times he will only work under duress, below it perhaps for slots he is keen to be out delivering. The bottom of each rectangle represents the legal minimum he is allowed to charge for his labour.

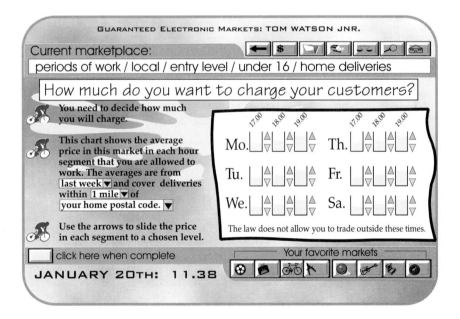

He might chose to maximise his competitiveness early in the week with a pricing level below last week's average. By dragging the pricing bar above the top line for all three periods on Thursday he could tell

GEMs he does not want to be in the market at all that evening, the TV schedule is too good. Because he is a probationer GEMs might only allow him to set out a timetable of availability for two weeks in advance; the software needs to see some proof of reliability before letting him schedule further ahead. If he turns out to be a rogue trader he could damage the system's most valuable asset: users' faith in the markets. Were he to prove unreliable in the first fortnight, by not logging on to check for work when he has said he would, for instance, GEMs would politely evict him from the marketplace. His jobs would be reassigned with costs borne by his bond and he might be told he can try again in 3 months.

Now, a screen asks for details of his bike's carrying capacity and whether he wishes to define local areas in which he will not work. Then it seeks to underline the seriousness of his new commitment.

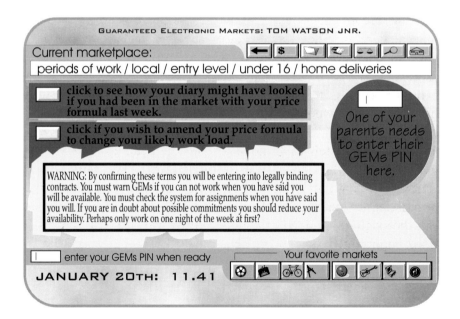

This could be many youngsters' first introduction to obligations in the unforgiving world outside home and school. GEMs should ease them in gently. Any bookings he wins in the following few days would be spelt out clearly. 'Go to 12 Station Road, ask for Mr Jones, collect casserole dish and deliver by 5.30 p.m. to Miss Smith, 17 Avenue Terrace', for instance. Maps could be provided along with estimated journey times. Market mechanisms such as codewords might come with expanded explanations and acceptable levels of service could be reiterated. The software might issue sporadic reminders, for example that standard contracts forbid bikes being chained to a client's property without permission or that deliverers are expected to carry their own padding for fragile items. A wise GEMs franchisee running this marketplace would see that the system allowed extra time for journeys, even above its normal allowance for cyclist speeds, to anyone entering through the under-16s template. Further facilitating the callow suppliers might be a facility allowing purchasers to say they wish to give priority to students of a named school for their household services. Parents could be persuaded to do this by teachers in weeks where they have new entrants making a first step into GEMs trading.

Any teenager choosing to begin working this way should accumulate a trading record that could amount to several hundred hours by the time they are 16. They would then have wide-ranging proof of reliability, independence, competitive trading and people skills to show insurers or college interview panels. Some students would want a more focused portfolio of evening or Saturday work and GEMs could, in time, help by providing templates for those hoping to enter specific careers. If the boy in the example above, for instance, had set his heart on working ultimately as an architect, he could call up a GEMs page that might show him his chances of finding immediate work or work experience doing home improvements or assisting with exterior work on building or landscaping. He would then come to formal training with thorough grounding in the practicalities of his chosen profession. More importantly perhaps, he should be sure that it really was the course for him.

Training: out of the classroom into the community

'There has been sustained demand for chefs in your area, click to see availability of training' is a message that might confront someone in their thirties idly shopping for a new career on GEMs. Having checked the appropriate market overview, to ensure there were not already hundreds of aspiring cooks in the pipeline, the user might cautiously pay for an initial 2 hour trial lesson to be scheduled into his diary. His tutor could be anyone with the required accreditation to teach catering skills, working freelance or for a college. If she was freelance, GEMs might only schedule her appointments when it could simultaneously hire a kitchen for teaching sessions. Commercial kitchen hire would be a new market realised by GEMs. It would be a means for perhaps a school or restaurant to generate income by renting out their facilities after hours: they are likely to do so only to tutors with flawless trading records. Tuition could be one to one or based on a class of stipulated maximum and minimum sizes: GEMs would ensure the availability of all registered participants. After one introductory lesson, the system could help both sides construct further periods of study, allow the pupil to buy a slot with an examining body and, assuming he could then input a 'pass' PIN, enter the market for lower-grade chefs.

Universities would be free to trade course vacancies in a GEM tailor-made for the purpose. They might want to build the flexibility offered by the system into personalized blends of work experience and conventional study. The responsiveness of a public markets system should ensure the end of skill mismatches and make a reality of just-in-time learning. It should ensure that uneven supply, like that in Britain where engineers able to fix washing machines and dishwashers can currently name almost any price they choose, is resolved.[11] It also allows for training in 'soft' skills too often considered uneconomic within the inefficiencies of the uncoordinated market. The girl who spends two hours after school every day walking dogs and feeding cats, for example, might use accumulated proof of that responsibility as a first rung on the ladder into a childcare market. With hundreds of hours of animal supervision on record she should be able to hire herself out as a mother's help, looking after children while under supervision from a parent in the house. Trading record proof of periods of volunteer work in a youth group would also help her career plans. Simultaneously she could be studying child welfare, first aid, cooking for children and maybe a tourist board-led series of evening classes and visits examining facilities for youngsters in her locality. That might put her onto a first step in unsupervised child care from where she would continue to be rewarded for her continuing investment in non-academic but thoroughly practical training. It would be very much in each GEMs franchisee's interest to promote depth and variety in the market for which they were responsible.

What impact would GEMs have on overall levels of work?

'When I was growing up, we used to read that by the year 2000 everyone would have to work only 30 hours a week and the rest would be leisure time. But as we approach 2000 it seems likely that half of us will work 60 hours a week and the rest of us will be unemployed.'[12] The writer, quoted in a study on the future of work, crystallizes the irony of employer-run software packages in the computer age. Such packages rigorously produce efficiency within their tiny segment of the economy. That tends to mean fewer workers, who develop a monopoly on skills, while the costs of rising unemployment are foisted upon other parts of society. GEMs, conversely, should foster equilibrium across the economy as a whole. It spreads the available work around and evens out inequalities, not by redistribution of wealth but by constant distribution of opportunity. It should be radically different from the way workplaces are set to move, as localized efficiency for employers continues to dominate the uncoordinated marketplace for work. A major study into employment environments found most US companies remain 'wedded to a low-trust, low-skill, authoritarian route to competitiveness'.[13] Annualized hours, for example, is an increasingly popular scheme that enables employers to pay for a certain number of hours from their workforce, who are then rostered, often at short notice, as the company requires.[14] GEMs would counterbalance the need for employers to extract increasing value from their workforce with the means for employees to exploit flexibility in industry for themselves. This is likely to include fewer hours of conventional work for many, creating new openings.

As a public markets system evolved, new patterns would emerge. Inevitably, there would be those who would lose their jobs because of efficiencies offered by GEMs. Factory payroll departments, for instance, could have a limited future. But most of those jobs could be judged under threat if the employer invested in a proprietary software package. In that case, however, much of the cost savings would go on licensing fees and computing consultants rather than to the firm. At least those who lose their jobs to GEMs should stand a chance of retraining for a former employer. If not, they should find a newly vibrant work market outside. Labour intensive provision of services could thrive in new areas at the expense of automated manufacture. Were caravan owners, to take one example, to start renting out their trailer homes for the 48 weeks they had previously sat on their driveways, there would be demand for delivery and maintenance that scarcely exists in an economy where so many mobile holiday homes are unused for most of their life. Even if all restrictions on employers and hirers were removed, it is hard to envision GEMs leading to full employment in a technological age. However it could end the dismal prospect of structural unemployment, entire households who have no work, barely remember employment and have very little prospect of any member ever coming off benefits. The system may not create employment for all, but it could at least spread realistic hope of work through all tiers of society.

10 GEMs and society: new initiatives made easy

Once a public market system is built there are additional social features that could be added at little cost. As well as creating an additional revenue stream for the consortium funding the system they would do much to promote social stability. These features delivered by a sophisticated but low-cost system offer advantages that a mass of individually targeted Internet sites could never achieve.

A national parallel economy

In 1932 the Mayor of Worgl in Austria, dismayed at 35 per cent unemployment in his jurisdiction, took the unlikely step of authorizing and printing his own currency for the town. As this money, backed by bank deposits of official Austrian schillings, intentionally lost 1 per cent of its value every month the new notes were circulated rapidly. Anyone holding them had every incentive to seek out traders already accepting the secondary currency or persuade newcomers to join the circle of acceptance. With a powerful disincentive for hoarders, the notes achieved a circulation velocity 14 times that of the national currency. Two years later Worgl was the first Austrian town to achieve full employment as citizens used their new scrip to improve houses, replant forest and engage their fellows for activities they could never previously have afforded. Two hundred Austrian communities had appropriated Worgl's idea before their Central Bank deemed such currencies illegal. The point proved in the Tyrolean town – that a well-run but restricted currency can dramatically stimulate economic activity – resurfaced in the 1980s. A therapist in Canada's Comox Valley, Michael Linton, tackled the problem of a falling clientele by issuing his own notes and persuading local traders to accept them in part payment. After 15 years of proselytizing, Linton has inspired hundreds of similar Local Exchange Trading Systems (LETS) around the world. His message is 'Anyone can start a currency and persuade people to use it'.[15] Carpenters can now be hired for LUPP tokens in Uppsala, Sweden; in Rotorua, New Zealand shopping will be done in return for RIBS vouchers; in Mexico City slum dwellers are being offered the chance to trade their labour with each other for Tlalocs. Notes issued by the majority of these regional projects are not backed by any tangible assets, it is the continuing faith of a circle of users that assures their value. This limits the scale of any one scheme. Linton admits 'As you get up in scale you get more fraud, more scam artists'.

GEMs could create its own money for users. Because the deals enacted would be enforced in the same way as any other transaction there should be no problems with defaulters. On joining GEMs each user might be awarded say 500 Parallel Official Economy Tokens (POETs) to sit in an account on the system. They would be digital only, with no validity outside GEMs, and paid over in tranches, perhaps every few weeks to avoid flooding the supply. Any user could then offer goods and services in return for POETs. This would be particularly tempting to anyone who was getting little business when charging 'real' money. The parallel economy points would have to be restricted in their usefulness or they would simply devalue the main economy. They would certainly only be available to personal, as opposed to company, users and might be limited to transactions within 1000 homes of the user's postal code, confined to low-level markets like local household services and second-hand goods from around the country. A user in a depressed area, for instance, might offer to do neighbours' washing for POETs, which she then uses to purchase counselling sessions or pre-owned VHS movies. She may even use them to purchase surplus food from a neighbour. All her deals would be underpinned by GEMs' mechanisms for deal protection and could be scheduled in her GEMs diary while a trading record of demonstrable reliability is being accumulated. She would no longer be excluded from economic activity just because her country's main currency is being deployed elsewhere.

How would the GEMs consortium make its money on this service? Initially POETs would be worthless but as the supply stabilized they could begin to acquire meaningful purchasing ability. At that point the system would offer an exchange, where POETs and the main currency floated freely against each other (Box 10.1). Wealthier users who had spent their initial 500 POETs would be unlikely to hire themselves out to earn more but they might scent a bargain in converting hard cash into the parallel points, then using them to hire someone, perhaps to dig their garden. The second currency should find a value that puts it well below 'real' money while remaining useful for labour-intensive transactions and perhaps second-hand goods. GEMs will take its cut from each of these contracts and automatically convert the POETs it gains back into the primary currency, at the going rate, through the exchange. It would be an uncertain cash flow until the parallel currency hardened but the benefits to the consortium of bringing the underclass into economic activity go beyond any immediate return. Someone who cleans neighbours' cars for POETs through the system and builds up a credible trading record might then enter the GEMs market for truck cleansing, being paid this time in hard currency. High-spending companies that can meet all their needs, including vehicle valeting, from ever-open and competitive markets, are likely to take the system more and more for granted. GEMs' progress to wide acceptance would come about from a constant search of ways to extend each marketplace. For users, POETs would provide stability against movements in the primary currency. The parallel points could not be traded outside the system or abroad, would not be available to companies and, because of their increasing supply, should have little value as a savings medium. They should continue circulating whatever wider economic conditions might prevail and could appreciate dramatically in times of depression in the outside economy.

Box 10.1

GEMS' EXCHANGE BETWEEN THE MAIN AND PARALLEL CURRENCIES

Like every other aspect of GEMs' day-to-day operation, the exchange between primary and secondary currency would be completely mechanical. The computer would be programmed to deal as if holding two pools of money, say $1m and 5 million POETs. As demand fluctuates it sets the price between them at whatever level will facilitate the maximum number of trades while keeping the two pools as close to their original level as possible. This would ensure liquidity, removing the need for an immediate counterpart with whom to swap currencies.

It is not only not-for-profit community schemes that have emulated that of the mayor of Worgl. Large consumer companies are widely expected to start issuing their own currencies to customers for online shopping. Someone holding American Airlines Advantage points after a series of foreign business trips, for instance, might be able to use them to purchase groceries online through a tie-up between the airline and a retailer. As these points are backed by concrete assets, the right to air travel in this case, they are much more desirable than community currencies. The *Wall Street Journal* has already labelled frequent flier miles 'a second national currency'.[16] Going further, individuals can trade loyalty points among themselves, perhaps even asking an employer for payment in points, which can then be sold online. Former *International Herald Tribune* correspondent David Brown has researched the potential impact of these privatized currencies. He concludes: 'The electorate's leverage over its own social and economic policy will then further erode... this will further heighten the dangers of systemic collapse'.[17] It is primarily the well off who benefit from tax-free trading in loyalty points, they are the ones who have both points and Internet connections with which to fully exploit them. But, as Brown points out, any damage done to the main economy by proliferating sidebar currencies will be borne by all.

GEMs would not make decisions about money supply and, following its doctrine of maximum usefulness, must allow users to trade both in community currencies and loyalty points. In South Africa, for instance, a householder looking for a coffee table might want to pay from her alternative currencies account. The country's GEMs system would show her tables most closely matching her requirements, converting each price from rand into say 'Johannesburg Johans' or loyalty points from the Pick'n'Pay supermarket chain at the going rate if asked. However, the system could not set a pool level between these extraneous currencies and the rand because that would involve management, rather than the market, assessing their value. Instead of an automatically calculated rate based on two pre-set pools, the exchanges would have to work on the lumpen principle of bid and offer. Multiple currencies for the electronic age is an idea that has its supporters who point out it would be equivalent to international trade between companies, who simply transact in a mutually convenient and stable denomination regardless of its country of origin. In reality it is possible governments will eventually try to restrict trading in loyalty points because of the destabilizing impact of multiple currencies being used to replace 'real' money by individuals in the top income percentiles. POETs, available to anyone through public access GEMs terminals and automatically restricted to pockets of the economy which hard cash has so often largely vacated, should have an opposite effect. Sealed within a system committed to transparency and widening markets, they could finally make the full promise of secondary currencies for the less well off an undemanding daily reality.

Community organisation

British statesman Edmund Burke called them the 'little platoons', people who find reward in grouping together to serve their community. At present the arduous administration and problems of overcoming a tendency towards social isolation make such projects hard work. It is easier, and often considered safer, for a youngster to play a virtual soccer game online in his bedroom than to organize a real team with his peers in the outside world. A GEMs system could breathe new life into communal activities, not through centrally directing resources and individuals but by extending its technology for running markets into social functions. The system would not initiate, it merely offers to organize. This would allow anyone willing to act as prime mover in setting up a drop-in for local people with mental handicaps, for instance, to call up a GEMs template showing the extent of unmet demand for such a facility locally. The template would then help him find a room and furnishings from the appropriate marketplaces before calculating a cost for the whole package for his proposed period. If grants were available, the system would match him with them; if not, a cost per user would be calculated. Finally GEMs could act as a bridge to potential users, who would sign a contract with the initiator that would be bonded like any other GEMs transaction.

Recent decades have seen considerable imagination applied to community ventures, spurred on by able people who find themselves released from downsized mainstream organizations. GEMs could do much to release this 'third sector' (after private enterprise and government provision) from the momentum-draining requirements of marshalling users and materials in an uncoordinated marketplace. A local minister setting up a weekend away for pensioners, for instance, would be able to do so with all the instant back-up and verification with which a currency trader currently moves millions around the world. So would a family wishing to start an Irish club one night of the week. Or someone instigating a system of 'Civic Guards', as pioneered in Holland, to schedule volunteers who will patrol public places in the locality so the general public feel safe using them. Collectively GEMs' social initiatives could lead to a re-birth of 'civic society'. If individuals start connecting with their neighbours and are able to easily sign up for a range of secure but very low-cost activities there might be less fear of walking the streets, greater pride in the collective environment and improving local facilities.

Grass roots initiatives to replace government provision

On a bleak evening four days before Christmas in 1844, the door opened on a remarkable new store in Rochdale, UK. Initial sales stock was limited to butter, sugar, flour, oatmeal and candles: the bare essentials for families blighted by endemic poverty during the darkest days of 'the hungry forties'. Crucially, the new emporium was committed to honest trading in the days before effective consumer legislation and was run for the benefit of its member shoppers, not to make a profit. It was the success of the Pioneer's Society store in Rochdale that assured a future for the British cooperative movement which went on to encompass affordable insurance, burial services, banking, education and wholesaling. It proved a point often eclipsed today by relentless focus on capital assets: entrepreneurial drive can extend far beyond the profit motive.

GEMs would allow local entrepreneurship to flourish, probably at the expense of centralized provision. Consider, for example, a trio of experienced state sector teachers demoralized by bigger classes and dwindling resources. A GEMs system could, if permitted, reorganize services like education: it might facilitate the three in establishing and then running their own school. Clearly, there would be enormous hurdles to be crossed with standards and commitments to be enforced at every step. GEMs might, however, offer a standard page for seeding a junior school that would follow similar steps to its templates for establishing all sorts of organizations. As setting up an institution for children would be, quite properly, among the most demanding of activities, it is worth describing the scenario in full. The funding mechanism here assumes British-style municipal education provision but it would as easily work in other systems: the key point is that scale of operation would no longer be important.

The group of teachers, perhaps gathered in one member's kitchen, would navigate to the GEMs marketplace for school formation and call up a market overview page. It might show that 50 parents, within a mile radius of the postal code they identified, have tried to move their 5–11-year-olds out of the existing school into something smaller without success so far. The teachers have a market. Before going any further each of them in turn must prove their identity to the system by entering their name and PIN: this also brings up their trading records for group inspection. Now the system asks them to decide on a headteacher, perhaps pointing out a legal requirement that it be someone with at least 10 000 hours complaint-free experience at the chalkface in junior schools. Additionally, they must nominate how much extra that individual is to be paid. After the longest-serving member of the group is nominated, GEMs offers a business contract that binds all three into joint liability for the venture, while their newly appointed boss is held to additional legal responsibilities. A crucial function of this contract, it would be pointed out, is to define the ethos of the new operation. Democratic social initiatives in the past have often failed because they had no means of embedding values to which potential subscribers either acquiesced or moved on to a more like-minded grouping. The British co-op movement nearly foundered on this rock as it became demonstrably successful. 'It appears to me wrong for persons to enter a Society with whose principles they disagree, and then destroy its constitution' wrote William Cooper, one of the Rochdale Pioneers.[18] It is at this point that the principles of the new school are laid down decisively. They will be inserted into any eventual contract with parents, changeable only by a vote involving everyone concerned.

Now the three each need an insurer who will provide the substantial financial bond from which any compensation in case of wrongdoing can be paid. Like all the GEMs insurance markets, the forum for educationalists' bonding matches details of the candidates' experience, previous complaints upheld and potential liabilities with formulae input by insurers pricing themselves into different niches in the market. Each applicant for insurance specifies how they wish to pay for cover and the system will find the best match.

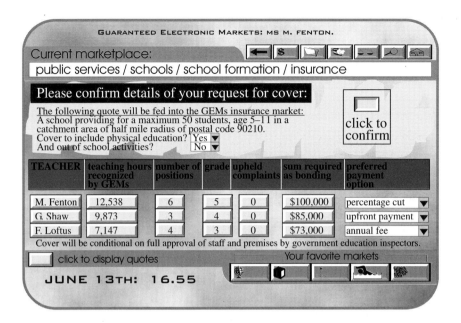

The insurance cover cannot be booked until some further procedures have been completed. GEMs simply needs to know that the three were insurable in current market conditions before continuing. Their next step is to locate a building. The GEMs franchisee running the template for school formation has input current legal requirements for a fledgling establishment and GEMs pulls together options from across its property market. Anyone selling property is offered the chance to answer detailed questions that determine whether their offering could additionally be made available in the schools template. For instance, someone putting a small office suite up for sale might be asked not only for room and outside area dimensions but also about the plumbing: are toilets and handbasins cemented to the building or only bolted? If the latter, then they can be easily replaced by child-sized facilities, for which GEMs can display the best price currently available in its sanitary ware marketplace and factor in the charges for such a job from local plumbers. Likewise, a suitable property that does not have the minimum space required for a playing field will be paired with the nearest sports facilities available for hire in that market. This process can sound prohibitively complex. In reality it would require a fraction of the computing power currently used daily by big banks to construct and trade exotic financial instruments around the world. Buildings, in the area the teachers have defined, that matched the requirements for a small school and were available for at least a two-year period would be displayed on a map.

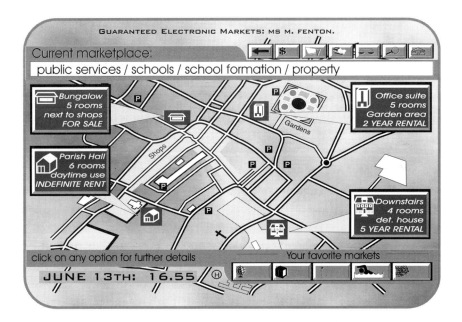

These are not properties that would normally appear in the market for education space. It is because savvy sellers have seen the advantages of answering precise questions that assess the suitability for school use that they appear in this context. Other questions for anyone putting property up for long-term rental or sale might be geared to assessing the building's potential for use as a doctor's surgery or community drop-in centre. No seller has to answer these non-essential questions in their contract but doing so increases the pool of potential buyers. It would also be in the vendor's interest to commission a survey of the property from a surveyor willing to put final gradings into GEMs against his PIN. They could then be browsed by any potential buyer.

Each of the available options is backed up by a details page about the property. After viewing these it might be that the teaching threesome decide that the ground floor rooms in a detached house are their best option. They could now opt for a 'purchased hold', paying the owner through GEMs to take his property out of the market for 24 hours until they have seen it. Simultaneously they tell GEMs to schedule a viewing in the seller's diary at his convenience and the group adjourns until after that appointment.

The following evening they reconvene having visited the suite of rooms and benchmarked it against a list of legal minimum requirements printed out from GEMs. They like the rooms and after haggling with the owner have persuaded him to discount his price to them: he inputs that instruction into GEMs which then constructs a provisional contract between the two sides. A further sum is transferred to the owner to allow for a new 'purchased hold' extending for another month. The teachers do not have capital to buy their potential school outright; they turn to GEMs for the best possible mortgage. As with the insurance, it will be found by matching specifics of price, surveyor's assessment, location and intended use against the pricing formula of providers. As well as offering that figure, the system now asks for precise details of modifications they need, then prices each in the appropriate market. The screen might look like this.

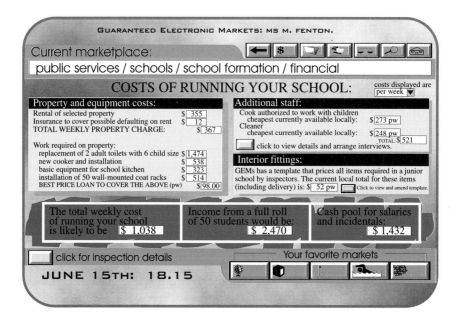

This would probably be as far as a new school could go without approval from the education regulators. Clicking to put their plan forward would schedule them into the local authority's diary for reviewing new school openings and give them a code-word to bring up all the details they had decided so far. Inspectors might, at the teachers' expense, spend a day interviewing them individually, visiting the proposed premises, and studying their conversion plans and costings as assembled by GEMs. If the venture passes this scrutiny it is then awarded an inspection PIN which, when entered into the template, allows the project to move into the next phase: recruiting students. Would education authorities be obstructive to start-up schools, to protect their empire of existing establishments? Central government would have to decide if it wished to encourage small schools: if so, vetting would have to be separate from administration of existing schools and clear, publicly accountable grounds for acceptance and rejection established. Additional grants might be made available through the system, perhaps to pay for inspection of potential enterprises.

A parent who tells GEMs they sought to move their child from an existing school in the area would be given the option of receiving a message from anyone licensed to operate a community alternative. The three teachers would now be able to activate this facility, throwing their combined GEMs diaries open for meetings with parents. As parents came away from their discussions with the entrepreneurial teachers they could call up the GEMs contract that would govern their child's education. This would set out the level of service to be offered covering hours of religious education, sports activities, facilities to be provided and so on. If the state allowed funding to follow a child to the school of choice, parents could then sign up and their youngster would be provisionally booked to spend his next term at the new enterprise. Once the required minimum had signed, all would be sent a message confirming their place, while purchase of the building, structural modifications and hiring of cleaners and caterers was activated. Once the school opened, GEMs would see that it was inspected regularly, the input of an inspector's PIN being necessary before pupils could be enrolled for each further term. Additionally inspectors' reports might be circulated to all parents as a term of their contracts with the teachers. As with any small organization trading in GEMs, there would be full flexibility to engage replacement teachers in case of sickness and to hire extraneous facilities. Innovative schools might use the public markets system to shop for, say, old people's homes in the vicinity that were looking for activities for residents and had clicked on 'would welcome visits to schools'. Children could then study oral history with pensioners, with GEMs scheduling their get togethers and arranging any transport required, perhaps drawing on funds for those specific journeys made available by charities to promote activities for the elderly. Specialist outside help could be bought in, perhaps with a local freelance nurse engaged for six Tuesday mornings to teach first aid or an experienced football coach hired for one day a month to train players for county little league trials. In all cases, GEMs would be attesting to the individual's solidity through a trading record and by status as someone verified by police as approved to work with children.

This changed model for education provision would not need central administration. The efficiencies of a market economy would dictate which institutions succeed and, because the schools are smaller and more evenly distributed, parents would have more choice about moving their offspring out of a failing institution. Inspection would be bought in a dispersed market that could expand and contract with demand. If teachers around the country preferred setting up their own neighbourhood schools to working in centralized education facilities and if parents enthusiastically supported those new ventures, there could be an exodus of students and staff from existing places of education. This is no concern of GEMs which exists only to bring the unbridled benefits of electronic markets to users, not to shape their impact. That task falls to elected governments. However, politicians who wished to encourage a newly realised efficiency for smaller schools might reflect that declining old schools could begin to sell their textbooks while renting out fixed assets, like laboratories and gymnasiums, to surrounding start-up institutions. Given the purity of the marketplace in which these transactions would take place, there should be little loss in the use of resources as the education system evolved. Community-based schooling with only two or three teachers per institution has been tried before: it is how education for the masses started in the UK with schools provided by church and parish in Victorian times. A demand for ever bigger places of learning emerged not from the needs of children but from the efficiencies of scale required to make universal provision, administered from above, cost effective in an industrial-age economy. Governments wanting to give their electorate the choice of returning to provision on that scale would need only to free parents to allocate the funds for their child's education. The market mechanism on GEMs would do the rest.

It is not just existing schools that could be affected by a grass roots revival. Local government services such as street cleaning could be taken over by locals, not in a voluntary capacity but as paid contractors who are answerable for any complaints. Suppose a town hall sectioned off its jurisdiction on a GEMs-provided map and invited contracts to regularly clean each square of the grid. This could mean agreements specifying that a contractor 'keep Station Road, High Crescent and Main Street from numbers 32 to 98 swept twice weekly with public litter bins emptied at least every other day'. The term of engagement might run for a month at a time. Anyone could bid for the part-time contract with the lowest tender automatically winning. Each winner would then have to put a sum in bond and be subject to adjudication at personal expense if their patch was not diligently tended. Any resident can complain through GEMs about the level of service. That might then be treated as a dispute with the cleaner, bypassing local officials. The market mechanism should maintain a high level of service: if a bad job is being done at a high price, someone else can undercut the current contractor next month. Local policy makers might choose that the rate being paid for each sector be made public on GEMs to increase this competition. Anyone who thinks they can do better for the money can then price themselves into next month's contract for that area. In the past, regional governments have shied away from engaging local people to provide local services because in the uncoordinated market it is almost invariably cheaper to contract-out a large area to a company big enough to possess expensive equipment and skilled staff. GEMs-empowered street cleaners would have the advantage of a pure market for trading second-hand bin trolleys, hiring brooms and shovels or engaging a street cleaning truck to pass through their sector for half an hour. A GEMs buyer's club among adjoining sectors could book the truck for a morning, with each contractor automatically paying their share of the cost through an individual agreement for the driver and equipment.

Social networks: using computers to increase human contact

The mechanisms that match buyers and sellers in electronic marketplaces could be adapted to unite those who want to set up a particular
group nationwide and those that want to join it. Someone wanting to
launch a mountaineers' ornithology club, for instance, or a recovery
network for Christian alcoholics, could call up a contract for club
formation. They would input a title for the proposed group, a brief
summary of its aims then a longer paragraph of description and
perhaps have some photographs scanned for a details page. Details of
any charges to be made on those who join, to cover production of a club
magazine or Internet site, perhaps, would also be required. The
founder's identity would be clear in the contract that any new member
signed and he would have to put a sum of his own in bond in case of
misbehaviour. Unlike the Internet, groups could not be set up by
concealed individuals who then abscond with the funds. Once initiated
by a user who was taking responsibility for its management, the club
would need to be categorized in a GEMs directory of groups available
for joining. Anyone interested could see the details sheet and sign a
joining contract. Meetings would then be arranged at times when the
maximum number of members had availability in their diaries and all
would pay a share of communal costs. GEMs would audit each club on
behalf of its members, showing in which markets the founder or his
approved signatories had spent funds and whether they had been allocated on a rational basis. If the joining contract specified a quarterly
magazine, for instance, GEMs would report to members how much had
been spent on printing and show that the treasurer had genuinely
selected the best value operator in the market that day and not just
opted to place the job with a friend's print works. Because many of
these clubs could be operating on a no charge basis, the system would
deduct a flat fee for this service but, assuming management adopt a
'penny post' pricing model sacrificing short-term margins to long-term
development, the sum involved should be small enough not to put a
brake on anyone's social life. The social networks facility on GEMs
could allow for evolution as flexibly as any of its markets. If two near
identical clubs are formed, for example, the initiators of both can
propose a vote for members on whether to merge. GEMs would

arrange the poll, while highlighting areas of difference in the two contractual constitutions that needed resolution. The social facilities available from a public markets system could be infinitely more reliable than anything offered on the open Internet with its lower grade levels of protection.

A particularly heartwarming social facility GEMs could offer, again for a flat fee, would be a friendship and dating function. Committed to fantastically sophisticated matching functions across thousands of varied markets, management would have little problem adding programming that brings together individuals by interests, locality and multiple additional fields. Likely to far exceed the pool of potential suitors, criteria in selection and cheapness of any agency outside the system, this function could be a killer application to attract many individuals on to GEMs.

Universal legal services

A GEMs system in mass use would be constructing millions of contracts a day for its users, each one underpinned by law. Why not spin off that facility into a feature, allowing users to write their own agreements and have them deposited in the GEMs registry of legally binding contracts? A home owner who agrees to sell half his garden to a next door neighbour, for instance, does not need matching with a buyer through the system. But he might want a contract specifying the extent of the land and the terms of any rights of way signed by them both banked on the system for an insubstantial fee rather than negotiated by the hour in a lawyer's office. (The latter option would of course also be available through GEMs.) Nearby a trio of builders agreeing to work jointly on a row of new garages might want a contract limiting their liability to each other. A comprehensive public markets system could easily include blank contracts which users then complete themselves, before depositing with the time and date of creation certified by the central computer. If this was deemed too casual, government may decide that signatories have to call up their contract and re-sign it a week later and then a month later before it is valid. That way they would have time to reconsider. Some businesses not selling their entire capacity on GEMs might still choose to impose the system's contracts on all deals. A small guesthouse, for instance, might invite a guest, who walked into reception and asked for a room, to sign a public markets contract for overnight accommodation, if he was a user. That would immediately clarify their relationship and facilitate the business's accounting by GEMs. Wills, house share agreements and affidavits about substandard goods or services could be created just as easily.

This facility could force government into new rulings on what constitutes an acceptable agreement between two consenting parties. Obviously a contract drawn up between two individuals committing to a bank raid or other criminal act would not be upheld in court. But what of prenuptial agreements, declarations of marriage by gay couples or a pact to split possessions and child custody between a long-wedded couple who have no wish to involve the divorce courts? At present these social contracts are expensive to instigate and carry little weight because they are dispersed. A GEMs registry would be more accessible and would show up numbers of any given type of social contract. This could lead to a situation where sheer weight of contracts signed led to pressure for a law underwriting their legitimacy being passed.

Electronic voting: 'participative democracy'

GEMs could transform the way citizens in its country vote. It could also allow them to have a genuine say on a far wider range of issues. Voting through the system would be a logical extension of its markets software but not one from which it could legitimately make any money. Even the most enterprise-focused countries would find it unacceptable to charge their populace for access to the ballot box. If voting through the system is to be offered, it must be a cost carried by the consortium, negotiated as part of their deal with parliament when setting up the operation.

How would it work? On election day the system makes a voting page available to every user, computing their constituency from its map of postal codes. Individuals tapping into GEMs at home, work or on a public access terminal then click against a chosen party, or rate a list of candidates in countries with transferable votes. Entering their secret PIN then sends that vote to the central computer where results are tabulated through the day to be released at poll closing time. The fact that an individual had completed his page would be recorded to forestall any attempt at voting a second time, but no record of the candidate he personally selected would be kept. The scores for each contender are compiled by GEMs' central computer without any reference back to who voted for them. A complication to this vision of a low-cost democratic utopia is the overriding principle that no one would ever be compelled to use GEMs: voters who want to walk to a local church hall, enter a booth and place a tick on a piece of paper must be free to do so. Losing sight of this principle would turn GEMs from a freely entered market system to a potential instrument of statist control, unacceptable in a democracy. The system's voting capability has to run in association with returning officers around the country. Each would have a GEMs terminal displaying the local electoral register. It is on this rather than the printed register that they mark who has been given a ballot paper. As individuals vote on GEMs they are removed from the display to local presiding officers, signifying they are not to be given a ballot paper at the polling station. When the polls close, electronic vote tallies are published immediately by the system to all its users; the paper count is then added for each constituency (Box 10.2).

Box 10.2

VOTING AS A BELL-WETHER OF TRUST IN THE SYSTEM

An electorate would only vote through GEMs if they trusted the system completely. A corrupt system might either falsify returns or reveal to officials how individuals had voted. The purity of a country's public markets system would be crucial to its economic and democratic well being and requires new forms of inspection. GEMs would be relentlessly probed both by outside organizations paid through a trust established by the consortium and by its own more technically minded users. Because the millions of lines of programming code driving the central computer are published openly and available to be checked (but not tampered with) by anyone with a GEMs terminal, conspiracy theorists could think up ways that data might be tampered with and confirm that it is not happening. Willing uptake of the voting facility by trusting users could be a useful target for consortium management to set themselves.

GEMs voting would be convenient and cost the state nothing. It need not be confined to election days. In Switzerland the value of national referendums has long been recognized. Collecting signatures from 0.7 per cent of a population of 7 million guarantees a national plebiscite on any proposed law. Anyone attracting 1.4 per cent of his countrymen to sign a petition can initiate legislation. Swiss political culture hands sovereignty directly to the people: when a Zurich newspaper reports 'The Sovereign has decided' it is simply saying the population have voted. GEMs could offer its users in any country the capacity to initiate Swiss-style referendums to which other users can choose to add their PIN signatures in support. However, its sheer convenience could lead to abuse. 'We get a lot of wacko things on the ballot' grumbles the governor of Oregon, one of the US states in which members of the public can initiate a referendum once a threshold of signatures has been crossed.[19] Any GEMs facility for petitions would need automatically to separate out the frivolous polls launched by users from the democratically useful. This could be achieved by grading petitions on offer by the number of votes, for or against, they had so far attracted. Thus anyone launching a petition, calling for the abolition of government rent controls perhaps, would have every incentive to also initiate a profile-raising campaign that should ensure the measure started to move up the list of polls available to users. GEMs would see that an individual only signed each petition once. The system would need a cut-off period after which a petition was removed. When drafting the act that launched GEMs, politicians would have to decide how far they wished to use it as a means of widening democracy. The potential for letting the public, or at least those who had enrolled with GEMs, stage a well-regulated poll could haunt them. How, for instance, would UK parliamentarians react to a definitive poll demanding the return of capital punishment? In the wake of atrocities there is inevitably evidence of an overwhelming desire to bring back hanging which the House of Commons has always resisted. One way to avoid this hysteria-fuelled rush to judgement in an age of effort-free polling would be to establish rolling referendums. The same question could be posed four times with perhaps a month's gap between each polling day. Those with an abiding concern for the issue would be likely to welcome the opportunity for a more measured sampling of public opinion, the uncommitted and media-frenzied might disqualify themselves by not bothering to cast a vote on each of the four days. GEMs' referendums should never be given the weight of Swiss petitions because they would perpetually exclude that segment of the population who choose not to use the system. However, if say 90 per cent of the populace have a GEMs account and 70 per cent of them consistently support a change of law, however abhorrent to parliament, it would take skilful dissembling by politicians to negate the impact.

A GEMs vote need not be national. Unions could ballot members on the system, with only those who had paid their subscription invited to vote. Clubs and democratically minded employers could do likewise. Most empowering of all, perhaps, would be community polls, displayed only to those who live within specified streets. For example two mothers living close to a patch of communal land could instigate a petition calling for pets to be banned from the grass so toddlers could play there in safety. They would word a question, define the street on which it impacted then launch a campaign among their neighbours. If a proportion of them, decided by government, voted and a sufficient number opted for the change of use GEMs might automatically pass the results on to local government. One of their officials would confirm that the question posed was fair and the new status of the contested land had now been enshrined in local legislation. The system would then collect subscriptions from any of the recent voters who wanted to contribute towards legally approved signage, then hire a contractor to install notices warning all comers that dogs were now to be walked elsewhere. Eventually this facility could lead to communities defining themselves. An area of many elderly residents might, if allowed, vote for a low noise ordinance. Zones with a large population of small children might collectively decide that they wanted their street car-free at weekends. Such polls might have to be reaffirmed every year; the decision would rest with local officials. In Glasgow, Scotland, residents of the council-run Langstone Place tower block were recently allowed to interview and rule on new applicants for apartments. Those suspected of drug dealing or antisocial activities are now rejected by a panel of locals.[20] It is a step that does have wider social implications but, if permitted by government, GEMs could allow countless other communities to take control of their destiny for far less effort. It might also allow for cost-effective voting for local officials, even to the level of school governors or hospital administrators.

Where would this world of newly reliable, instant, popular decision-making leave politicians? In Switzerland, few electors know the name of their premier. The culture of *subsidiarität*, whereby decisions are made at the lowest practicable level, makes him or her a far less influential figure than foreign counterparts. The politically active Swiss citizenry, though, has strong cohesion without a high profile leader to unite them: despite having four main languages spoken by its population the country has been stable for centuries. Other nations, where democracy is increasingly defined by adversarial politics driven by personalities, would probably not want to lose that capacity for a clear sense of leadership. But the progressive centralization of power in several first world countries in recent decades could easily be reversed as a public electronic markets system was taken up. It might demonstrate that a politically empowered population led to a more content and stable society.

User boycotts: forcing the supply chain

Any GEMs user could list companies or individuals who were not to be presented to him as trading options. A motorist who was not satisfied with the durability offered by a particular tyre company, for example, might click on 'I do not wish to have this seller's products offered to me again'. If a public markets system were truly committed to offering its users every benefit of which the technology is capable, however, it would empower buyers further. Users could be offered a 'current boycotts' page. Here they could list ingredients they preferred to avoid in their purchases or companies with whom they had no desire to trade, even indirectly. Ecologically minded consumers could tell this page, for example, that they wished to punish agrochemical giant Monsanto for its enthusiastic propagation of genetically modified crops. They would be telling GEMs that when shopping in food-related marketplaces they want priority in matching given to any supplier whose contract attests to no Monsanto involvement in their output. Any seller could call up the boycotts page and transfer an automatically generated clause confirming this commitment to their standard sales contracts. Were one of these sellers found subsequently trading with the boycotted company their new-found customers would all be automatically compensated from funds in bond. GEMs has no input into which companies are listed on the boycotts page of course, but market overview information will show sellers how many potential buyers are giving preference to manufacturers who have purged their supply chain of, say, Monsanto produce.

This facility could put buyers back in control of market regulation rather than abdicating responsibility for industrial processes to negotiations between big business and government. The resources of global corporations, combined with an ability to play governments off against each other, are, many believe, diminishing politicians' ability to act effectively as arbiters of the public interest. 'I am not sure' British Agriculture Minister Jeff Rooker is reported to have told government conservation agencies seeking a moratorium on gene modification 'that we are in the driving seat'.[21] Individual consumers certainly are not: modified food is rarely labelled in supermarkets because it originates so far down the processing chain. With a GEMs boycott gathering momentum, however, individual farmers might see advantages in decisively switching away from the merchants supplying seeds from boycotted companies, inserting the appropriate clause in their contract and making their harvest more valuable to processors who now wished to act likewise. If public distaste for biotechnology was overwhelming, as some surveys suggest, it would be mass market consumers who decided the fate of companies involved, not lone regulators.

11 GEMs' impact on parliament: technologically literate politicians and small government

British Prime Minister Tony Blair has famously joked that he has trouble finding the on switch for his official laptop computer. Bill Clinton came up with a similar quip for reporters at the launch of his government's electronic commerce policy statement. This affected naiveté would probably not be a vote winner in a country where a significant section of economic activity was happening in GEMs. Politicians would need to understand the dynamics of electronic markets, including the dizzying speed with which they can respond to events. In October 1997, for instance, the London stockmarket launched its SETs share dealing service with a speech from Chancellor Gordon Brown who, in the course of his remarks, appeared to suggest diminished enthusiasm for European monetary union. As his talk progressed the enormous SETs screen behind him progressively turned red as dealers used their new-found technology to immediately sell shares in companies reliant on the European market. When the frenzy abated, stock prices had been pushed way below their true value. Consumers given similarly fluid markets may conceivably respond in the same way to a report criticizing perhaps a specific make of car. Parliament, like the ruling bodies of Stock Exchanges, would need to decide whether the more illogical aspects of market forces were to be tempered with trading limits. They might, for example, rule that the price of any tangible asset on GEMs is not allowed to drop more than 15 per cent below its previous average in a 24-hour period, to put a brake on panic selling. Alternately they might opt for 'capitalism red in tooth and claw'. GEMs would not force any ideology on governments, merely give them a new forum in which their convictions can be applied.

A government launching GEMs would need to decide how much responsibility it was willing to abdicate to market mechanisms. Some regulatory issues might be better resolved by individual GEMs franchisees working to cultivate buyer confidence than by edicts from central government. In the UK, for instance, policymakers have repeatedly tussled with the question of whether nannies should be regulated or whether, as one official report put it, an enforced code would create 'a false sense of security' for parents.[22] A guaranteed market for childcare would sideline these quibbles, automatically building in ongoing checks to a depth far beyond that feasible in the uncoordinated marketplace. Parents would still be free to hire an unregulated nanny, through a newspaper classified advertisement perhaps, but they might ask themselves why she had decided not to trade in the very convenient, but heavily vetted, market on GEMs. Regulation currently puts an enormous cost burden on economic activity: supervision of financial services alone in the US costs over $700m a year according to studies by the London Business School.[23] With automated checking of market entrants and enforcement of deals, GEMs would not require anything like this level of policing (Box 11.1). As government regulators started clearing their desks, central administrators could be doing the same. In the USA, 15–20 per cent of the cost of healthcare is estimated to go on administration.[24] But in a GEMs environment, hospitals and health providers could trade their services on a day-to-day basis. A 50-year-old user requiring physiotherapy, for example, could be given a PIN by his family doctor which allowed him to decide on a supplier and have GEMs schedule the appointments as available. No one need predict demand for these services or oversee the premises on which they are given. Once insurers or state health services attach payment to the patient all provision can be left to the market which would have full overview information to ensure demand and supply attain rough equilibrium at the best possible price. It may lead to hospitals shrinking to core functions as staff who do not need operating theatres or centralised equipment shift to self-employed status.

Box 11.1

POLICING THE MARKETS IN GEMS

Each GEM would be self-policing. Sellers' claims are not evaluated by anyone, instead compliance relies on 3 C's: customers, competitors and consumer groups. Suppose, for example, a camping equipment manufacturer releases a new line of rucksacks in the appropriate GEM and types in that the product is '100 per cent waterproof'. A first buyer to discover it was not would instigate a complaint and, if successful, receive recompense according to the publicly known scale for misleading claims in that market, double the cost of his back-pack perhaps. However, if hundreds of the rucksacks have been sold, competitors or consumer groups might initiate tests and, if the bag's repellent qualities are not 100 per cent, launch a complaint of their own. If the case against the bag maker has foundation, and the waterproofing claim has been untrue throughout a long production run, the company will experience the punitive effects of cumulative contracts. GEMs will automatically access its month of stored contracts with buyers of that model and send them all a warning about their purchase plus compensation from the camping suppliers' bond. Would competitors endlessly complain without justification about each other? There would need to be rapid judgement by trading standards officials and perhaps a three-strikes-and-you-are-out rule for wilful complainers. The kind of preventative policing that can so encumber existing routes to market should not be required in this bonded environment.

Politicians around the world are already aware of the potential for online efficiencies in the delivery of government services. This aware-ness has spawned multiple computer systems at enormous start-up cost for the taxpayer. At time of writing, for instance, the UK government is having to explain embarrassing overruns in a scheme called BA-Pocl that will eventually computerize welfare payments at a price in excess of $1000 million.[25] Nearby, civil servants in the agriculture ministry are setting up CTS, the Cattle Tracing System to record movements as live-stock are bought and sold.[26] Elsewhere officials are grappling with a late-running system that should one day simplify tax calculations.[27] All these projects and their related expenditure in the uncoordinated online marketplace would be irrelevant with a fully functioning GEMs system. It could pay benefits, register cattle as they changed ownership and constantly compute individuals' tax liabilities. As provision of official services came to be governed more by the transparent GEMs marketplace, and less by coteries of administrators, problems of accountability should diminish. The Pentagon, for instance, has been criticized for the opacity of its accounting, but if it were purchasing through GEMs, and choosing to release its auditing on the system to Congress, any missing millions could be quickly tracked back to the individuals concerned. Other countries who have a problem, not with official ineptness but with full-scale corruption, could likewise find a solution in public electronic markets. Civil servants might be told they can buy only through the system and be given assigned levels of purchasing responsibility then have their record of transactions made public to all users. GEMs need not release full details of course, simply showing that a certain amount was spent in the market for uniforms by someone in the police procurement division and attesting that the deal for which he opted was the one offering best value for his requirements at the time. His specifications could be made public, to ensure they were not skewed to favour a particular supplier, and the state of the market that day recorded: were there sufficient suppliers to ensure real competition? As the smallest of deals would be open to automatic scrutiny, the favouritism and incompetence that can tarnish an entire government should disappear. While dishonourable politicians would be unlikely to welcome this facility, as online technology spreads it is possible it could be forced on them. The World Bank for instance might one day make the launch of a GEMs-style system, with its facility for transparent government accounting, a condition of any financial bail out.

Government control of a GEMs economy: precision and imagination required

The telephone played a pivotal role in the 1929 Wall Street crash. No one had anticipated its capacity for allowing sell orders to snowball. Governments launching GEMs would need to exercise some foresight about the broad effects it could unleash. They might feel that, instead of a traditional industrial policy, they had a role in promoting sectors that offered new sources of employment, for example. Tourism is one obvious category. Inbound visitors to the country of operation could open a GEMs account and assemble personalised itineraries for travel, accommodation and activities, each component of which would be found in a market moving towards direct payments to individuals and away from corporate coffers. The traditional levers of government control over a democratic economy would remain unchanged by GEMs but they should each become much more responsive to policy decisions.

Tax and social policy

Taxation of transactions across the Internet is currently a fraught issue. At which end of the deal are goods dispatched from one US state to another charged sales tax? How is tax calculated when a Swedish customer orders clothing from an Australian company? Can retailers follow banks in moving their computers to offshore tax havens to escape revenue officials? Unlike the global complexity of controls on uncoordinated electronic trade, a GEMs system would be national and could immediately calculate current tax payable on each transaction. Consortium management would need to ensure this ease of collection did not tempt policymakers into using GEMs as a cash cow for higher taxes, which would price users off the system. A more intelligent use of public electronic markets would be to drop the revenue department's take from very specific transactions. Politicians might do this to achieve social ends: lowering the tax on lorry and driver bookings between midnight and 6.00 a.m. for instance, to ease road congestion or allowing parents of a registered disabled child to buy a quota of clothes, in the appropriate size, every year free of sales tax, to reflect their increased costs of care.

Selective tax rates could also be used to tempt traders out of the grey economy. The untaxed money-in-hand sector has expanded around the world three times as fast as official economies in the last three decades.[28] It now amounts to some 15 per cent of the cash turnover in developed nations. Enticing thousands of hairdressers, plumbers, drivers, builders and catering staff from the fringes of criminality and on to the system would be a rich prize for both government and management. Politicians might drop tax rates in these markets on the pragmatic grounds that a small cut from 15 per cent of gross domestic product is better than no cut and that society, as a whole, has much to gain from cleaning up the grey market so that crime detection can focus on a remaining hard core. As it downsized government, GEMs should reduce public spending. The resulting leeway for policy makers could be applied in many ways through the system. They might, for instance, want to reflate particularly depressed areas by zoning tax payments, allowing anyone living in specified postal codes 25 per cent off their employment tax. This zoning need not be as crude as previous attempts, where residents on one side of a street often find themselves paying local taxes well above those of households they see out of their front windows. If politicians define an epicentre to be given full tax relief, GEMs could graduate the percentage outwards over a variable radius.

GEMs does not demand this kind of sophisticated taxation policy to become workable. But a government choosing to ignore its potential would be opting for very blunt supervision of their economy in a new era. Bold politicians might one day go further in harnessing the system's capacity to collapse the criminal economy. It would be a radical step indeed, but if underground drugs were made legal and their supply (heavily restricted, of course) moved on to the system, an entire infrastructure of sustained crime would cave in. The social ramifications would need thinking through in great detail but for GEMs the operation of a restricted sector would be routine. The system's marketplace for explosives, for instance, might only be accessible to buyers with authenticating PINs to prove their status as licensed quarry blast managers plus verification from an approved employer. Their every purchase would be recorded for public safety officials who could set limits on the amounts that could be bought. Similarly, a heroin addict, once registered with a drugs counsellor, might be given a PIN enabling him to purchase a small personal supply, day by day, as long as he continued submitting to supervision and getting new PINs. Legitimate sellers could sell in this market in transparent competition with each other. It might be that the supply side is restricted to established pharmaceutical companies because they have experience of distributing controlled substances. They would obviously not be allowed to promote their new product range. This market should end the 500 per cent or so street mark ups typically enjoyed by many dealers.[29] Would the implied imprimatur of respectability increase drug use? Its immediate effect could be to destroy any channel for recruiting new users. As existing addicts realised they could find their fix much more cheaply on GEMs, they would be likely to enroll with a counsellor and then purchase controlled amounts from a supplier trading on the system. Not only would long chains of profit-taking intermediaries be broken but the sector would be working on a customer pull model, rather than having thousands of small sellers around the country motivated by high margins to push their product on to new customers. Once a hard drug began trading at commodity prices in a transparent market limited to supervised buyers and suppliers, it should be relatively easy for government to stifle current levels of growth in the sector. Auditing the supply would become precise to the last milligram.

Unlike the uncoordinated Internet marketplace, it would be virtually impossible to commit a crime on GEMs. Markets would only be written for legal sectors of the economy and, as each deal is enacted through a contract provided to both parties, it would be difficult to launder money without leaving an incriminating audit trail. The disposal of stolen goods would be similarly affected. As opening a GEMs account requires high-level proof of identity and every transaction involves a contract that is copied to both parties, only the dimmest racketeer would choose this route for his underhand activities. However, this automated enforcement should be the extent of GEMs' role in the fight against crime. What it must not do is spy on its users. For example, the system could, on request, compile earnings accounts for every user, simultaneously calculating their tax owed on each transaction. At financial year's end one click would send this statement to revenue officers, perhaps accompanied by a signed declaration from the individual testifying he had not earned any money outside the system so they were a complete record. A transfer of the appropriate funds to the tax authorities could be authorised with a few more clicks. However, it would be crucial that GEMs' management do not allow any user to be coerced into deepening his reliance on the system. An individual who wished to file a paper tax return would be free to do so, even if he had traded exclusively in GEMs that year. If tax authorities queried his figures they could not have access to his accounts page on the system, which would be available only to him and which he could choose to destroy irrevocably at any time. It may seem inconsistent that GEMs, a system predicated on enforcement of honest trading, would stand back and allow a user to commit a crime by destroying his true accounts. But it is on a par with another principle implicitly accepted in most advanced democracies: photographers and television crews covering, say, a rowdy demonstration do not hand over unpublished material to police, even though it may identify perpetrators of criminal behaviour. It is preferable that some miscreants go unidentified rather than communications media lose their independence from state bodies. Revenue officials, dubious of a paper return from a GEMs user, could obviously call up market overview archives to show what he would have been likely to be earning at the times stated in his area. Such information would be in the public domain. Tax authorities might choose to offer a discount to anyone filing their system accounts as a tax return and then concentrate their enquiries on those who do not, but they could not snoop on GEMs users' details.

Environmental policy

Thousands of Berliners belong to a scheme called *Stadtauto* (city car). In return for a joining fee, deposit, monthly charge and usage payments calculated by time and mileage, they can use hundreds of cars based at dozens of sites in the city. Members make a phone call to establish the identity of their nearest vehicle, then use a pass key to open a kerbside deposit box for the ignition keys. They abandon their transport at journey's end. 'A lot of people like the idea that there's no hassle, no trouble and no responsibility', according to the manager of one of more than 300 such schemes, born of Germany's green movement.[30] Proponents reckon that each city car removes four privately owned vehicles from the roads. This sort of venture would have much to gain from public electronic markets. First, the pricing and car location process could be made much more convenient; second, the fixed pool of cars could be supplemented by individuals letting their car out, perhaps during their two weeks of holiday, into contractual chains of drivers each with an impeccable trading record. Whoever managed the car pool would have overall responsibility for the vehicle. Finally, city car schemes could be extended to cover much longer journeys. If a family required one way transport from Berlin to Nuremberg, for instance, a German GEMs system could automatically price the vehicle into an immediate return journey then arrange transfer between drivers, or via a local 'holder', with identifying code-words. It may be that this facility would become indistinguishable from the GEMs car hire market if thousands of dispersed owners were to decide to let out their vehicles when not required. Government could do much to encourage this activity. Tax breaks would be one step, so would GEMs terminals and reserved parking places for communal cars around city centres. Kerb-side boxes could be opened with PINs issued seconds earlier by a public access GEMs terminal at the car park. A couple who went to the theatre in one car might drive home in another, then deposit it on the rank near their house. The PIN they use to open the key deposit case on a nearby lamp post might be wired to another terminal that automatically registers the car's new position and the end of their hire. None of this would require particularly advanced technology, just government will.

Other low-cost, eco-friendly transport options that would become much more practicable in a coordinated marketplace include Middle Eastern-style shared taxis, summoned immediately via a GEMs display on the driver's dashboard and particularly valuable for regular journeys such as school runs. For shorter trips involving children, GEMs could, of course, draw up and underpin rotas of parents to walk from a neighbourhood to the school gates. Other environmental schemes particularly suited to public electronic markets might include a marketplace for squatters, allowing responsible inhabitation of temporarily empty buildings, or an urban greening initiative where scraps of land are identified for grants that local people can access to spend on approved plants. Once a small group of neighbours had accessed the money, signing contracts to accept responsibility for planting their purchases, officials from the grant provider would be able to use their copy of such contracts to check that the work had been done.

A sophisticated tax structure could help to consolidate deliveries, reducing road use. If the rate on a local delivery journey was highest for a one drop-off assignment and lowered for each additional job accepted through GEMs, automatic calculation of prices that include tax should ensure that, in a case where all local deliverers were pricing themselves equally, the first one to win an assignment for an hour hence would then collect other jobs in that vicinity, ahead of rivals. It would be up to government whether to distort the market for environmental ends.

Recycling could be driven by the GEMs market mechanism, rather than central administration. If aluminum cans, for instance, were made to carry a deposit repayable at the recycling plant, as is the case in some countries already, a market that moves their supply towards the smelter should develop organically. A family with perhaps 40 cans, accumulated in a bin under their sink, might put them up for sale with a couple of clicks in GEMs. Bought in a competitive market by a local 14-year-old who comes round to pick them up, crush them and add them to his hoard in the garden shed, they are then sold to a consolidator who will only collect once the teenager has 1000 cans, and so on. A chain in which each member subtracts their share of the value of the deposit ebbs and flows with the supply of cans. This is the kind of low-level market, largely infeasible with current overhead-heavy trading, that GEMs could originate.

Officially imposed quotas, too, could evolve from those rigidly imposed restraints on individual traders to market-driven controls across a whole industry. Trawlermen out at sea, for instance, landing their nets to discover an over-catch of plaice could use their GEMs terminal in the wheelroom, linked to land by a mobile phone, to purchase other boats' plaice quotas for that day. If plaice is easy to catch, the rising quota price should tempt a proportion of trawlers to stay in port and make their money on quota sales from a wide open market. Similar transfers between countries given a limit on polluting emissions have already been proposed. GEMs would roll out this kind of facility, like so many others, to individual traders.

People on benefits

Public electronic markets could easily handle social security payments for claimants willing to use the system. In time the system might even automate the process of deciding who is paid what. A GEMs user wishing to claim benefits could release their tamper-proof availability for work and pricing records to social security staff. If it is clear he has found bonding, then offered his services for sustained periods in active markets at minimum wage levels without finding work, he is obviously a temporary victim, rather than a shirker. If his claim is legitimised, state funds can be transferred to his account in successive weeks. In addition they might be earmarked for spending in specific markets on GEMs, food, transport and rent, for instance. This would benefit those claimants currently prone to extortion attempts on the day funds are moved into their account. Should he choose not to open his records to officials, GEMs obviously would not permit any surveillance of his activities on the system and even allow him to wipe his records, if he wished. Would this facility encourage traders to claim while working in the cash-in-hand economy? By releasing their records they would show that they had genuinely been available for work in GEMs and had been checking regularly for assignments, the non-completion of which would have resulted in fines being deducted from their bond and eventual expulsion from the system. More importantly, if the levers of tax and regulation had been adjusted to entice people into legitimate GEMs trading, there should be little incentive for buyers to hire, say, a car mechanic for cash. They would be ignoring the contracting and bonding mechanisms that would ensure a job well done, and any price advantage would be minimal. Once a GEM for car repairers achieved critical mass it should find pricing equilibrium at a level below which only cowboys were willing to trade.

The allocation of funds to the unemployed could be made automatic if politicians set up formulae for calculating allowances according to previous availability for work, circumstances and area of residence. Applicants would then fill in a GEMs template to learn of their entitlement, which would then be paid over as decreed by the formula. A PIN issued by the local doctor might be required if sickness payments were sought. This would be an area of enormous sensitivity. The consortium running public electronic markets would have to see that the system was constantly apart from government. Even a suspicion that they acted as an arm of the state could damage business prospects for GEMs systems in other countries. Despite the loss of the small fee subtracted from every payment, it would be very much in management's interest to see that a robust core of sceptics claimed their benefits the old-fashioned way.

This vision for electronic commerce aims to offer all citizens the right to trade on their own terms within a secure market. That capability could be extended to the lowest tiers of society, who may need extra help achieving the self-sufficiency that should be available from GEMs. Take, as an example, a former decorator who had hit a bad patch in his personal life and who repeatedly failed to turn up for bookings the system had found him, sacrificed his bond and he had been automatically banned from GEMs trading for 6 months. Instead of sitting idle on benefits, or trying to find work in what could be a very restricted market outside the system, he might join a closed GEMs market, overseen by social workers or perhaps a charity. Buying and selling in this forum would be open only to a local circle of people in a similar position. Although barred from selling in the wider market-place, they could engage each other to cut lawns and to do shopping, house cleaning and countless other tasks that would require adherence to a diary of commitments. Payment would be either in points, valueless outside that specific market, or in parallel economy points if a charity could persuade better-off users to donate them. GEMs would not dilute their value by doing so. By demonstrating consistent reliability in this market, the former decorator should find it easier to re-obtain an insurance bond when he is allowed back into the wider marketplace. To further widen the experience of participants, anyone overseeing these closed markets might persuade selected local people to tell GEMs they specifically wanted to hire from the closed market. The system would make it clear the trader they hired was not bonded and the trade could not be guaranteed.

12 A country with GEMs in a global economy: international advantage

Around 500 BC, the Kings of Lydia achieved dominance of their region by inventing money to replace direct barter of goods. In the 1980s, Singapore automated all export/import paperwork on a computer called TradeNet and became the busiest port in the world in terms of shipping tonnage. Countries that use technology in unique ways to develop their economic workings have often done well. A nation with fully functioning public electronic markets should be able to stand aloof from trends that other nations will have to accommodate in the age of linked online economies. New efficiencies and a galvanised domestic economy could create unequalled appeal for investors that transcends short-term considerations, such as interest rates or business cycles. The nation would, for instance, be particularly attractive to inward investors. Take, for example, a Korean company debating where to set up their European manufacturing facility. If, say, Spain had a GEMs system the company could open an account in a Madrid bank, then a GEMs account, based perhaps at their Spanish lawyer's address. Before leaving Seoul, they might access GEMs on the Internet and use their account to book an office suite and hire bi-lingual secretaries willing to work particularly long hours. Long-stay accommodation for a forward team and dependable support for their domestic lives could likewise be arranged in minutes. After putting purchased holds on various production facilities for hire on the system, then selecting a site, they could engage highly flexible staff, in their hundreds if necessary, to start work the following Monday. If there were a shortage of skilled workers, fitters qualified to work on a certain make of machine for instance, the company's demand would show up on market overview screens studied by mechanics around the country, who should then be able to click their way to the training required.

Might the Koreans be deterred by the competitiveness of the market in which they would be selling output from the new factory? If Spain was unique in its development of GEMs and the company planned to distribute across Europe, the advantages of purchasing and manufacturing in an efficient coordinated marketplace while selling in a price-heavy, relatively uninformed, uncoordinated equivalent could be overwhelming. As European integration proceeds, a nation willing to go it alone with public electronic markets alongside its adherence to all EU agreements on Internet trade could emerge as disproportionately attractive to foreign investment. Members of NAFTA, Mercosur or other regional trading pacts could be in a similar position. Individual companies in the country with GEMs would be equally equipped to extend their efficiencies abroad. A Spanish yacht maker, for instance, could send out a diaspora of representatives equipped with laptop access to GEMs over the Internet. Sitting beside a Cayman Islands millionaire, one of them would be able to input requirements for the construction of the desired craft for immediate costing. With not only company facilities but materials, additional labour and a delivery crew available for contracting instantly, the millionaire could have all his requirements competitively costed, timetabled and contracted during one visit to his poolside.

How would a country with GEMs interact with a globalizing economy? The existing online economy is dominated by US firms, who generated 85 per cent of global Internet revenues in 1997 even though only 62 per cent of Net users are thought to be Americans.[31] Because most households in the USA enjoy free local phone calls the country is likely to remain at the forefront of Internet take up for some time. Despite this dominance, there is currently widespread agreement between governments world wide about the need to encourage online transactions. Within four months in 1997, Europe, the USA and Japan issued separate policy documents focusing on the coming digital economy.[32] All three agreed broadly on a key principle for the trading revolution: government's role should be minimal, confined to the bare necessities of enacting unified new laws in cases where industry self-regulation did not work. The corporations driving the new technology are to be left free to decide how it develops. Freed from geographical restraints, companies trading digitally can site their computers anywhere in the world and still reach a global customer base. Countries with strong traditions of social welfare partially paid for by corporate taxation are unlikely to find favour with these nomadic institutions. As many commentators have already pointed out, collectively they are likely to play governments off against each other and base themselves only in the most capital-friendly havens.

Many see this lifting of national restrictions for businesses as a good thing. Both *Business Week*[33] and *Wired*,[34] the monthly bible of digital aficionados, have written approvingly of the 'long boom' anticipated from the descending prices and increased productivity of online business. From the perspective of their readership this is probably a reasonable long-term economic assessment. Elsewhere, however, a down-page news report in August 1998 shows the wider implications of these changes. British wine merchants Victoria Wine and Thresher are to close 300 shops and shed 1500 staff as they merge. The cutbacks come not as a result of traditional merger efficiencies or poor sales but because 'their online shopping profits have never been so good'.[35] Increased unemployment, caused by digital shopping, accompanied by low taxes, to placate the companies involved, form a potentially explosive social cocktail.

A GEMs country could stand back from this race to the floor of social provision. Instead of trying to tempt international money by minimizing negatives, it should be able to offer distinctive positives. Social and economic stability, corruption-free trading, low government expenditure plus a responsive and motivated workforce could be some of the points to be talked up by trade delegates. The social order and lower public spending that should accompany a GEMs system would give politicians room for manoeuvre that might be used to further protect their population from the economic buffeting of 'hot' money flashing around the world. Chile, for example, has experimented with minimum investment periods for outsiders to engender stability, but few Western countries could risk alienating the financial markets by acting likewise. If public electronic markets were to deliver their full potential, their country of operation would have a unique proposition for investors that could add considerable long-term value to its currency. Politicians need not live in fear of upsetting the markets.

Invisible trade, too, could benefit. Unless government decided otherwise, any foreign company could trade in the GEMs country by setting up a subsidiary. A Turkish hotel owner, for instance, might choose to sell his rooms in a Belgian public markets system rather than *en masse* to one of the country's tour operators. As soon as he had found insurance, or provided his own sum to go into bond, he could be in the market. Were other East Mediterranean hoteliers to do likewise, the Turkish tour companies may find it advantageous to open a 'brass plate' subsidiary in Brussels and start buying rooms for domestic tours departing from Ankara or Istanbul in GEMs, rather than over the phone. The longer a country could retain a monopoly on public markets in its region, the greater the advantage to be gained. A problem for politicians might be that foreign manufacturers were able to gain a toehold in the economy, previously denied to them. If they are able to undercut domestic suppliers in a pure market, the government might opt for protective tariffs.

As national cultures homogenize, with the continuing spread of global entertainment and cross-border business, GEMs could offer a tantalizing but intangible asset: national pride. Countries around the world have 're-branded' themselves in recent years. This project would create a sustainable difference beyond shallow perceptions: a sense of governmental purpose, rising above the confusing uncertainty that few doubt will engulf us as the unfettered digital economy really builds momentum. To quote a slogan of Silicon Valley's Palo Alto Research Center in 1970: 'the easiest way to predict the future is to invent it'.[36]

Notes to section two

1. Hugh L. McColl Jr quoted in David Greising *et al.*, Trillion Dollar Banks: are megabanks – once unimaginable, now inevitable – better for customers, the nation's economy or even for the banks? *Business Week*, 27 April 1998, electronic edition.
2. Doing Business, *Business Week*, 31 August 1998, p. 55.
3. Edmund Mierswinski quoted in March of the Banking Behemoths, *Observer*, 19 April 1998, p. 5.
4. Barbara Wood, *E. F. Schumacher: His Life and Thought*, Harper & Row, 1984, p. 363.
5. *Wealth of Nations* (1776) Bk 1, ch. 10, Pt 2.
6. www.monster.com
7. www.peoplebank.com
8. Interview with the author, 4 August 1998.
9. How the Land Lies During Interviews, *Daily Telegraph*, 18 June 1998, p. A6.
10. *Voyager*, British Midland Airways in-flight magazine, September 1998, p. 43.
11. Analysis: Jobs and Pay, *Guardian*, 16 July 1998, p. 11.
12. Thompson P. and Warhurst C. (eds) *Workplaces of the Future*, Macmillan, 1998, p. 18.
13. Ibid. p. 9.
14. Open All Hours, *Commercial Motor Magazine*, 16–22 April 1998, p. 36.
15. Interview with the author, 3 September 1998.
16. Evan I. Schwartz, *Webonomics: Nine Essential Principals for Growing your Business on the World Wide Web*, Penguin, p. 140.
17. David Brown, *Cybertrends, Chaos Power and Accountability in the Information Age*, Viking, 1997, p. 116.
18. John Pearce, *At the Heart of the Community Economy; Community Enterprise in a Changing World*, Calouste Gulbenkian Foundation, 1993, p. 18.
19. Governor John Kitzhaber, quoted in How Far Can we Trust the People? *The Economist*, 15 August 1998, p. 41.
20. Drug Tower Tenants get Power to Ban Dealers, *Observer*, 26 July 1998.
21. George Monbiot, Gene Prince, *Guardian*, 9 June 1998.
22. Melanie Phillips, They say they reject a register of nannies because Mr Blair doesn't want a nanny state. Is this a joke? *Observer*, 12 July 1998.
23. Missionary Government, *Demos Quarterly*, 7, Demos, 1995, p. 47.
24. Peter Kellner, We can Pay, But What About the Cost? *Observer*, 12 May 1998.
25. Alexander Garrett, Why Everyone's Keen to Take a Swipe at Plans for a DSS Card, *Observer*, 9 August 1998, Business p. 7.

26. Keeping Tags on Cattle, *Daily Telegraph Connected*, 12 August 1998, p. 6.

27. EDS Humbug, *Private Eye*, 4 September 1998, p. 9.

28. *Thriving in the Shadows, The World in 1998*, Economist Publications, 1987, p. 16.

29. England's Green Unpleasant Land, *Observer*, 9 August 1998, p. 8.

30. Joachim Schwarz quoted in Car Sharing Means Less Jam Today, *Guardian*, 6 March 1996.

31. Interactive Media in Retail Group, *Electronic Commerce in Europe – an Action Plan for the Marketplace*, 1998.

32. *A European Initiative in Electronic Commerce*, April 1997; *Towards the Age of the Digital Economy*, MITI (Japan) White Paper, May 1997; *A Framework for Global Electronic Commerce* (US) July 1997.

33. The 21st Century Economy, cover story, *Business Week*, 31 August 1998.

34. The Long Boom, cover story, *Wired* (5.07), July 1997.

35. Check Out Hassle-free Online Shopping, *Guardian Editor*, 29 August 1998, p. 14.

36. Antony Sampson, *Company Man: The Rise and Fall of Corporate Life*, HarperCollins, 1995.

The battle for public markets: electronic trade becomes politicised

The German philosopher Schopenhauer wrote that truth 'passes through three stages. First it is ridiculed, then violently opposed. Finally it is accepted as being self-evident.' He could as easily have been writing about campaigns aimed at persuading governments to instigate new infrastructure for public use. Because Schopenhauer's stage three has now so obviously been reached with services such as postage, nationwide rail links, water and other everyday services, originally initiated by government, it is easy to lose sight of their earlier phases. The campaign for universal flat-rate postage for instance started in the UK and was widely derided by those in authority. Parliamentary commissioners who finally agreed to consider the idea were told by the British Postmaster General that 'of all the wild and visionary schemes which he had ever heard... it was the most extraordinary'.[1] Toll road and canal companies in the UK, who eventually realized parliament was serious in its consideration of acts to spur railway growth, were appalled that 'whereas all were free to use the roads... the villainous new railway companies would hold a monopoly of the traffic on the iron roads which they proposed to build across England'.[2] Playing on the conservatism of a little-travelled public, they invoked fears that cows would stop giving milk, as fiery machines blazed by killing the grass and stopping farm animals breeding. More ridiculously still they suggested 'ladies would have to travel through tunnels with pins in their mouths to stop anyone kissing them'.[3] Ten years later, when a crusade for centrally provided clean drinking water was underway, its opponents had refined the art of opposition to infrastructure proposals. Having overcome collective incredulity at politicians offering a vision for their industry, the existing supply companies in Britain bought a newspaper, the *Daily News*, in which they relentlessly attacked the individuals advocating a mass water network.[4] The possibility that electronic trade might also be developed for social benefit could follow a similar three-phase progression. Were a clear strand of opinion to emerge that wanted public electronic markets underpinned by government, it could lead to the first campaign for mass infrastructure in a developed country in living memory. The Internet, the most recent example of a centrally initiated infrastructure, was inaugurated without public debate by Pentagon chiefs. Before that, broadcasting was directed towards mass usage by governments on both sides of the Atlantic amid little significant opposition, possibly because the companies who were to be its main victims remained complacently in a Schopenhauerian phase one. As late as 1946, Darryl F. Zanuck, head of Twentieth Century Fox and Hollywood opinion leader, believed '[television] won't be able to hold on to any market it captures after the first six months. People will soon get tired of staring at a plywood box every night.'[5]

This section looks at the possibility that the evolution of electronic commerce might become a dominant political issue. Should development be left to short-term commercial forces, with perhaps a little backstop regulation, or would Guaranteed Markets be made available to all who want them? The first route already has its priorities clear: it is driven very much by a vision of super service for a generation of restless online buyers. 'Right here. Right now. Tailored for my idea of useful or cool. Dished up the way I like it. Stripped to the core, that is what the new consumer's expectations are', writes consultant Regis McKenna, author of *Real Time: Preparing for the Age of the Never Satisfied Customer*.[6] But individuals are multifaceted and often want more from life than instant material gratification. They also seek intangibles, such as a stable society, personal empowerment and richness of experience. These social factors do not necessarily flow from a world in which formidable new technology is developed primarily to woo the most rapacious customers. The first chapter of this section explores the possibility that e-trade with no accompanying vision from government could become its own worst enemy, causing inequalities and market distortions likely eventually to provoke a backlash against the technology. Assuming individuals in their capacity as voters, rather than customers, will eventually become a force in the trading revolution, the next chapter outlines steps politicians might take to instigate electronic markets for mass benefit. Likely opposition to such a move is discussed in the chapter that follows. There are valid concerns to be raised in response to the idea of government-initiated markets, not least the undesirability of one operator being awarded certain advantages by the state and the perilous consequences of any system failure. These are examined. So, too, is the possible reaction of powerful organizations who would have much to lose as an economy atomised. A final chapter in this section asks which countries would have the most to gain from launching a first public electronic markets system.

13 Could there be a backlash against electronic shopping?

The disproportionate benefits of online trade for large sellers

US phone company AT&T used to run a seductive commercial in which two young women, dismayed at the shortcomings of their hard plastic sunglasses, set up in business making a more pliant alternative. Although the mechanics of manufacture present no problem, their newly founded company, Rubbereyes, cannot find retail distribution. In despair, they turn to AT&T Web Site Services, start selling over the Internet and enjoy swift success. This notion, that Net selling will, by its nature, create one level playing field in which a small newcomer can immediately reach world-wide consumers, has been enthusiastically propagated, not least by companies who would like to see every corner store and lone trader setting up a website. The reality, however, is shaping up very differently. 'People say there are no limits to channels on the Internet. But that's not the limiting factor here. The real limits are how to get through to people and get their attention', explains one commentator.[7] The number of online enthusiasts who will enter, say, 'sunglasses' into Internet search software then laboriously peruse even a few of the 190 000 sites returned at time of writing is diminishing sharply. Instead, interactive shoppers increasingly call up a 'one stop' site that allows them to shop with a manageable number of pre-selected retailers. These Net 'portals' are widely seen as the way forward in Net commerce because they simplify a range of online facilities, including shopping. With millions of users visiting a typical portal every day, the operators can sell their virtual real estate to the highest-bidding retailers. A regular visitor to the Netscape Netcentre, for instance, who clicks for finance information will find the subsequent display favouring the product range of Citibank. The US institution is reported to have agreed to payment of $40 million over three years for this prime cyber-space location.[8] Other portals offer customers the facility to search product databases of several partner retailers in search of their require-ments. Without one of these expensive relationships, restricted to big suppliers who keep the number of virtual storefronts manageable, outfits like the fictional Rubbereyes will probably find benefits of the new marketplace pass them by. To quote *Fortune* magazine: 'launching an e-commerce site without a Portal partner is like opening a retail store in the desert. Sure, it's cheap, but does anybody stop there?'[9]

It is not just issues of visibility that are beginning to conspire against small traders in the uncoordinated marketplace. Another problem arises from the changing role of computers in organizations. In its early days, business computing was seen merely as a way to cut costs by automating administration. Now intricate exploitation of information is at the core of many corporations' activities. The bigger the enterprise, the more intelligence it possesses and the greater sophistication with which this can be applied. In 1985, the airline People Express was an early victim of this potential. Running a strictly no-frills service and undercutting major carriers, the company was for a while the fastest growing in the US. It was SABRE, American Airlines' enormous order-taking system, that largely reversed their growth. Using the system's vast reserves of data on load patterns and pricing sensitivity, American began to offer dozens of fares for any one departure, automatically changing the mix in response to demand until the gate closed. Seats that could only be filled with backpackers willing to accept travel restrictions were priced below People Express rates, while high-revenue generating business travellers were still sold expensive open tickets. Within a year of SABRE being unleashed in this way, People Express, with no market insights on a comparable scale, had lost half their market share. The company was sold off in 1986.[10]

Today, it is not only information about market sensitivities but details of individual customers that offers added leverage to those who possess it in enormous quantities. US retailer JCPenney, for instance, holds records on 98 million customers including particularly detailed records on the transactions of 17 million store card holders.[11] In the early days of vast databases this information could have been processed through online analytical processing (OLAP) software to answer questions such as 'what were our five top selling lines last year?' or 'how many customers closed their account with us in the last six months compared to the first half of the year?' That simplistic interrogation has now been superseded by complex 'data mining' capabilities that predict behaviour. Store chiefs can ask 'which customers are likely to switch their accounts to a competitor in the next six months?' or 'which additional products are most likely to be sold with a purchase of men's shoes?'[12] Desirable individuals whose spending traits suggest they are in the process of switching to a competitor can then be targeted with lower prices or extra services. Any male footwear buyer can be offered the additional purchases that he is most likely to accept. Corporations using these predictive tools keep their findings to themselves but there is little doubt of their efficacy as they continue to mature. A 1998 presentation from Swiss Bank Corporation, 'Using Data Mining to Identifying Behaviour', showed how such systems can teach themselves: drawing together strands that mere humans in the marketing department may have missed.[13] The resulting leanness of operation and understanding of the marketplace extracted from bigger and bigger data pools are crucial drivers towards ever larger corporations.

AT&T's idealized two-women-and-an-idea business would probably suffer additionally for its lack of a recognized brand name. Unlike three dimensional shopping, which at least imbues traders who set up a premises with some measure of solidity, the online buyer cannot see behind a web site. There could be a keen and professional outfit waiting to despatch his sunglasses or a group of fly-by-nights who will take his money and disappear. It is always a temptation to confine credit card details to known names that have been around for some time. Certainly, fledgling brands are emerging on the Net but they increasingly represent a new big name, not a diversity of small traders. Amazon.com, for instance, became a force in book retailing in just a few months but it is one monolithic organization that displaced others slow to understand the winner-takes-all potential of Net trade. Few industry leaders will be so slow in the future.

This landscape, where big players are able to lever their strength in the old economy to near domination of the new, will be set in stone when interactive home shopping graduates from the complications of Internet access to less intimidating two-way television services. You cannot create a web site of your own on a TV set. Nor can companies not approved by the broadcaster offer their wares. *Information Strategy* magazine reports 'broadcasters are prepared to fight tooth and nail rather than use digital television to give their viewers direct Internet access'.[14] The technical requirements of retailing by interactive television form an additional barrier to entry. Because they demand richness of broadcast content that can be manipulated by a user who has no significant processing power in his set, such sites will cost between $800 000 and $1 600 000, according to one software company already geared up for this market.[15] Viewers must then be confined to these sites, not free to seek out bargains from cheaper operators. The intention is to retain viewers and their spending potential within a 'walled garden', explains a senior executive at the ironically named Open TV, a company providing underlying operating software for two-way television.[16]

As a highly convenient and reliable new marketplace on interactive television sets is unrolled for the exclusive benefit of powerful retailers, market diversity will diminish further. In the bricks and mortar world of, say, travel agency anyone could still set up their own high street premises and draw some customers from the existing operators, by virtue either of a niche specialization or catchment area. The first advantage is not sustainable in the digital age; if a niche is worth having, the Thomas Cook store on Open interactive television can enter it immediately. They no longer need additional salespeople or display space. The uniqueness of a catchment area disappears likewise; Thomas Cook's Open front end becomes the nearest, most convenient travel agent to anyone connected to the system. Walter Forbes, an early visionary of online shopping and former chairman of Cendant Corporation, one of its undoubted success stories in terms of consumer take-up, has predicted a shake-out of companies selling online 'which will make the restaurant business look stable'. He believes fewer than 15 companies will end up making 80 per cent of online sales.[17] The worst consequences of this 'closing of capitalism' are suggested by recent actions of supermarket chains in the UK. Having underpriced and out-convenienced a former tapestry of neighbourhood stores, the now unchallengeable chains responded to their new playing field by ruthlessly controlling suppliers, increasing margins to the point where British shoppers pay a third more than those in Germany or the USA, and becoming a significant force in political lobbying in an attempt to maintain their *status quo*.[18]

There will always be specialized suppliers who find a niche and develop a level of customer relationships with which no large player can compete, a site selling art deco lamps to appreciative enthusiasts for instance. But if the new very attractive marketplace is left to develop with no wider vision than immediate commercial considerations it is likely to emerge as a platform on which the bulk of activity flows through large corporations. Unlike the paternalistic firms that signified national achievement in previous decades, tomorrow's big players are likely to be increasingly unpopular. They will certainly be free of the need to employ anything like the numbers they have in the past. The consequence of cheaper goods and hassle-free shopping could be dramatically increased unemployment. In Britain, to take one example, over 10 per cent of jobs are retail related. Interactive shopping needs only offer a small advantage to tip high streets into the beginning of a downward spiral of increasing relative prices and reduced ranges, accompanied by progressive job cuts. But even this scenario does not reveal the full extent of the social and economic damage new trading technology could conceivably cause if left purely to the uncoordinated market.

Market force: the black arts available to online marketeers

The business elite currently driving the trading revolution enjoy a rarefied life. As they relentlessly pursue new frontiers in profitability, dealing with the highest levels of the aggressive companies who fund their activities, they are in danger of developing values that may not play well once they become more widely recognized. 'A battle is imminent' averred a 1998 statement from Britain's well respected Interactive Media in Retailing Group 'to own the consumer and to control these new channels to them'.[19] In other words it is not enough to be a powerful player, the aim is then to distort the electronic marketplace. The phrase 'owning the customer' was much in vogue in e-commerce publications and presentations in late 1997 and early 1998. It translates as controlling the information that a consumer must give about themselves as part of an initial transaction to see that they subsequently have little incentive to shop anywhere else. This should be presented as a benefit offered by your company. An airline, for instance, to which you have told your credit card details plus seating and meal preferences for an initial ticket, then automatically applies them to every future flight booked on their site. If you are in a hurry you are likely simply to book with them rather than shopping for a better fare which might entail repeating the information to a second carrier. Additionally, the company owning the information can contact the customer with offers based on past patterns of purchase. More advanced programming is being developed by other sellers hoping to reap the same benefit. A marketing newsletter tells the story of North Carolina-based Textile/Clothing Technology Corp. who have introduced a scanning device in stores that can pinpoint more than 300 000 points on the body using an array of cameras. Once measured, a consumer can then order personalised garments from the company. The newsletter notes 'the challenge facing [the company] is making sure the customer can't walk away with measurement data that can be carried to a competitor and used successfully'.[20] In the GEMs model, by contrast, this kind of personal data could be input by any user, in this case with a tape measure or through a device attached to the system by someone charging for its use, and harnessed by them to shop around at will.

Facilities like body scanners do not come cheaply and for maximum profitability need to be concentrated on customers who have plenty of money to spend. This is no longer difficult to achieve. The practice of charging richer customers lower fees to retain their business has long been practised, among credit providers for instance: it is becoming both widespread and more finely honed. An emerging science, Customer Value Management, enables individuals to be assessed by a company's computer for their profitability to the firm. Instead of the market as a whole supporting a certain standard of service for everyone, as has previously been the case, a firm's resources can then be targeted at the well off. The leading evangelists of this movement are Don Peppers and Martha Rogers who run a Stamford, Connecticut, marketing consultancy and published the seminal *Enterprise One to One: Tools for Competing in the Interactive Age* in 1997.[21] They advise companies to segment customers by profitability potential, present and future, so someone identified as a student, for example, might have low value for a furniture retailer but is worth cultivating for their spending potential after graduation.

At the bottom of the Peppers and Rogers metric are 'below zeros' or BZs, consumers who 'will probably never earn enough profit to justify the expense involved in serving them. Every business has some of these customers, and our objective should be to get rid of them.'[22] The duo admit 'dealing with BZs is definitely a ticklish problem',[23] not because of any social concerns but for fear of a public relations disaster. Their book documents the story of First Chicago bank whose goal was 'to find a gracious way to help its unprofitable customers become some other bank's unprofitable customers'.[24] The solution: to charge clients with little money in their accounts more for certain transactions.[25] Doing so did eventually contribute significantly to reduced costs of operation but the tactic was spotted and made headlines. As Customer Value Management tools become increasingly sophisticated, there are fewer examples of such a blunt approach to the dumping of undesirable customers and less chance of the companies doing so facing the public scrutiny suffered by First Chicago. Peppers and Rogers are not fringe thinkers, embarrassing to mainstream electronic commerce developers. In 1997 IBM was giving away a sponsored edition of *Enterprise One to One* at conferences in Europe: in 1998 Oracle, a big supplier of business software, announced a global partnership with the duo's consulting firm.[26]

Pioneers of the trading revolution are putting considerable effort into refining Customer Value Management tools that enable their computers more subtly to assess the worth of any customer. This process will become easier still as trading moves online and, once again, it favours large companies with an extensive customer base. One 1998 survey found as many as 40 or 50 per cent of retail customers are actually not profitable.[27] With online sellers no longer needing to maintain a minimum level of service the underclass are likely to find they are discreetly earmarked for expulsion by many service providers. Crucial to this ruthless new approach to marketing is the ability of those operating sales channels to compile information about their customers and trade it with other providers. 'We'll all have to get used to the fact that there will simply be less privacy' writes *Wired* magazine in their *Encyclopaedia of the New Economy*.[28] Automated marketing techniques feed on details of individual lives which are being gathered from increasingly ingenious sources. An advertisement in Britain's *Direct Marketing* magazine for March/April 1998 offers to sell a database of 'affluent home improvers'.

The firm offering the data, Glenigan Direct Marketing Solutions, has had no dealings with these householders: it has gleaned their status from 'planning applications nation-wide'. As early as 1995 a report into the future of electronic commerce warned 'it is now possible to assemble a profile of an individual that draws upon quite disparate sources of data – health care information, consumer purchases, banking habits, movies watched, travel and dining habits gleaned from credit card transactions and so on'.[29]

Means of collecting this information continue to advance, driven by the competitive advantages of new marketing methodologies. A Colorado-based company, Earthwatch Inc., has launched the first commercially accessible spy satellite. It allows marketing departments to purchase detailed photographs of homes, perhaps clocking what make of car sits on the drive or whether they would have space for a backyard swimming pool.[30] Insensitive use of personal data can undisputedly provoke hostile sentiments from consumers, *The Economist* has reported on one woman who tried to break her relationship with a supermarket chain after receiving an automatically generated letter reminding her it was time she replenished supplies of tampons.[31] Online trade bodies are aware of these concerns and have responded with groupings such as TRUSTe which allows subscribing organizations to display an award mark in return for signing up to principles that protect shoppers' privacy. A weakness here, as the trade magazine *Future Shopping* notes, is '[the] possibility that policies might change after the data was collected'.[32] It is not clear how these self-regulating schemes will evolve as electronic commerce concentrates on to interactive television channels. It may be hard for governments to rule effectively on online privacy, as information can so easily be moved around the world to offshore 'data havens' by unscrupulous operators. Once again, a GEMs system would offer a different approach, assiduously protecting its users' information within a closed network. More importantly it could remove much of the incentive to collect personal details by any other route. Buyers in GEMs would automatically find their best value deal instantly, there would be little point incurring overheads to build a relationship with them unless they expressly wished to form that bond (Box 13.1).

Box 13.1

GEMS AND USER PRIVACY

GEMs would have an unequivocal approach to confidentiality. The system invites constant inspection to demonstrate it is simply not capable of collating details of an individual user's activities or preferences. Standard contracts include a 'no unsolicited communications' clause which a seller can remove at the risk of turning away potential buyers or a buyer can remove if they want to be kept informed by a particular seller. Information about a user's trades could only be accessed with a court order. Suppose for example a distraught wife rings the control room of a future Brazilian GEMs system at 1.00 am to say she knows her spouse has booked accommodation in Rio that night and she needs to know the address because their daughter has had an accident. That may be the case, alternately she might suspect him of entertaining a mistress and be planning to go round and spoil the party. That is not a judgement, between the man's absolute right to privacy and his likely wish to be informed of a familial catastrophe, that GEMs staff would be empowered to make. If the wife wants his records on the system opened she must obtain a court order, possibly over the phone from a duty judge, which will include a PIN. This becomes the equivalent of a launch code in a missile bunker, allowing staff to open the man's record of most recent contracts which are sent blind to the judge's terminal. It would be his decision what information is revealed to the wife. A message is automatically left for the husband telling him what has happened.

The potential impact of uncoordinated electronic commerce on society

The early days of technological revolutions have often been economically intoxicating but socially damaging. Even as Britain ascended to domination of global manufacturing on the back of the Industrial Revolution, small children were learning to work 12-hour days in her factories. Philanthropists who questioned this were blankly assured that a need to remain competitive forced factory owners to extract maximum value from the families they housed. Only after the inhumanity of the revolution became inarguable were Factory Acts, limiting the age of employees, forced on grudging industrialists who collectively tended to believe their new vista of wealth creation should advance without hindrance. Some electronic trade gurus have shown themselves dangerously prone to the same view. It may yet emerge that the trading revolution will likewise add to the sum of human misery even as it delights economists and investment analysts. No-one seriously disputes that the move to an online economy will destroy jobs, for instance. Hardware supplier Cisco, one of the early giants of Net selling, has saved itself a reported $363 million a year and the need for 1000 employees by automating its order taking through a web site.[33] Its customer companies, too, save on labour costs because there is no paperwork or payment procedures. The hotly contested point is: will new avenues of work emerge to replace the retail, supply management and finance jobs now being decimated? In the short term there is little shortage of employment for computing personnel but this may only be a temporary bonus as companies switch to new technology and then settle down to years of updates by a skeleton staff. Two journalists on the German news magazine *Der Spiegel* analysed the underlying trends in developed world employment for a book and concluded that eventually 20 per cent of the workforce will suffice to keep the economy going. The remainder will be perpetually surplus to requirements.[34] Defenders of the new online economy, however, point to a sustained growth in service industries, particularly call centre operations. Assuming they are correct and this booming sector will ultimately cancel out the downsizing in other industries, what quality of employment will it offer?

Customer care in a world where companies enjoy unprecedented computing power demands a very different salesperson from the traditional ambassador for his employer. A 1998 UK report described call centres, the fastest growing employment sector in the British economy, as 'the ultimate form of industrial tyranny'.[35] Serried ranks of operators are usually expected to complete between 100 and 150 near identical calls a day with only seconds between them.[36] The operations manager of one such centre for the British Halifax Direct financial services company explains, 'there is no button pushing, the system dials and as soon as the call goes through it is routed to a free agent. This means agents can maximize the time they spend talking to customers.'[37] Dialogue is read from a computer screen which is where the intelligence of the system resides. A website for Graham Technology, one of the companies supplying call centres boasts their GT-X software analyses the result of each call as input by operators and '"learns" which scripts are most effective in terms of results and the minimum number of steps to complete the transaction'.[38] Monitoring employee productivity in this environment presents no problems; 'the tyranny of the assembly line is but a Sunday school picnic compared with the control that management can exercise in computer telephony', surmised the report's authors.[39] Rate of calls and their duration for each worker on a shift are routinely collated, the actual words spoken can be taped for later analysis. The efficiency demanded by many centres dictates that staff dare not take coffee or lunch breaks away from their desks for fear of rebuke.[40] Despite one in four British call centre operators being a university graduate, there is virtually no hope of promotion: performance is monitored for senior management by the central computer with only a handful of supervisors required.[41] Is there a danger of this conveyor belt communication being a turn off for customers? Human warmth can be made part of the script. A former call centre operator, writing to a newspaper in February 1998, attested to the tiring nature of her work, which demanded a new call be answered within a second of the old one finishing and added 'if you didn't get in the "closing salutation" you would be assigned to retraining'.[42] This new role for business computing, as day-to-day driver of the organization, with closely monitored humans carrying out its decisions, can only increase as software developments like Enterprise Resource Planning penetrate further into the market.

Despite this maximized productivity, call centre operations are expensive, which makes them vulnerable. One US survey puts the average total cost of each call at $3.21.[43] A medium-term threat to call centre jobs comes from mass migration away from the phone towards screen-based shopping through interactive television sets. Customer service need not suffer in this new environment. Programming that mimics a human dialogue when potential customers type in their individual enquiry is already well developed. E-mail a few lines to Insure Direct in the USA, for example, asking for a quote on motor cover and its computer will communicate back and forth in an individualised conversation.[44] Because the firm have shaved that $3.21 off the cost of each interaction they may well be able to offer a lower price than elsewhere.

Guaranteed Electronic Markets could offer a long-term alternative to mind-numbing and insecure work in call centres and other lowly business functions. A country with GEMs would enable its citizens effortlessly to seek their own mix of work, including time at a call centre on their own terms if they wished. Take as an instance a young woman who currently answers the phone for a financial sector employer: she may have initially been attracted to that post because of an aptitude for figures and a desire to help people. With GEMs on her side those factors would provide far wider choice. She might for instance hire herself out as a coach for schoolchildren having problems with their arithmetic, as a financial planner for local enterprises or as an expert in very particular investment vehicles whose knowledge can be bought over the phone by the hour. In each market she would be scheduled according to personal priorities, have every incentive to upgrade her qualifications and reap the rewards of a stable trading record. If pickings were lean, she could additionally enter the market for general clerical work signifying a willingness to work in call centres. Her life could be enriched in this way once politicians offered a vision for electronic commerce to run alongside the current exploitation by corporations. The point is not that governments have any inherent duty to provide richness and variety of experience for their electorates. Simply that it might soon be a vote winner to do so. It is also worth considering that the bright young woman reduced to conversations parroted from her computer screen for 40 hours a week is contributing a fraction of her economic potential to society, compared with a motivated and flexible trader spanning several markets as she responds to ever-changing local conditions.

In many sections of society people who work in call centres are regarded as the lucky ones: they have a job. The long-term unemployed are not a topic that merit much discussion at e-commerce conferences. As one round table put it, 'we don't need what they have and they can't buy what we sell'.[45] But in most developed countries these people have votes and they may not like what they see as the online marketplace begins to bite. Unable to afford the hardware for Internet or interactive TV shopping, and of little interest to sellers even if they could, they are likely to be meeting their needs from what remains of high-street retailing after it has been progressively vacated by the better off. The lingering demise of shopping centres could remove what is often the last safe community space for many. Social provision can only be restricted in an era where governments must compete with low tax regimes to entice foreign investment and keep their own companies competitive on the world stage. Realistic hopes of a job are already folklore in depressed areas of first world countries. In the UK, for example, nearly

40 per cent of the tens of thousands of 16-year-olds who leave school without significant qualifications fail to find work or further training.[46] The grey economy becomes a continued temptation for these young people, further depriving state services of tax income and increasing the fear of the lawless world beyond their front door that others perceive.

What can governments do to improve quality of life for their electorates if they decide to go with the current flow of online developments rather than offering their own vision with a GEMs style system? Few commentators dispute that multinational businesses are already becoming more powerful at the expense of national politicians. Some argue this is a good thing, because at least businesses have a sense of direction and tendency towards efficiency. But the story of the Canadian parliament's conflict with the Virginia-based Ethyl Corporation in July 1998 illustrates the fears behind the opposing view. Ethyl manufacture MMT, a fuel additive thought by some scientists to be a dangerous pollutant.[47] After a debate the Ottawa parliament voted to ban the substance in April 1997. Under the terms of NAFTA (North American Free Trade Agreement) however, Ethyl sued the government alleging unfair barriers to trade had been raised. With little chance of upholding their judgement, Canada's legislators capitulated to the corporation and agreed to pay the firm $13 million in compensation. The framework of NAFTA is similar to that of the, as yet unrealized, Multilateral Agreement on Investment or MAI which will, many believe, allow big businesses to shape a global marketplace suiting their priorities in the online age rather than the concerns of national governments. Defeated in April 1998, the MAI is scheduled for a new round of preliminary negotiations with a view to becoming international law in the future.[48]

The sum of bleak projections in this chapter may not be the outcome of a mature uncoordinated online economy. It could be that the portal model does not last and Internet shoppers find ways of traversing all sorts of sales outlets with total faith in the results. Interactive TV shoppers might then successfully demand access to the untamed Internet so they can do the same (thereby destroying the business model for an entire sector). Either the US model of industry regulation or the European belief in enforced restraint may resolve issues of privacy. And high quality jobs for the masses could emerge from a source as yet largely unforeseen. If this were to happen, GEMs could be no more than the final step on a road towards wide-open online marketplaces. If, however, the trends at the time of writing converge further, we could be heading for a two-tier online economy. The well off will eventually enjoy handy, secure and low-cost access to large suppliers who fight for their custom. An underclass, who are at best tolerated by operators of the new channels, will have to contend with poorly developed buyer–seller matching services on the Internet, in which the buyer has to beware at every stage of the transaction. In this case underpinned public markets would offer a completely alternative route.

It is possible that the voracious computerisation of capital flows, order taking and product marketing may contain the seeds of its own collapse. In *One World Ready or Not: the Manic Logic of Global Capitalism*,[49] journalist William Greider compares the new economy to a powerful runaway machine rampaging through countryside with no one at the wheel. As that machine builds momentum it is difficult to see who will enjoy any sustained advantages from its progress. Large businesses? Initially yes, but in the longer term they could see their customer bases truncated as more and more people are excluded from significant participation in economies. Company executives? But the marketplace is increasingly unstable; mergers and acquisitions often result in scant respect for valuable career histories and the pressure to deliver increasing returns can be inescapable. It is telling that personal counselling services for senior executives are mushrooming.[50] Owners of capital? In an acute irony it is often the individuals being downsized and marginalized who provide the money, through pensions and savings, with which fund managers are working so pitilessly to obtain the best return. Customers? There will be those so enamoured with falling comparative prices and immediate gratification but untroubled by the wider state of society who will welcome uncoordinated e-trade even after any pernicious effects are clear. But GEMs would also offer lower prices, across a far wider range of markets. Those who hold principles of non-government intervention higher than social conditions could start to become a minority.

Would financial companies, retailers and service providers really offload staff while targeting only well-off individuals for sales, thereby ultimately shrinking the number of people who are economically active enough to be potential customers? Could a whole industry charge into new technology with so little consideration for its wider long-term effects? It has happened before. A few decades ago equipment developed for submarine warfare allowed fishing boats to precisely locate shoals of fish, which could then be instantly scooped up in a new generation of super nets. It was pointed out at the time that once this became commonplace the biological diversity on which trawling's future rested would be compromised but individual skippers reasoned that the big picture was someone else's problem. As the previous vagaries of deep sea netting gave way to trawlers leaving port for a precise destination at which point they simply harvested a boat load of marine life and returned, governments found themselves unable to prevent an impending crisis. The problems were similar to those that will face any parliament trying to rein in e-commerce. If Iceland had successfully commanded its trawlers to stop hauling cod out of the North Atlantic those fish would simply have ended up in boats bound for Newfoundland. By 1992 the targeting and gathering efficiencies of trawling technology had laid waste to fragile food chains and left entire species commercially extinct. Governments and the industry finally agreed to implement quotas, which saw boats around the world decommissioned while communities wait for the previous diversity to re-establish itself. The comparative richness of our economic life could conceivably be demolished by paradigm-shifting technology as inexorably as was the diversity of species on our fishing grounds.

Government's response to maturing e-trade

It is the contention of this book that the future of online commerce is going to become a subject of sustained public debate sooner or later. Multinational businesses and their consultants should not be held as villains in this scenario. They exist, as firms always have, to pursue profitable opportunities as they arise. Corporations have no mandate to restrict their potential in pursuit of amorphous, off balance sheet, social objectives. It is governments who will eventually have to face the problems caused by selective new efficiencies in commerce. They could opt to constrain the technology, but national restraints risk being counterproductive in a globalised arena. Industry self-regulation would avoid the need for legislative action but, as with the world's trawler captains, it may take epoch-defining calamity to unite participants on this course. Another option would simply be for governments to accept they can do more than sit on the sidelines of the trading revolution and put a system of Guaranteed Markets in place, while leaving global business channels to go their own way. *Information Strategy* magazine, aimed at a corporate readership, examined the possibility of GEMs in February 1998 after an interview with this author. 'If any government did seek to intervene in the market in such a way there would be very loud howls of protest from some very powerful companies' they wrote in an editorial headed 'Behave or else…'. It continued: 'but what is the alternative? If governments adopt a completely *laissez-faire* approach they risk leaving themselves and a large number of their citizens completely powerless.'[51] It would be a brave parliament that began outlining a social vision for electronic commerce, but one motivated by understanding of a changed world rather than ingrained ideology. The notion of public electronic markets transcends philosophies of left or right. True, it would require fleeting government involvement in the initiatory phase but any rightist condemning the concept as left wing for that reason must attach the same label to Margaret Thatcher's Channel Tunnel project. GEMs' immediate beneficiaries would include the currently poor but they would be elevated not by handouts or centrally imposed restrictions on the well off. Instead closer equality would come from the chance to participate in what could be some of the most uncompromised free markets the world would ever have seen. Crucially, those markets would no longer be protective of big players. The broad aims of Karl Marx might be achieved by the philosophy of Adam Smith.

History suggests there is an inevitability about new technology being channelled towards maximum social benefit by policy makers. Debate can be fierce but it has a tendency to cross party lines. For example, 150 years ago an arch priest of non-government intervention, Nassau Senior, considered problems of sanitation and proposals for public water supply in Britain before writing 'with all our reverence for the principle of non-interference, we cannot doubt that in this matter it has been pushed too far'.[52] Another infrastructure scheme, universal flat rate postage, was introduced by a Whig (centre party) parliament in the UK but nurtured, and defended from attacks, by its Tory (rightist) successor, then, once it was seen to work, initiated by governments of all hues around the world. Railways, roads, telephones and broadcasting spread across the world as public infrastructure, with governing ideologies able only to speed or delay their introduction by a few years. Notable exceptions, South

Africa's resistance to the liberalising potential of television until the 1970s for instance, hardly halted that medium's otherwise relentless advance and only increased the apartheid regime's isolation. It might take only one country to successfully demonstrate the benefits of officially underpinned electronic markets before they started to spread to other nations. There are some countries in which public debate has become too calcified around unquestioned belief that government inactivity is always the preferable option for GEMs ever to be launched. Other nations could be more pragmatic.

14

How a government could instigate GEMs

The act that launched a GEMs service would need plotting in immense detail to ensure it achieved its desired effect, an outcome that can never be guaranteed. The US Telecommunications Act of 1996, for instance, was intended to open the telephony market to a wide range of sellers but instead encouraged big players to consolidate.[53] In the case of GEMs, the aim would be to shape a viable business opportunity for the winning consortium while ensuring benefits of trading technology were spread as widely as possible. Once the official protection for a potential system and its accompanying obligations had been crafted and a winning consortium selected, the goals both of parliament and the consortium would be very similar. In a democracy, both would need the new markets to grow while having every reason to continuously assert their independence from each other. Even in countries where many utilities are state run it would be undesirable for parliament to control a GEMs system: the technology has social implications that puts it on a par with broadcasting rather than water or electricity supply. Furthermore, politicians around the world have proved themselves spectacularly inept at articulating a consistent vision for large computer projects. Past evidence suggests that, once a vision is outlined, it is the private sector that should make it reality. Both sides of the pact should adhere to a fundamental principle of GEMs: taxpayers do not fund the project and no one is ever to be forced to use the system (except in the context of a professional relationship at the behest of an employer). Another absolute is that the launch not be predicated on any attempt to restrict the non-GEMs world of online commerce in any way. There would not, for instance, be a repeat of the French government's effective outlawing of Teletext to protect a nascent Minitel online service in the 1980s.

Politicians would probably be tempted to launch part of a GEMs service rather than the full system, which could unite so many powerful opponents. They might opt for a system that trades periods of work, for instance, but lacks the critical mass and software efficiencies of other sectors. That is to risk being a national also-ran if other countries move to full underpinned public electronic markets. A consortium that is looking to a future building additional countries' GEMs-style facilities would be rightly cautious of such an opportunity, particularly if they were expected to obtain a return using the 'penny post' model of radically low pricing. A parliament truly committed to the full GEMs vision would need to instigate changes that would run through to every nerve end of government. The first politicians along this road would suffer the hardest battles; once a first country had a system in operation, later entrants would at least have a map to follow. However a consortium serious about GEMs might treat the first country in which it wins a commission as a loss leader, to be allocated additional spending so the markets evolve more quickly.

What do governments have to offer a winning consortium?

The package of benefits enshrined in law for a winning consortium should include:

- 'Must carry' status with high visibility, mandated on the nation's television platforms. This would be akin to the British government's decision to award key multiplexes (channels) on its digital spectrum to the established broadcasters on the grounds that those organizations are crucial to national culture. Where a very low number channel was no longer available, GEMs would be assured of a prominently flagged position in the main programme guides.
- Contracts on the system to be legally enforced with GEMs specifically absolved from ever being judged a counterparty in any deal enacted between its users. The courts would need to uphold contracts drawn up by the system and accept its mechanism for freezing monies until resolution. Further, court officials around the country would accept disputed transactions forwarded automatically by the system and input judgement on their GEMs terminals, so that the system could apply any fines awarded.

- Pump priming of the markets. All government buying, selling and staff rostering goes through the system in its initial stages. If the prison service is buying bread, for instance, it shops first in GEMs and has to justify a decision to then buy elsewhere on grounds of better value. Hospital staff are scheduled through their individual GEMs diaries, which they can control with the same flexibility as any other user. If they do not wish to connect to the system at home, they could of course use a terminal at work.
- The system is allowed the highest levels of encryption and legal protection of users' privacy because of its near crime-free status.
- A raft of miscellaneous legislation that acknowledges the safety of trading in a GEMs environment would also be required. As the insurance function is so important to the new marketplace, for instance, the rules on who can act as an insurer might be relaxed. For example an individual with $200 to invest for a week might put it in GEMs bond and sell the cover to someone at the opposite end of the country who was hiring herself out to iron neighbours' clothes during that period. So long as she did not exceed say five bookings that could be all the cover for accidental damage to garments she would require: her trading record would automatically rank the statistical likelihood of an insurer having to pay out for her negligence. With freeing of regulations, the GEMs capital market could instantly show investors where their most profitable opportunity for a chosen level of risk was to be found across the entire spectrum of demand for money. Likewise lawyers need to be enabled to work across the board on a no-win no-fee basis (Box 14.1).
- State agencies would also need to be made ready for the system. The driver licensing authority for example would need to start issuing PINs generated by GEMs with its paperwork: it should not be a difficult process, their computer could obtain the codes through a link to the GEMs machine.
- The new system should be given stringent protection for its interface with users, just as banknotes usually have legal status above other copyrighted designs. Online services who try to confuse the public by passing themselves off as GEMs would be treated as forgers.
- Legal backing for the system's relationship with banks so it can credit and debit users' acounts. In countries without a reliable financial infrastructure the system may itself need authority to act as a bank for users.

Box 14.1

THE ROLE OF LAWYERS IN A GEMS DISPUTE:

Verifiable lawyers who chose to offer their services on GEMs could be automatically allocated cases according to their pricing formula or, if prices of many individuals and firms converge, randomizing software. They would act for groups of aggrieved purchasers. If, for instance, a trader delivering parcels is unacceptably late on his round, the senders of every package in his van can be banded together by GEMs and all their contracts passed to a legal services provider trading on the system. This would be provided for in each of their contracts for delivery although they could, of course, remove the clause. The wording would specify a level of trading record for lawyers to which complaints would be passed. If the parcel operator denied culpability, a lawyer needs to be able to take the case on without having to contact each individual counterpart to see if they were willing to pay an upfront fee.

- One further possibility: governments might agree to use their control of taxation to tempt people on to the system. The advantages of increasing market turnover, attracting activity out of the grey economy and ease of collection could arguably offset a reduction in rates for GEMs transactions.

A winning consortium would be assured of a monopoly on this package of benefits for a specified period, perhaps fifteen years. In return they would have to comply with conditions enshrined in their tender document, designed to spread the benefits of the new marketplace as widely as possible.

What concessions might politicians extract from a winning consortium?

Government's priorities in a GEMs launch should be to ensure that full benefits of the new markets are available to anyone in the country who wishes to use them, while giving existing businesses sufficient time and information to adapt to their impact. In addition to their set-up costs for the system core, a winning consortium might find their agreement with parliament stipulated the following:

■ The successful companies fund a given number and geographic spread of GEMs terminals in public places around the country. These should be efficiently used; unlike, say, web browsers, a GEMs' interface would not be a source of entertainment. Apart from browsing for purchases, most users should primarily be checking their work diaries and printing details of any contracts they had secured, a process taking minutes. (A micro-charge for printing could, of course, be deducted from their account.) One terminal in perhaps the bus station of a depressed area might service 120 people a day. Many of them could be daily users of that machine each running a range of GEMs businesses, perhaps undertaking to log on in search of assignments before a certain time every weekday morning.

■ Restrictions on increases in the commission charged to users so the consortium could not abuse its position. This should not hamper potential earnings from the project: merely ensure they have to come from continued growth in usage. This, coupled with a fixed term on the agreement, could counter any tendency towards undynamic complacency in the consortium.

■ A clear timetable of roll out for individual market sectors is published in advance, so the transition to GEMs trading can be predicted. An accountancy firm specialising in sports club clients, for instance, would be entitled to know when the system's market for football ticket sales with its automatic auditing would be unveiled. Policymakers might chose to enforce this timetable with fines for the consortium if it was behind schedule. The interlocking nature of GEMs markets would dictate a reasonably rapid launching order: the usefulness of a market in sheet glass for instance would be limited without an accompanying forum in which specialist transport was traded, that in turn would be dependent on active general haulage and driver hire sectors. Similarities in software requirements might also influence the order in which sectors are made available: once a market in shipping domestic goods abroad was written, perhaps with customs routines for purchasers automated, a similar market in air freight could be ready almost immediately.

■ Full transparency of operation to enable constant inspection of the system.

- The consortium might have to provide certain non commission generating facilities such as voting and perhaps local friendship matching without charge to users.
- Although the consortium is likely to be made up of international companies running the core GEMs hardware and software, parliament could insist that the individual markets are run by franchisees who would all be nationals. (The details of a proposed GEMs franchising system that would allow for organic growth is contained in Appendix two.)
- Additionally, government might want to tie the launch of GEMs to other online initiatives, the provision of nationwide e-mail perhaps. These might be run on the GEMs core computers using the system's networking but should be operated by other companies to avoid unjustified centralization.
- Automatic tax collection on the system but always at individual user's discretion. The consortium might be required to pay for interface with government legacy computers that provide up-to-date information on tax rates for transactions in any given market. Once that was achieved a newly directive scale of taxation across countless sectors of the economy could be applied. Assume, for instance, policymakers had specific economic aims in the market for taxi journeys. They might perhaps drop the rate of purchase tax on off-peak bookings by a user who was registered as a schoolchild, or charge a lower percentage on journeys involving multiple pick ups or encourage trips to local high streets with reduced tax on trips from less than a mile away. To discourage drunk driving there might be a tax free hour as people are leaving bars to go home. Multiple permutations would be calculated automatically by GEMs for each booking across the market with rates varying daily if that was the wish of lawmakers. A taxi driver taking assignments through a simplified GEMs terminal on his dashboard might for instance call up end of day accounts that looked like this.

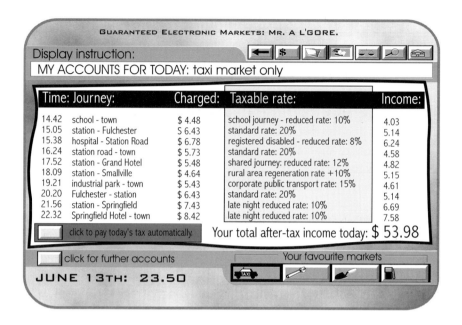

GUARANTEED ELECTRONIC MARKETS: MR. A L'GORE.

Display instruction:

MY ACCOUNTS FOR TODAY: taxi market only

Time:	Journey:	Charged:	Taxable rate:	Income:
14.42	school - town	$ 4.48	school journey - reduced rate: 10%	4.03
15.05	station - Fulchester	S 6.43	standard rate: 20%	5.14
15.38	hospital - Station Road	$ 6.78	registered disabled - reduced rate: 8%	6.24
16.24	station road - town	$ 5.73	standard rate: 20%	4.58
17.52	station - Grand Hotel	$ 5.48	shared journey: reduced rate: 12%	4.82
18.09	station - Smallville	$ 4.64	rural area regeneration rate +10%	5.15
19.21	industrial park - town	$ 5.43	corporate public transport rate: 15%	4.61
20.20	Fulchester - station	$ 6.43	standard rate: 20%	5.14
21.56	station - Springfield	$ 7.43	late night reduced rate: 10%	6.69
22.32	Springfield Hotel - town	$ 8.42	late night reduced rate: 10%	7.58

click to pay today's tax automatically.

Your total after-tax income today: $ 53.98

click for further accounts

Your favourite markets

JUNE 13TH: 23.50

The taxi operator has no need to study these accounts of course, he can simply set his basic pricing structure and tell GEMs to calculate the tax on top to arrive at a price for each assignment. Nor need he even click to release payment to an Inland Revenue account. If he wishes it could be transferred automatically through the day.

15

Opposition
to public markets

Since the dawn of commercial computing, millions of jobs have been lost to successive new technologies. The pain involved is generally regarded as an unavoidable part of progress: as one commentator told *Business Week* in 1993, when cheaper software for clerical and administrative functions was becoming widely available, 'people who don't add value are going to be in trouble'.[54] A full-scale GEMs system would be but the latest encroachment of computerization on previously established ways of doing business. A crucial difference, however, would be the status of its victims: corporations and executives rather than humble office workers. Will they accept their fate as thousands of past employees were expected to and resign themselves to irrelevance? They might not and they would have ample scope to resist. A GEMs service should not be initiated without full public debate. That would ensure the legitimacy of government involvement in a launch and, as a bonus for the consortium behind the system, heightened public awareness. During this phase the proposed system would be vulnerable to attack on several counts. Like all previous major public infrastructure projects, it would push existing technology to its limits in a leap of faith that initially may not stand up to aggressive probing. Historians would recognise the pattern. In 1845, for instance, work began on Britain's Chester to Holyhead railway with a 5-mile gap in the plans because no one knew how the plunging gorge of the Menai Straits was to be bridged. A race for solutions led finally to the invention of box girders, which could bear all required loads, even as lines leading to the gorge were being laid.[55] In the case of GEMs, it would not necessarily be the functions performed that would stretch existing know-how but the scale on which they might have to be delivered. It is worth pointing out, however, that the system could start small and grow, launching simpler markets first and leaving its equivalents to the Menai Straits problem until later. Additionally, those convinced the project was infeasible might need to be reminded that it would be the consortium, not taxpayers, who would bear the impact of failure.

Debate over Guaranteed Markets tends to invoke five often repeated arguments in opposition. Each will be considered in turn.

Points of opposition

■ **Government does not need to get involved in electronic commerce. If there is demand for a service like GEMs, market forces will ensure it emerges**

'Intelligent agent' software, which takes details of an Internet shopper's requirements and searches thousands of sites for the best price, is expected to have an increasing impact on online retailers. Many believe that consumer demand for this function will overcome currently formidable resistance from retailers and the portal sites that charge sellers for high-visibility positions. Some argue that if advanced 'shopbots' (shopping robots) become reality, and start roaming the whole gamut of web sales sites on behalf of buyers, everyone will instantly get the best possible deal and GEMs would be unnecessary. Others point to a panoply of buyer–seller matching services emerging on the Net. These consumer-orientated services often adopt the language of a wide-open market but remain restricted to favoured sellers. In the USA, for instance, 15 per cent of cars are purchased through the Net from far wider pools of vehicles than any one dealer site could offer, but services like Autobytel and Microsoft's Carpoint offer autos from mutually exclusive pools of dealerships, who pay to be listed and collectively offer only a fraction of the country's available cars at any given moment. In the UK, SCOOT allows Net users to type in their location and a service they seek, a plumber perhaps or a Pizza delivery firm, to get details of a nearby trader returned. The beginnings of an unbiased marketplace which can be freely entered? No, SCOOT earns its money on fees from the companies it lists and makes a speciality of collecting data on consumers who use its service. As their Corporate Communications Manager explained in a presentation to retailers 'once we recognise [the individual computer an enquirer is using] we can start to log their interests. If we'd seen that they'd asked about details for mortgage brokers and then for removal men – we might justifiably push offers relating to DIY. ...I'm sure that even greater possibilities will appear, to help you effectively market to your customers'.[56] Companies have little incentive to take on the gargantuan investment and uncertain prospects of growing a neutral, fully functioned electronic marketplace running on wafer-thin transaction charges: there are better short-term returns from what appears to be an open market but is actually a vehicle for client sellers.

It is worth repeating the advantages a fully enabled GEMs system would have over intelligent agents and existing services: the simplest possible market entry for sellers, authenticated trading records enabling reliable individuals and companies to selectively trade with each other, arbitration backed by frozen payment to instantly underpin any deal and interlocking markets that can pull together a personalised contractual chain at once. All this delivered not by a patchwork of software packages each with their own incompatibilities and value adding business models but in one simplified system that has been committed to user privacy, utility pricing and ever-widening ranges of sellers. Only a national parliament has the clout and legitimacy to shape an opportunity for one potentially dominant marketplace to rise from the online bedlam, then force its operators to invest in its full potential for an inclusive economy. Only government can write the laws that would underpin and promote an atomization of economic life. There are certainly those who find such a step unthinkable from the perspective of prevailing ideology: that is not the same as saying it could never work.

There is widespread recognition in electronic commerce circles that users want a simplified and convenient online marketplace. That is the force behind home shopping through interactive television, which is scheduled to deliver anything but a marketplace open to all sellers. Nevertheless, services like Open, Autobytel and SCOOT are undoubtedly useful and offer a huge improvement on old ways for consumers to meet their needs, but they should not be mistaken for the full potential of an online marketplace.

■ A GEMs service would create an unacceptable monopoly

The computer age has a natural tendency towards monopolies: a point made many times by Microsoft, the world's biggest company by market value, when justifying its 95 per cent share of personal computer operating system software. Everyone wants to have programming compatible with the bulk of existing users. The controversy over Microsoft as monopolist stems from the company's attempts to leverage dominance in one sector into others. Its chief technologist, Nathan Myhrvold, for instance, told the *Wall Street Journal* in 1997 that Microsoft hopes eventually to take a cut from every Internet transaction using their technology.[57] The uncoordinated marketplace does not dispel monopolies in the online world. What is more, it gives companies who achieve that position enormous market-controlling power. A GEMs operator backed by government would admittedly start with advantages no other online service could match in the country of operation but would pay for that privilege with a mass of unique obligations, annulling its potential for control. They would include an inability to extend into additional areas and the sacrifice of normal commercial secrecy to transparent accountability. All this would be enforced with pitiless inspection. Nor would GEMs be a Microsoft-style mammoth but a consortium of companies running a minimal core operation while individual franchisees oversee the marketplaces. Although united by a financial need to develop the system, it is difficult to see any ideological certainties that would bind together such a diverse group of participants. Unlike software houses, GEMs could do nothing to 'lock in' its users: there would be no cost for them to start using the system and little time required to learn its interface. Any user could disengage at any time and switch to other online channels without having to write off an investment in time or money.

The power that goes with dominance in outside industries would be denied the GEMs consortium: the economy running on their machines would be controlled, as in the outside world, by government, who could be made further accountable if they enabled GEMs' referendum capabilities. Additionally, a public market system meets the economist's test of a 'useful monopoly': someone seeking, say, a fur coat demonstrably benefits from access to one universal, dependable exchange showing a full range of second-hand and new options, rather than having to track down multiple forums and evaluating the offers therein. The indisputable advantages of having multiple suppliers from which to choose should not be confused with the more debatable benefits of being forced to hunt around a slew of marketplaces to find them.

GEMs' opponents would probably invoke images of 'big brother': one massive core computer that knows exactly what individuals are up to and when they are logging in. It is a valid fear. In 1996 San Fransisco based I/PRO was forced to abandon its plan to set up a central repository of individual's details on the Net with a view to sparing them the need to re-enter data every time they began a relationship with a company online. Centralized pre-registration through one company proved unacceptable to most users. But large computer systems harvesting information about us are now a fact of life, although the extent of the data they are allowed to reap is still being debated. At least in a GEMs system there would be stringent checking by a wide range of bodies to demonstrate that the system could not make improper use of the information it held and was unable to retain any details on a user who decided to close his account. If ever there was mass loss of faith in the system it would probably be followed by an exodus of users who would leave no trail behind. The system's power would be theoretical rather than exploitable. In the early days of broadcasting it was pointed out that the companies being licensed to transmit would have enormous power to create unfounded mass panic at will. Like GEMs operators in the case of privacy betrayal, it is something they could only ever do once and has never happened on a significant scale.

Arguments about the impact of failure in the central control room of a mature GEMs service have a firmer basis. Such disasters can happen. In late January 1990, AT&T, the USA's dominant telecommunications provider, experienced long-distance switching breakdown as a result of one logic circuit faltering in their central computer, the world's biggest. With a 9-hour break in service, the day the US phone system died is legendary among computing experts.[58] Existing large trading systems are coy about their particular failure rates although SABRE, the biggest, is known to have very occasional short periods of non-availability.[59] Prolonged gaps in service are less likely: SABRE's core computer is in a bomb-proof, concrete-lined bunker which can survive on its own air water and power for up to three days in case of above-ground holocaust. Instantaneous back ups are another route towards fail safe operation: the Reuters' 2000–2 currency market system, for instance, runs on hardware now in London Docklands that relays every deal immediately to other computers in Geneva and Singapore. Should London fail for any reason, trading can be switched seamlessly to far-away machines. Despite this, Reuters admit there has been a handful of brief gaps in the service.[60] The impact of crashed technology on a marketplace that has become reliant on electronic trading is demonstrated by the July 1998 chaos among worldwide currency dealers after Reuters's rival, the Electronic Broking Service, stalled. Non-availability led to '20 minutes of mass panic' and 'raised concerns about the widespread use of electronic matching' according to a trade newsletter.[61] It would be facile to promise GEMs could never fail or to minimise the consequences of any gap in service. But the consortium should commit itself to the array of technologies known as fault tolerant computing, which increasingly offers what professionals call nine fives reliability: full service 99.999 per cent of the time. Like SABRE, military-level security at the core should be an indisputable condition. If fears of down time became an issue, a scale of fines might be instigated, payable by the consortium for any breakdown and distributed perhaps as a few pennies to the accounts of 25 per cent of users chosen at random.

■ **Big corporations are vital to national advantage**

Behind the latest cheap headline about CEO compensation, this argument goes, are valuable organisations that if weakened could leave a country uncompetitive. GEMs would be a move into a new economic model, the effects of which cannot be fully predicted but which is likely to deliver new sources of international advantage, primarily efficiency of trading, a flexible workforce and cheapness of resources. The firms likely to be first hit by public electronic markets would be in service industries such as financial provision. These companies are already being rapidly transformed by computerization, from pillars of community and employment provision to amorphous computer networks overseen by a diminished cadre of executives. A GEMs system would deliver to the national economy the efficiencies these globalizing organizations currently stand to gain from moving online.

Manufacturers should feel the impact of GEMs later. In the first country in its region with GEMs they could enjoy purchasing labour, services and some materials in a very efficient marketplace, while selling under less competitive pressure elsewhere. Might they find themselves under attack at home from imports now able to go instantly to market? It would be up to government whether to erect tariff barriers but without them imports would certainly be able to go more rapidly into distribution although they could be overpriced relative to domestic production.

■ A GEMs system would be an employment killer

GEMs would probably create new work opportunities and redistribute existing work as it effectively removed transaction costs from the economy, encouraging money into more rapid circulation. The jobs it undercut would almost all be those vulnerable to computerization anyway; if GEMs was not the threat, a proprietary software package would be.

■ Citizens in a GEMs country would be restricted by shopping in a national rather than international marketplace

Internet shopping would not come to an end after a first GEMs system was launched. Users of national public markets would still want to shop globally for novelty, for needs from niche markets and for digitised products like software or music, which can come dependably from around the world as well as via GEMs sellers. More entrepreneurial Net shoppers may see a role in arbitrage between the worldwide market and GEMs and then start a home import business. Anyone can sell anything in GEMs (with the exception of legally restricted markets). A user in Saudi Arabia, for instance, who noticed a particular brand of Cuban cigars could be ordered cheaply from Havana over the Internet might purchase 10 boxes and then sell them in his country's GEM for tobacco products. He adds value to the final transaction by putting up the GEMs bond that turns a difficult-to-find, precarious Internet purchase into a solidly underpinned and very convenient deal. Because the import market has atomized, GEMs shoppers should enjoy a far wider range of foreign goods in this way.

It is sometimes argued that consumers will always want to shop in an online, branded environment. Opponents should not assume the logical corollary of this view: that GEMs' interfaces would be functional and unimaginative with uniform presentation across all sectors. It would be the ever-changing offerings of any number of sellers, mass market and exclusive, that would make the GEMs market for, say, sportswear a constant source of interest. There would, of course, be nothing to stop shoppers purchasing in whatever online forum they wished, but once they started comparing prices they would be likely to find the branded sales channel was a good place to browse and GEMs the best place to buy.

Likely tactics of the opposition

Individual corporations come and go but, as a community, big business can fight tenaciously for its future. A GEMs project, once it was taken seriously, would antagonize virtually every significant power base in a developed economy. Crucial opponents would include the established media, who might fear a diminished role for advertising in a world with pure markets available to everyone. This could make it difficult for pro-GEMs arguments to enter circulation. If the debate over merits of institution-led 'old' capitalism versus atomized 'new' capitalism were confined to rational analysis of the benefits and risks inherent in both, there would probably be a swing in public opinion towards GEMs. Recent history of localized infrastructure projects suggests intelligent debate may not be the case: distortion and emotionally loaded arguments could be used to obfuscate the true issues. When the Los Angeles Chamber of Commerce, for instance, responded to demand for comprehensive public transport with a plan for an integrated rapid transit system centred on downtown, opponents dubbed the scheme 'socialistic'. As such it was deemed unpalatable and killed. An 'astonishing defeat' according to the episode's historian.[62] Years later the city has to cope with a legacy of medical, social and planning problems following an over reliance on cars but it at least avoided the spectre of active government! Officially initiated public electronic markets would be particularly prone to this kind of emotional pigeon-holing whereby even a scheme's potential beneficiaries might be convinced of its undesirability without any exposure to reasoned discussion.

Were sustained grass roots support for government intervention to create GEMs to emerge, this kind of tactic could be employed wholesale, as has already been the case with corporate opposition to the environmental movement. In the USA an anti-green movement first emerged with far right authors who, for example, claimed environmentalism stood for a new religion which was 'anti humanity, anti civilisation and anti technology'.[63] This coherent philosophy of attack provided the foundation for a sophisticated movement against a movement: the Wise Use organization. 'The public will never love big business. The pro-industry activist group is the answer to these problems' leader Ron Arnold told a gathering of Canadian forest industries representatives in 1988.[64] Explaining his tactics in a later newspaper interview he added that the most effective way of defeating the environmental movement is 'by taking their money and members' with another movement.[65] Wise Use appears to be an ecologically sound organization; opponents see it as nothing more than a misleading front for voracious industrialization. The growing influence enjoyed by Wise Use and its corporate supporters became clear in 1994 when the group stopped the anticipated ratification of the United Nations agreement on biological diversity in the US Senate with a barrage of opposing letters, calls and faxes.[66] Similar tactics can be seen in tobacco giant Philip Morris's 'whitecoat project': the establishment of a network of scientists throughout Europe paid to cast doubt on the dangers of passive smoking while appearing independent.[67] British salt producers adopted a similar ploy to counter links between their product and stomach cancer, successfully removing salt consumption from the list of points in official health advice.[68] Anyone campaigning for underpinned public electronic markets would be wise to brace themselves for well-funded opposition claiming to represent a wide constituency and for a succession of experts, only some of whom will have started with an open mind, asserting that the project is unrealistic or undesirable.

Moral panic has been productively deployed against infrastructure proposals in the past. The telephone was denounced as occultist because it brought disembodied voices into the room. Clergymen sympathetic to canal and turnpike road companies described early railway locomotives as satanic because of their propulsion by fire. One small aspect of a GEMs operation that may be inflated by opponents in search of similar hysteria is the potential it would offer to adulterers and relationship dabblers by GEMs' local friendship-building facilities. Public markets should be predicated on a conviction that elected politicians, not system managers, decide what areas of trade in a country are available to citizens. If prostitution is deemed permissible by legislators in the country of operation, for instance, there should ultimately be a GEM for sexual services, in which providers can enjoy the protection and freedom from touting for business available to any other trader on the system. However, GEMs could widen such market activity unless restricted by government, a potential boon for the proposed system's detractors. (Conversely, of course, the system may lead to increased prices in the market by making so much alternative employment available to the supply side.)

The sheer ambitiousness of the system could be another profitable area of attack, with every mistake along the consortium's learning curve given crisis coverage. If there were to come a point when opponents realized they were losing public sympathy they might shift to a campaign for a limited system, or lobby for alternative government schemes that would provide a compromise with corporate interests. Firms that currently oppose any involvement by national policy makers in the new economy might start advocating projects like Singapore's Approved Cyber Trader scheme, which bestows concessionary tax rates on companies deemed to be using electronic commerce for officially sanctioned economic ends. Full-scale acceptance of such schemes might pare down the potential abuses of electronic trading capability among big players; they would not deliver an atomized economy. Other firms might demand government issue of digital certificates to prove individual identity and increase security in the uncoordinated online marketplace. There is no reason why such schemes to help those who wish to shop outside GEMs should not be launched alongside an eventual system. The project aims to increase choice, not stifle any other form of marketplace.

Another tactic to watch for would be the pre-emptive strike. In spring 1996, for instance, the local US telecommunications companies petitioned the Federal Communications Commission demanding a ban on technology enabling Internet users to make international phone calls between computers at local rates. Few people at the time were aware the technology existed.[69] A further alarming trend for GEMs' proponents is meetings between corporate interests and governments in secrecy. The Multilateral Agreement on Investment, a set of statutes to protect international money flows, for instance, was initially negotiated in three years of almost total secrecy. Politicians could find themselves under enormous pressure to quietly acquiesce to elegantly worded agreements actually designed to prevent their citizens ever discovering the full benefits electronic markets have to offer.

The luxury of fully explaining public markets' potential may be denied to those who seek a newly inclusive capitalism. Advocates of GEMs-style systems might need to focus on communicating three simple messages: using the system would always be a matter of choice not compulsion, it would cost taxpayers nothing despite being government initiated and it would not involve restricting existing channels to market in any way. While braced for a particularly vituperative battle they could console themselves that similarly bloody conflicts, by the standards of their day, were fought before the need for mass public transport, postage and water provision became self-evident. Historically, no new technology has been indefinitely withheld from widespread public usage because of resulting damage to powerful institutions of its time. Infrastructure proposals have always won, ultimately.

16 Which countries would have most to gain from a GEMs launch?

The potential unpopularity of a raw online marketplace in the first world notwithstanding, GEMs is unlikely to be launched in a developed country. It is in 'second world' nations that the opposition to such a move by government could be most readily overcome. The possibility of GEMs in a far off country might be enthusiastically supported by investors who would bitterly contest the same project on their home ground. Unlike, say, online entertainment applications GEMs can operate with very basic displays to users and would not require substantial bandwidth or advanced technology in terminals. The personal computers with 486 processors now being piled into skips across Europe and the US and the copper wire discarded for high-density fibre optics could provide the spine for a usable, if not particularly glossy, GEMs in a developing nation. Many of these countries are propagating the awareness and technical backbone required for a GEMs service. Internet access and usage is accelerating faster in developing countries than elsewhere.[70] In China, for example, twice as much fibre optic is now being laid as in the USA, encouraging the number of Net accounts to double in the first half of 1998.[71] The Prime Minister of India (which has an existing middle class of 200 million people) has set out to reverse his country's slow take up of the Internet with a national task force designed to make the country 'an Information Technology superpower'.[72] Brazil is now committed to growth through privatization deals to create commercially driven infrastructure. With a favourable government any of these countries could achieve much from launching a first GEMs service.

It would be in a country plagued by a bandit economy that underpinned electronic markets for mass use might have the most dramatic impact. Take Russia as an example. Since the country's banks closed for a 'technical break' in August 1998 an estimated 75 per cent of transactions have been in the form of barter, even between companies. It starves the government of tax revenue, is inefficient and extremely time consuming. A Russian textile factory, for example, will routinely make 50 to 60 deals a month with suppliers of meat, footwear, jewellery, furniture and concrete blocks employing a 'hunt-and-gather' team to locate potential swaps.[73] GEMs should be able to staunch the underlying problems that created this catastrophe: state and private corruption, financial scams and capital flight. Assuming a system had been set up in August 1998 with all the inspection protocols and guarantees of democratic independence already outlined, it should have begun to stabilize the economy almost immediately. With terminals around the country provided by a foreign consortium of GEMs companies, individual Russians could have started to trade at grassroots level, selling their produce for instance with providers of delivery or storage emerging in other GEMs. Because of low computer awareness among nationals the system might have a specially simplified interface in its early days. Market consolidators could have started to buy in rural areas and supply in town with no administration or central planning required to kickstart activity.

Initially the medium for this trade would probably be GEMs' own parallel currency, sealed from big institutions and speculators and eked into supply as users increased. The system's currency exchange may then be trading in a reverse situation to that expected in a first world economy: the rouble almost valueless against a Russian equivalent of POETs (Parallel Official Economy Tokens). Low-level economic activity for ordinary people would thus be separated from the currency crisis, creating breathing space for officials. A second stage might be ensuring the nation's natural resources such as oil and metals are sold on the system with downstream processing being driven by open market efficiencies. With core exports moving solidly through the economy the Duma would then have to persuade other firms and state institutions to trade on the system, foregoing backdoor deals and crony capitalism for pure markets in which every transaction can be instantly audited if the parties are willing. As big players moved on to GEMs roubles should approach parity with parallel economy points and overtake them in value once major capital providers domestic or international began using the GEMs money markets. The mafia, which has blocked so many past attempts at reform, should find it difficult to stall this process. Core soft-ware would have been written overseas not by tainted local suppliers, inspection would be international. Big crime would be as handicapped as large service companies in an atomized economy made up of countless, ever-changing, underpinned small deals rather than dominated by large transactions. Tax collection could become immediate with infinitesimal sums transferred to government coffers as part of each sale, although any tendency towards over taxation that could price people off the system would need to be contained. Politicians would not be immune from this clean-up imposed on economic life by GEMs. Official purchasing and hiring could be made open to scrutiny, perhaps with the system proffering an 'automatically audited' symbol on official contracts to show they represented the best value purchase available at the time. More fundamentally, government would have to decide whether to submit itself to public approval by allowing GEMs voting, dependent on system penetration and take-up. If they did use the system to endorse their own legitimacy it could be the final step that brought foreign funds back into what should now be a lean and durable economy.

To see how sensationally an economy can be lifted out of total wreckage by stabilizing domestic money supply, as GEMs could do uniquely with its limited currency for users only, it is worth looking at the launch of Germany's deutschmark in 1948. In the rubble of wartime defeat, as in modern day Moscow, the black market dominated with 8 hours of an average worker's toil required just to buy an egg in the legit-imate shops. Paid work was, in any case, barely available so stores remained empty as financial anarchy prevailed. The new currency, given out in allocations at Post Offices, reversed the situation immediately. As one contemporary politician who had struggled with earlier attempts to resolve the problems wrote: 'I'll never forget the impression when I walked through the city on the Monday after the currency reform and saw goods in the shop windows once again. In this unforgettable moment I realised for the first time that a stable currency and liberal economic policy belong together'.[74] A decade later the mark was one of the world's most sought after currencies. Marshall Aid money from the USA was a vital part of that process but it was stability induced by the launch of a virgin currency that allowed the benefits to filter through the economy. Now that the currency controls of 1940s Europe have been replaced by global 'hot money' flows the only way to achieve similar impact could be through a sealed system of computerized transactions, available exclusively to nationals.

The mechanism for this economic revival would have involved no financial outlay for Russia. Costs of hardware and some public access terminals would be met by a consortium wanting to launch GEMs. Would such large scale investment in a crashed economy be viable for those companies? They would be gambling on enthusiastic take up by the populace and progressive 'GEMification' of economic life, making a future flow of commissions on every transaction in a newly-hardened currency worthwhile. For a country of the size and natural resources of Russia, that could be a worthwhile prize. Once a first GEMs was launched, further systems in additional countries would cost little to develop beyond the costs of dedicated programming, such as mapping software and charges involved in recruiting franchisees and setting up hardware. Would national pride be dented by inviting a consortium inevitably featuring foreign companies to build a new economic framework? Most second world nations already pay overseas companies to print their banknotes and are finding they must turn to foreigners to computerize banks and government departments. Eastern Europe, for instance, has widely promised exclusive monopoly rights to foreigners for years to come in key areas of telecommunications. This has been judged the only way to obtain lasting investment.[75] The core software at the heart of the new system would probably be transnational in its roots but each country with GEMs should have its own core computer on national soil for security reasons. Market front ends should be run by a national franchisee each aware of the multiple local sensitivities in his area of trade (Box 16.1). Unlike the Internet, interfaces would all be in the local language(s).

If a race between countries to roll out the benefits of public electronic markets developed alongside the existing contest between companies racing to control the new infrastructure, there could be worldwide realignment. For a possible indication of the outcome it is worth looking at power plays in the financial sector, which has been both global in its competition and dependent on true electronic markets longer than any other area of trade. Countries that had little to offer but a willingness to adopt the full force of electronic markets have shown an ability to overtake centres of trading previously regarded as impregnable. An example: Frankfurt's financial futures exchange, the DTB, adopted

BOX 16.1

GEMS AND NATIONAL SENSITIVITIES

The GEMs consortium should not seek to impose one uniform marketplace on the world but develop core software that can then be amended by franchisees. Some emerging market countries have traditions of cooperative capitalism at odds with GEMs' ruthless enforcement of each deal for instance. The Chinese diaspora throughout south east Asia is marked by a willingness to seal agreements at the highest level with nothing more than a handshake. It is difficult to see how automated markets could incorporate this valuable role for trust in a society across the board but government might decide to preserve that culture perhaps by allowing unprotected deals in certain sectors. Other regional traits that would not sit easily on GEMs include Islamic banking. With strict adherence to scriptural injunctions against charging interest, predominantly Muslim countries might require more complex financial instruments in a basic loans market.

unbridled computerised markets while its London counterpart loftily opted only to move its 'open pit trading' system online at hours when their physical trading floor was closed. As successive trading contracts moved to Germany, The London International Financial Futures Exchange has spent millions trying to catch up with the cheapness and convenience which so spectacularly benefited Frankfurt.[76] There are several large countries with plentiful natural resources and a reasonably educated workforce kept low in world rankings by corruption and monetary instability. A coherent government vision for electronic markets might enable them to overtake nations mired in adherence to the online *status quo*.

Notes to
section three

1. Douglas N. Muir, *Postal Reform and the Penny Black: a New Appreciation*, The National Postal Museum, 1990, p. 46.
2. L. T. C. Rolt, *Victorian Engineering*, Penguin, 1970, p. 20.
3. D. P. Titley, *Machines, Money and Men: An Economic and Social History of Great Britain from 1700 to the 1970s*, Collins Educational, 1969, p. 80.
4. S. E. Finer, *The Life and Times of Sir Edwin Chadwick*, Barnes and Noble, 1970, p. 410.
5. David Milsted, *They Got it Wrong! The Guinness Book of Regrettable Quotations*, Guinness, 1995, p. 191.
6. Published by Harvard Business School, 1997. The quote comes from the Mc-Kenna Group web site. www.mckennagroup.com/realtime/rt/rt_primer/primmer001.html.
7. Media journalist Alfred Balk quoted in Radio Days All Over Again? Today's wannabe Web stars can learn from the past – 75 years to be exact. *Business Week,* 27 August 1998, electronic edition.
8. Portal Play, *Information Strategy*, September 1998, p. 10.
9. J. William Gurley, The Soaring Cost of E-commerce, *Fortune*, 3 August 1998, p. 165.
10. Case study 9-490-012, *People Express Airlines: Rise and Decline*, Harvard Business School, revised 14 September 1993. Quoted in Jerry Yoram Wind and Jeremy Main, *Driving Change: How the best Companies are Preparing for the 21st Century*, Kogan Page, 1998, p. 23.
11. Evan I. Schwartz, *Webonomics: Nine Essential Principals for Growing your Business on the World Wide Web*, Penguin, 1997, p. 108.
12. The examples used come from Follower of Fashion, *Ovum Update,* Ovum Consulting, January–April 1998, p. 4.
13. Increasing Customer Loyalty through Knowledge Management, conference, London, 10–11 March 1998. Presentation by Dr Michael Wolf, Executive Director, Swiss Bank Corporation.
14. The Walled Garden: Interactive digital television could offer widespread access to the Internet. But broadcasters are not keen, *Information Strategy*, October 1998, p. 9.
15. Kenneth Helps, Managing Director of Cabot Software. Phone conversation with the author 22 September 1998.
16. The Walled Garden: Interactive digital television could offer widespread access to the Internet. But broadcasters are not keen. *Information Strategy*, October 1998, p. 9.

17. Consolidation on the Internet, *Internet for Business*, September/October 1997, p. 10
18. Adam Nicholson, The view from Perch Hill, *Sunday Telegraph Magazine*, 4 October 1998, p. 78. Also Peter Hitchens, Superstores are turning our cities into ghost towns, *Express*, 28 September 1998, p. 13.
19. IMRG statement 'E-commerce and the Universal Network', part of the notes for Online Delivery '98, held 11/12 February 1998, London.
20. Martha Rogers and Stacey Riordan, Building Learning Relationships with Mass Customized Clothes, *Inside 1to1*, 16 July 1998, p. 1.
21. Currency Doubleday.
22. Don Peppers and Martha Rogers, *Enterprise One to One: Tools for Competing in the Interactive Age*, Currency Doubleday, 1997, p. 104.
23. Ibid. p. 127.
24. Ibid. p. 127.
25. Confirmed in e-mail exchange between the author and Thomas A. Kelly, Public Relations Division, First Chicago, September 1998.
26. Bob Dorf, M1to1/PRG launches global partnership with Oracle, *Inside 1to1*, 21 October 1998, p. 1.
27. 1998 survey by Mercer Management Consulting quoted in *Inside 1to1*, 15 July 1998, electronic edition.
28. *Encyclopaedia of the New Economy*, *Wired* reprint, 1998.
29. The Aspen Institute, Colorado, *The Future of Electronic Commerce*, 1995, p. 35.
30. Mike McDowall, Big Brother Brokers, *Direct Marketing*, March/April 1998, p. 38
31. Market Makers, Some of the Most Familiar Ways to Market Consumer goods are Proving to be Costly Failures, *The Economist*, 14 March 1998, p. 87.
32. Wendy Grossman, Who's Watching the Webwatchers? *Future Shopping*, September 1998, p. 12.
33. Business at Net Speed, *Business Week*, 22 June 1998, p. 72 and Online Computer Sales. Dell and Cisco: leading indicators? *Electronic Commerce Briefing*, January 1998, p. 13.
34. Hans-Peter Martin and Harald Schumann, *The Global Trap*, Zed Books, 1997.
35. David Metcalfe and Syue Fernie, Hanging on the Telephone, *Centrepiece*, 3(1). Quoted in Remote Control of the High Street, *Guardian*, 2 June 1998, p. 17.
36. The Human Answering Machines, *Guardian Jobs and Money*, 26 July 1997, p. 2.
37. Alec Maycock, operations manager of Halifax Direct quoted in It's all in the call for a little extra, *Information Week*, 10–23 December 1997, p. 62.
38. Graham Technology website wwww.gtnet.com. Extracted on 20 May 1998.
39. Quoted in Employees at the Mercy of Company Bugging Spree, *Daily Telegraph Connected*, 21 May 1998.
40. Paul Thompson and Chris Warhurst (eds), *Workplaces of the Future*, Macmillan Business, 1998, p. 176.
41. The Human Answering Machines, *Guardian Jobs and Money*, 26 July 1997, p. 2 and Paul Thompson and Chris Warhurst (eds) *Workplaces of the Future*, Macmillan Business, 1998, p. 128.

42. Sarah Adamczuck of Bristol writing in the letters page of the *Guardian*, 24 February 1998.
43. Variable Compensation Helps Keep Call Centers Buzzing, Mercer Consulting, www.mercer.com/usa, extracted 10 September 1998.
44. Bob Dorf, The One to One Insurance Policy, *Inside 1to1*, 16 April 1998, electronic edition.
45. David Bollier, Rapporteur, Charles M. Firestone, Program Director, *The Future of Electronic Commerce*, The Aspen Institute, Communications and Society Program, 1995, p. 41.
46. Fine line between a role and the dole, *Times Educational Supplement*, 28 August 1998, p. 7.
47. George Monbiot, Running on MMT, *Guardian*, 13 August 1998, p. 16.
48. Larry Elliott, Move to revive world pact, *Guardian*, 10 September 1998.
49. Published by Allen Lane, The Penguin Press, 1997.
50. Simon Caulkin, Pity the poor CEO. Those share options are to die for – literally, *Observer Business News*, 23 August 1998, p. 7.
51. Behave or else..., *Information Strategy*, February 1998, p. 13.
52. *Report on the Sanitary Condition of the Labouring Population of Great Britain* by Edwin Chadwick 1842. From a new introduction to the report by M. W. Flinn, University of Edinburgh Press, 1965, p. 39.
53. Robert W. McChesney, Digital Highway Robbery: where is the 'competition' the Telecommunications Act was supposed to provide? *The Nation*, 21 April 1997, electronic edition.
54. *Business Week*, 14 June 1993. Reprinted in Caroll Pursell, *Heat,* BBC Books, 1994, p. 197.
55. L. T. C. Rolt, *Victorian Engineering*, Penguin, 1970, p. 28.
56. Miranda Cleverdon, Corporate Communications Manager, Scoot UK, speaking at the Non-Shop Shopping conference, London 17 September 1998. The same speech was originally to have been delivered by Marc Lynne, Internet Manager of Scoot.
57. *The Electronic Commerce Briefing*, June 1998, electronic edition.
58. David Brown, *Cybertrends: Chaos, Power and Accountability in the Information Age*, Viking, 1997, p. 201.
59. Phone conversation with Peter Heath, Countrywide Public Relations, SABRE's spokesfirm in the UK, August 1998.
60. Peter V. Thomas of Reuters Transaction Products, London, e-mail to author, 5 October 1998.
61. Price Glitch on EBS Raises Debate over Automation, *fxweek: the global business of foreign exchange newsletter*, Waters' Treasury/Risk Group, 6 July 1998, p. 1.
62. Mike Davis, *City of Quartz: Excavating the Future in Los Angeles*, Verso, 1990, p. 122.
63. R. Arnold, *At the Eye of the Storm: James Watt and the Environmentalists,* Regnery Gateway, 1982, p. 248. Quoted in Andrew Rowell, *Green Backlash: Global Subversion of the Environment Movement*, Routledge, 1996, p. 10.
64. Andrew Rowell, *Green Backlash: Global Subversion of the Environment Movement*, Routledge, 1996, p. 13.
65. Interview with *The Toronto Star*, ibid., p. 14.
66. Ibid., p. 30.
67. Clare Dyer, Tobacco company set up network of sympathetic scientists, *British Medical Journal* **316**, 23 May 1998, p. 1555.

68. Marie Woolf, Food Firms Twist Science to Minimise Dangers of Salt, *Observer*, 7 June 1998, p. 15.

69. Evan I. Schwartz, *Webonomics: Nine Essential Principals for Growing your Business on the World Wide Web*, Penguin, 1997, p. 188.

70. The Internet and Poverty. Real Help or Real Hype? *Panos Briefing 28*, The Panos Institute, (TBC) 1998, p. 2.

71. Godfrey Linge (ed.) *China's New Spatial Economy*, Oxford University Press, 1997, p. 55 and China's Net Population Doubles, *The Industry Standard Intelligencer,* vl. 32, 11 September 1998, electronic edition.

72. Quoted in the National Taskforce website: http://it-taskforce.nic.in/.

73. Sharon LaFraniere, An Enemy of Russian Economic Reform: Barter, *The International Herald Tribune*, 4 September 1998, p. 1.

74. Count Otto Lambsdorff, former leader of the Liberal Free Democrats quoted in David Gow and Denis Stuanton, Arrival of euro marks end of a golden era for Germany, *Guardian,* 20 June 1998.

75. Why tortoises won't win: A slow but steady approach to modernising the telecoms sector had served the region well through the course of the 1990s. Now it is time to speed up the process, *Business Central Europe*, September 1998, p. 39.

76. Jill Treanor, Liffe turns for help to bring back glory days, *Guardian*, 8 September 1998, p. 19.

How might businesses respond to the rise of public electronic markets?

This section assumes that what many might see as a nightmare scenario for established businesses has become reality. After public debate a country has decided to launch a GEMs-style facility. It has been efficiently constructed and launched then embraced by a grateful populace who increasingly trust the system for a widening range of transactions. As usage increases the operating consortium is ploughing further funds into new software features and market-widening activity. What do large businesses do now? The GEMs project is emphatically not anti-business; any left-wing government who viewed it through such a prism would be likely to cripple their economy. GEMs' only concern is to provide a comprehensive trading platform open to any seller: consumer choice in this new marketplace then decides winners and losers.

It could be a mistake to underestimate the potential reach of such a system. Certainly, it could not compete with those providing the highest levels of personal attention at the top end of the market nor with shifty 'back of a truck' deals at the bottom. But there is a broad middle of the spectrum of transactions for which it should provide better reliability, range, convenience and price competition than other means of trading. Companies with exceptional customer relations, however, would probably not be threatened. The Italian mail order clothiers, for instance, whose selling point is that their size 40 dresses will fit a size 44 woman would be unlikely to see an exodus of customers to a GEM for womenswear, where enforced standards of truthfulness could lead to painful revelations. Other brands who are particularly cosy with their purchasers include Jack Daniels whiskey whose web site offers personalised interaction with staff and lavishly produced displays.[1] Even with the brand cheaply available in a GEM for alcoholic drinks there are likely to be customers who would prefer their buying experience wrapped up in a personal online exchange with a fellow whiskey enthusiast, rather than as a functional transaction in the public markets. The key impact of GEMs would be in removing any automatic benefits currently gained from owning trading infrastructure: the system would make that infrastructure universally available. At time of writing, for instance, Federal Express have a policy of giving their biggest customers automated shipping and invoicing facilities that, among other functions, group packages for nearby destinations together for cheaper shipment. GEMs could do this for any user in its parcel deliveries market. It would then be up to FedEx whether to input a GEMs pricing policy and accept parcels through the system, but the full infrastructure required for a parcel despatch market would now be available to anyone with a van who had cleared the verification hurdles required (Box S4.1).

Could it be worthwhile for firms to find ways of reaching the customer in places where public markets would not be on hand? Certain mobile phones in the USA, for instance, have a 'car breakdown' button that instantly connects the caller to American Automobile Association (AAA) headquarters from where a mechanic can be despatched. In the uncoordinated market for car repairs at present the simplicity of this concept has real appeal to users and allows AAA to circumvent local competition. But if GEMs flowered in the way past communications infrastructure has done it would not be long before mobile phone makers were offering handsets with instant connections to GEMs. With perhaps four programmable buttons an owner might set the first to access his GEMs account and immediately book the nearest available experienced car mechanic to his location at the time, a second for use if suddenly working late could tell GEMs 'book a high grade babysitter who I have hired previously for four hours from 6.00 p.m. today' and so on. The phone's display might then confirm transaction details. Once the new marketplace gained momentum it is likely to be futile trying to set up channels around it unless they were based on a shopping experience so rich and distinctive it outweighed the value and convenience that could have the bulk of the population seeking additional ways of connecting to GEMs.

Box S4.1

THE GEMS PARCELS MARKET

Any GEMs user could tell the system they have a package to despatch, say from Chicago to Manhattan. They would then be asked for a timeframe: clicking on 'immediate' would ensure a place on the next available flight that had space for sale on the system and the arrival of the most promptly available courier to take it to the airport, while a New York courier was lined up to await arrival. If a cheaper, more leisurely, journey was acceptable, GEMs would look for the lowest-cost departure for packages of that size and weight and ensure the deliverer whose pricing formula made them the best value for that assignment collected, possibly as part of an afternoon's worth of pick ups around the city. If cheapness was the overriding consideration travel between the cities might be by road, in which case the parcel could be carried by a one-man-and-a-truck operator who aggregated packages from couriers all over Chicago. Every provider in this market would need extensive bonding because of the security implications of their work; they would be unlikely to get it without an incontestable trading record. The system would allocate a code number to each package that shows who was responsible for it at any given time in its transit. Open to thousands of providers and with trends in demand freely available, this market should be both more responsive (because its pool of couriers and potential hubs are larger) and cheaper than any one of the existing big parcel companies.

An immediate response of many companies to a GEMs launch could be a retreat from areas of trade that were reaching commodity prices on the system towards more exotic value-added services. Once electronic markets became key to global money exchange, for instance, the big banks virtually surrendered trade in mainstream currencies to new entrants and concentrated on rarer denominations such as the Yugoslav dinar and more complex financial products that defied easy categorization for electronic trading. That would be one battleplan for a company faced with a GEMs launch. Some other suggestions follow. Most of them contradict thinking about how to succeed in an uncoordinated online marketplace.

17

Innovation becomes decisive

Constantly experiment with product range

The existing online marketplace is concentrating economic power and diminishing the variety in mainstream outlets. Under pressure from globalizing retailers, for instance, consumer goods manufacturers led by Proctor & Gamble are slashing their ranges to focus on a smaller number of key products standardized for marketing to the world.[2] Advertising and brand building would still be beneficial in a GEMs selling environment, although not crucial. However, speed to market would be so fast and demand data so freely available that the range of products available to GEMs users is likely to be constantly refreshing itself. Big companies would be foolish to respond with nothing more than a small number of unchanging lines when brand extensions or new merchandise could be painlessly tried on thousands of waiting consumers.

The following example shows how a fictitious, fast-moving consumer goods manufacturer might launch a chocolate candy bar product on GEMs. A launch process that would currently involve trade promotion, consumer awareness raising, commitment to pre-ordained production runs and a mass of distribution agreements could take the brand manager less than twenty minutes in the public markets. Assuming his employer already had an account on the system and he was authorized to input new products, his task would start in the market for confectionery distribution.

Told that he wants to launch a new product, GEMs begins with a request for basic details. Once he has finished typing it looks like this.

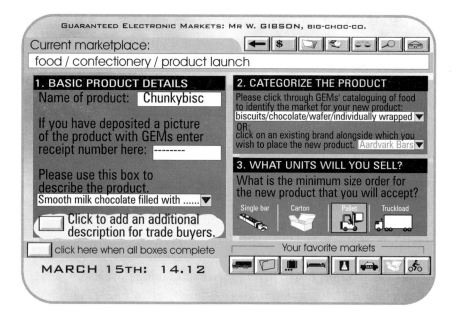

The market for confectionery sales would be available to home cookery enthusiasts with a kitchen table full of sweet cookies they wanted to sell locally that afternoon as much as food multinationals. GEMs asks for the size of units to be sold so it knows whether to proceed with a very simple list of questions for a home baker who probably would not have standardized biscuits, or a more complex formula for a major supplier. It now knows it is dealing with the latter who will only sell pallets of output, that the product is to be called 'Chunkybisc', and proceeds with questions that would be crucial for trade buyers.

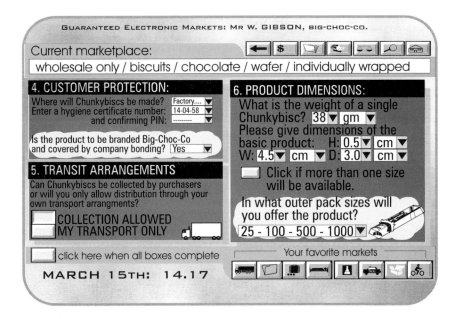

Sales in GEMs could be driven by consumer pull rather than manufacturers pushing their products through a distribution network. It is asking if their brand manager wants to limit distribution of Chunkybiscs to the company's own vehicles or whether he is willing to allow anyone who has bought a sufficient quantity of the product to arrange their own vehicle for collection. The latter keeps the price competitive because GEMs can compute a delivery price independently from a wider marketplace and construct a contractual chain with the haulier for a buyer, it is also more flexible. Some basic information is now needed so distribution through multiple operators can be arranged.

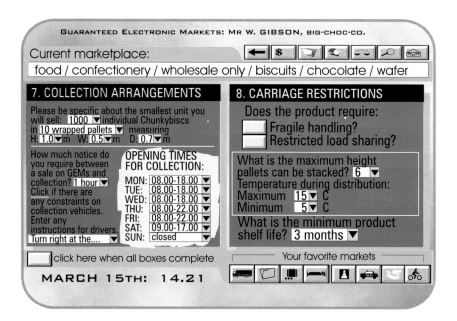

Now the system needs a pricing formula. That can factor in overall demand for chocolate bars: making Chunkybiscs expensive in a slack market for instance when only a minimum production run was likely to be sold. Or it can drop prices according to size of order, previous history with a given buyer, postal code of purchaser and so on. GEMs also needs to know parameters for supply. It could be as simple as saying there will be 2000 pallets a day available for the next four weeks but a more sophisticated service is available. The brand manager can in effect tell GEMs his variable costs knowing the system will constantly alter the price to buyers to maximize profitability. How many bars does he need to sell to make it worthwhile running the production line? Having reached that figure, does he then want to sell more competitively still? Like all individual user information on the system these details will not be available to anyone working for GEMs or released to anyone else.

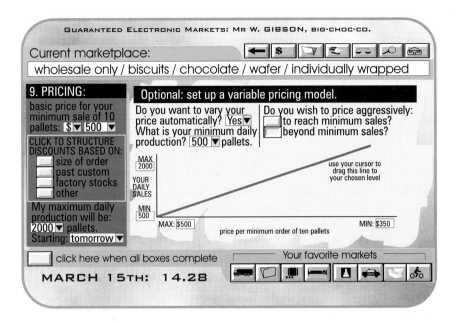

Now the brand manager is asked for consumer information: for example, what are the key ingredients, does the product contain specific substances to which some individuals are allergic, is it kosher and is it suitable for home freezing? Then GEMs asks if the product is to be made eligible for users who have boycotts in force. If this page is not filled in Chunkybiscs when re-entered on the system by wholesalers, retailers, buyers club organisers and other re-sellers will not be displayed to individual users with an applicable ban in force. It might be, for instance, that 2 per cent of regular biscuit buyers in GEMs were punishing the Nestlé food group for alleged bad practice in marketing baby milk to developing countries. The brand manager would have to decide whether to banish any trace of Nestle output from his supply chain and allow a clause in contracts with buyers to that effect or to write off that segment of the market.

GEMs could offer unparalleled marketing opportunities without compromising user privacy. It might for example offer individual users the option of accepting messages according to their consumption patterns. These would be sent blind by sellers. In this case there might be thousands of individuals around the country who purchase more than say five chocolate bars a week and have told GEMs they are happy to receive unsolicited messages so long as they contain a relevant free product offer. After studying market overview information for past take up of such offers in this sector, the brand manager might chose to activate a message to these people that tells them they qualify for a free Chunkybisc. If they click to accept it, their details are released to the company, which is then contracted to deliver a biscuit. Next time those who accept browse the chocolate bars in their GEMs grocery store Chunkybiscs would be prominently displayed, making a first purchase especially easy. With faith that his new launch is genuinely innovative and likely to have a lasting hold on consumers' affections the brand manager might select some variation of this option.

He has now provided GEMs with the essential information it needs to launch his product in the marketplace. Before offering a contract, it can provide a snapshot of the likely impact of Chunkybiscs on the confectionery market. First it feeds his product details and pricing formula into stored overview data from that sector to show how the new entrant might have performed, given demand for chocolate bars without an established brand name and price levels over past weeks. Then it uses the same data to predict immediate demand for Chunkybiscs.

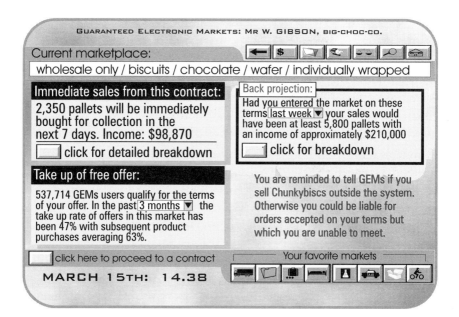

GEMs could include a facility for buyers called 'wait-and-purchase' whereby a maximum price for a given commodity is entered and the system buys automatically when the right deal becomes available. In this case there might be wholesalers or caterers on the system seeking individually wrapped chocolate bars within size, price and availability criteria met by Chunkybiscs: they would account for immediate sales within seconds of launch. Happy with these projections the brand manager clicks for a contract in which all his commitments just entered are embedded. His assurances will pass through the distribution chain to consumers. Because this leads to potentially enormous liability GEMs might have been told a more senior manager at the company has to countersign such agreements with his PIN before release.

Consider expansion into previously unthinkable sectors

With market entry and distribution this simple there should be little problem competing in new sectors. A company making paper cups, for instance, which had formerly only had relationships in the food services sector might launch disposable paper vases in the GEM for florist accessories, cautiously building up production as orders came in.

Service industry innovation might acquire a new importance

With access to the marketplace removed as a source of competitive advantage and the need (as opposed to emotional desire) for branding nullified by mechanisms that make every deal reliable, innovation is likely to become a key differentiator. The problem then becomes the speed with which a competitor could launch a me-too copy through GEMs. For manufacturers this is less of a problem. They can patent the processes and protect the descriptive trademarks behind a launch. In other sectors government could do much to encourage innovation by strengthening patent protection as they unroll an enabling act for a GEMs service. They might even allow service companies to protect their ideas from competitors for a given period.

The US government has made tentative steps in this direction already by granting patent protection to Internet service Priceline which has a distinctive way of matching buyers and sellers, initially on airline seats. This kind of protection for an idea rather than a technology could be extended. A week-long coach tour of South Africa's wine country for example is clearly not a concept that could be owned by any one travel operator but the same tour operated for the benefit of kite-flying enthusiasts with all equipment provided might be. As with existing patent law the onus could be on the pioneer to register his idea and take action against violators, but putting the laws in place would further ensure the vibrancy of the new marketplace by rewarding innovators. Financial service providers might find increasingly imaginative packages were the only way they could add value compared to the system's own loan matching. If those ideas were protected there could be even greater flexibility in the money marketplace. The cataloguing on GEMs would need to keep pace with the full diversity of offerings in each sector, the way this might grow organically is discussed in Appendix two.

18

Prepare to let go of customers

'Customer owning' would be an option, but would probably not be worthwhile

Any seller in GEMs could stipulate favoured buyers for whom he will drop prices. This could be automated so that, for instance, someone designated a member of a furniture store's loyalty programme would always have cheaper prices displayed. But they would be shown to the customer seeking a new armchair alongside those of multiple other sellers. As she narrowed her search down, by defining perhaps style of chair, pattern of material, then cost and availability with delivery charges for each option already calculated, the chances of the store being in her final selection would be increasingly slim. It would probably be more beneficial to orientate the company towards market overview information, trying to predict trends and 'own' a niche: individually tailored leather armchairs perhaps. Instead of outlining a pricing formula for one product the company specifies a rate at which it will build chairs of different sizes. These options, on as yet unbuilt items, are offered to every buyer whose requirements they match with the details sheet giving a delivery timetable and emphasizing the benefits of made-to-measure seating.

There would be little point in taking on the costs of communicating with a customer base for basic provisions. The manufacturer of Chunky-biscs in the example earlier, for instance, would harvest the names and addresses of individuals who had clicked to receive a free sample, but sending them a letter to cross-sell a second product would probably not be productive if competitors were offering easy click samples of their new creations. The same might not, however, apply to sellers of high-value items. A car maker, for instance, might offer a free test drive to

GEMs users who last bought a new vehicle on the system two years previously and were willing to take marketing messages containing an offer. (All GEMs messages would be bound by a contract so anyone originating the equivalent of unsolicited junk e-mails would be identifiable, with damaging consequences for their bond and trading record.) Car makers could follow up accepted road tests with postal or e-mail inducements to prospective purchasers but they would do so knowing several other test drives were probably only a click away. A manufacturer might instead focus on promotions made uniquely easy through GEMs contracts: lending a new model to qualified potential buyers for a week perhaps.

Expect a rise in ideological customers

A significant proportion of personal investors now opt for funds with an ideological bent. Likewise, GEMs users faced with a much wider marketplace than before might choose to complete sections in the system's user questionnaire that identify personal affiliations and allow them to be used as a means of prioritizing options in all markets. Devout Christians for instance might tell GEMs they will always favour suppliers who provenly donate to church causes and specify belief as a requirement when hiring staff on the system. An ethnic household might demand a similarly affirming political stance from sellers. This could be how emotional value is added to products in the wide-open marketplace. It might lead to a situation where, say, a shampoo production line is run one month by a firm that has genuinely positioned itself as pro-life in the abortion debate and the next by a similarly sized enterprise that meets requirements set out by pro-choice customers. There would be little point in either owning the line, it could be hired according to precise demand through GEMs, but they might be buying identical bottles to fit the machines and shipping the same ingredients. Illogical? It may be, but GEMs has no remit to iron out idiosyncrasies in consumerism.

19

Exploit the flexibility now on offer

Reassess the importance of a fixed supply chain

Order processing between manufacturers and their supplying companies was one of the first areas of business to go electronic. The now ageing technology known as Electronic Data Interchange turned *ad hoc* orders by e-mail into on-screen forms from which information could be extracted by the computer at either end for billing, transit details, stock management and so on. Later attempts to cut costs by creating more efficient supply chains led to the creation of electronic markets in which buyers were limited to large corporations whose presence made it worthwhile for sellers to invest in the software for that market. General Electric (GE), for instance, set up the Trading Process Network (TPN) through which they bought more than a billion dollars' worth of goods and services in 1997.[3] Other substantial purchasers including utility giant Con Edison now use the TPN to meet their needs. For the sellers a recurrent problem is how to integrate the demands of TPN with their in-house computer systems, so that information can flow seamlessly around the company.

The advantages GE and Con Edison gain from being big enough to set up their own marketplace in which potential suppliers must invest would be lost in a country with GEMs. Any regular purchaser, whatever their size, could personalize a template on the system listing the materials needed to keep a production line or home workshop fed. This could involve auto ordering if desired. So, for example, a chicken farmer who bought 500 additional birds on the system in the morning might find a truck load of feed from the cheapest supplier automatically arriving in the afternoon. Would purchasing in an open marketplace be preferable to buying from a small number of approved suppliers? The latter option would of course be available to GEMs users but the newly enabled capacity to shop from the entire marketplace in a few keystrokes could ensure unprecedented efficiency in supply. In the 1920s General Motors (GM) was the world's most integrated company, owning the manufacturers of 70 per cent of its automobiles' components. Despite this unique leverage on the supply chain William C. Durant, father of GM, insisted each of the owned firms sell half their output outside the company. Unable to luxuriate in assured sales the subsidiaries remained competitive on price and quality.[4] Any company with a strong trading record of supply in GEMs would have attained Durant's standards for the same reason.

GEMs could facilitate a tendering process for companies supplying non-standardized goods. Sign makers, for instance, could click through a list of specialities – stonework perhaps or three-dimensional displays – and highlight the ones in which they were interested in building a business. They would then tell the system how quickly they undertook to respond to enquiries: one working day, for instance, in a given week. (The time could be changed at will, being lengthened during busy periods, for example.) A design company that wanted say an illuminated figure constructed on behalf of a client would go to the GEM for signs and click on 'customized neon', immediately the system would specify response times to which suppliers had contractually bound themselves: perhaps a dozen firms willing to produce a quote in six hours, a further twenty to do so by the next day and so on. The buyer then types a description of the sign they want made and it is circulated to the selected suppliers who can phone or e-mail for more details before coming back with a price that, together with a newly agreed description, is sealed in a contract offered by the system.

Start rostering employees and assets on the system

There will be many companies who choose not to sell output in the new marketplace. Even so, they could use it for staff and resource management. Take for instance a house-building company. Their best workers would probably find themselves able to sell their services effortlessly in GEMs and would be the most tempted to leave an erstwhile employer. But by allowing staff to set pricing formulas and work more flexibly even while hiring themselves out elsewhere (employer confidentiality being a requirement in every contract they sign) the firm should retain at least a part share in their brightest stars. They might give GEMs a ranked list of their approved employees and ensure the best were offered periods of work first, the list could be supplemented by new recruits, for whom the system would search endlessly, who may be only willing to work on a part-time basis. It would require a different mind set for those used to pushing out weekly rosters compiled by software on a manager's desktop computer. But the flexibility in fixed costs offered could be a buffer against winds of change as the market for house purchasing moved to GEMs.

GEMs should offer users a 'shadow trading' facility whereby they can input details of an asset into the system plus a pricing formula but not enter the market. Managers can then see the worth of that item. A house builder for instance could 'shadow trade' their mobile crane on GEMs and see the pattern of bookings they would achieve if they were actually offering it on their stipulated terms. It might be in this finely tuned market that the cranes could be earning hire charges at times not required by their owner, even that they would be worth more rented out than employed on the house builder's own projects. The same could be true of production lines, distribution vehicles and fixed purpose buildings.

Be prepared for the business to erode to a core activity

However much the market atomizes there will be functions that can not be performed by individuals. A diving school, for example, that had previously employed ten instructors would probably find them migrating to GEMs where they could sell their services without overheads and according to an ever-changing willingness to work. But those newly enfranchised instructors still need equipment for pupils: providing and maintaining it could be the school's new *raison d'être*. For some firms, information will become their new product: selling a paperback recommendation service, for instance, rather than offering it as a marketing package with book sales. Or offering a 'we help you move' service based on local knowledge instead of selling houses.

Sellers who currently capitalize on confusion in the uncoordinated marketplace by bundling goods together for the convenience of buyers might find they were no longer adding value when all the components of an enquiry could be pieced together by the system. A camera seller for instance offering 'free' rolls of film with a particular model could find it made him uncompetitive. He would of course be able to promote the offer on his details page for that camera but the cost of films would be likely to push him down the price rankings for that model. Any user wanting a new camera and say six film rolls for next day delivery could input the two requirements in precise detail and have the two components from disparate sources with delivery priced alongside any bundled offers. However, in a widening marketplace, it may be that consumers become much more demanding about, for instance, the brand of film they require and find bundled offers too inflexible. Knowing what kind of cameras to sell and maybe offering separately bought after-sales packages would be the business focus, not inventing marketing offers.

In some sectors a supplier may even choose to abdicate the need to plan their exact offering in the market. In long-distance bus travel, for instance, most operators will select destinations and enter their seats for sale at given departure times. Travellers who require immediate confirmation of journey details would be matched with those suppliers. Other more leisurely travellers might tell GEMs something like 'book me a seat from Delhi to Agra at some point next Monday and confirm the details by Friday. Once it had 50 such commitments to purchase, the system might band them together then hire a vehicle and driver with a collective contract. They would simply be in the GEMs for coach charter, offering the best value for times and distance on the day in question.

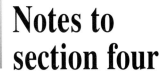

notes

Notes to
section four

1. www.jackdaniels.com
2. P&G's Hottest New Product: P&G, *Business Week*, 5 October 1998, European Edition, p. 58.
3. Business at Net Speed, *Business Week*, 22 June 1998, p. 3.
4. Peter Drucker, The End of Command and Control, *Forbes Global Business and Finance*, 5 October 1998, p. 61.

Electronic markets as a public utility

The world has been here before. A potent new technology is being exploited but only for restricted commercial advantage. Meanwhile, problems that it could address if made more widely available worsen. In the 1840s the technology was water pumping; the problem, epidemics caused by poor sanitation. Now electronic trading is being used primarily for new efficiencies in marketing while economies around the world become exclusive and inefficient. This is not a 'them' and 'us' argument. Just as no amount of wealth in Victorian England could create a barrier against airborne diseases that started in the poor areas so the impact of disintegrating social structures in the technological age can not be reassuringly compartmentalized.

Victorian advocates of mass water supply faced many questions about their unfamiliar concept. What rate would be charged for each cup of water? How would people who worked irregular hours store their share of water for use late at night or early in the morning? Who would be responsible for telling users when the product was safe to drink? It took some time for the sheer simplicity of the proposed service to be widely understood. Water was to make a transition from its status as a costly, laboriously collected and sparingly used resource to an abundant commodity, unthinkingly available at high quality around the clock in every home. A similar point needs to be made about Guaranteed Electronic Markets. Although indisputably complex in their inner workings, their role in a user's life would be elementary. With a few clicks on a TV remote control the service would allow individuals and companies to buy or sell anything instantly at the best possible price in a huge market-place that anyone was always free to enter on their own terms.

Despite making small units of production uniquely efficient, a GEMs system should have absolutely no ideological agenda. If automatic weapons for instance are legal in the country of operation there will be a GEM for them run by a committed franchisee with a pressing incentive to grow the market. Those who oppose guns would find the system equally useful. They would be only a few clicks away from joining a boycott of any firm in the armaments business or forming a solidly administered group to lobby for tighter gun laws. GEMs itself would be, like the World Wide Web, telephones or the money supply, simply a platform for diverse activity across a pluralist society. Its only agenda is to provide all the features of electronic trade to anyone who wants to use them. While the system would need to be built by big companies they would do so on the basis which corporations currently build our roads. Once finished a new highway is handed over for use by all drivers according to their individual priorities, not annexed for the advantage of the companies that built it.

A GEMs system would require vigilance to ensure its subservience was unwavering. It is not impossible, however, to construct a legal framework that creates profitable opportunity for electronic markets as a lowly public utility with the potentially pernicious applications of such powerful technology thoroughly eliminated. When centralised water supply was advocated, for instance, a key worry for many was the damage that an operator could inflict on an entire city with a phial of poison. Such an event has not happened during the century in which aggregated water provision has become the norm. Equally it should not be supposed that because a GEMs consortium could theoretically wield significant power it would put the opportunity for a once only megalo-maniacal act above commercial considerations and abuse that position.

Will the vision in this book become reality? Not immediately, certainly. The economic entities that dominate uncoordinated market-places will not go quietly and have multi-tentacled patronage that binds most of us to the *status quo* in some way. There is, additionally, a fear of managed change: a view that adverse social impact of new technology adopted by corporations is 'inevitable' whereas government initiation is an abhorrent interference in natural events. Faith in free markets runs deep. Paradoxically it is likely to be appropriated by organisations who, having become winners in the free market of today, are determined to stop a much freer market emerging for tomorrow.

Despite this resistance to planned transitions it is worth asking what the alternative to GEMs-style systems is. Electronic trade for corporate benefit is now on the march. Already we can see how electronic markets have made world-wide capital flows ultra-efficient. It is now often more effective to put funds into financial instruments divorced from economic reality, tradable only between bank computers, than to invest in workers, companies and communities. Money is leaching out of the tangible economy, which is overhead ridden, imprecise and unresponsive, towards a near-pure marketplace for world-wide capital. If the destabilizing impact of global money currents is to be diminished, governments face a choice. Either they band together and somehow disable the current efficiencies of capital movement or they elevate their populations' individual trading potential to the same effectiveness. GEMs should destroy a cardinal concept now underpinning the world economy: that money works most effectively for its owners when aggregated into enormous blocks. Once a public electronic markets system reached maturity it could push funds into highly efficient, rapid, atomized circulation.

Existing e-commerce companies – the firms who would logically build GEMs – are unlikely to be enthusiastic advocates of low margin, unknowing, universally provided electronic markets. They may yet repeat the fate of mainframe computer manufacturers in the 1970s and 80s. The notion of personal computers was beyond the corporate vision of these companies, run as they were by men who had devoted their lives to creating basement-sized hardware. Once PCs took off, former behemoths found themselves marooned in a backwater. New technology has always flowed towards maximized usefulness and cheapness, with little regard for the tenets of those who progressed its development. A conviction that 'the trading revolution will be decided by companies alone, governments are irrelevant' could one day seem as naïve as the view, once widely held, that the then powerful telegraph companies could stop the telephone being born. If policy makers can initiate the benefits of electronic trade for less cost and on a wider scale than private companies alone then, history suggests, that is what will ultimately happen.

appendix
one

Principles governing GEMs

The benefits of a Guaranteed Electronic Markets system would be balanced by its potential to become the most sophisticated pervasive technology in history. In years to come there could be countless systems claiming to bring the unexpurgated advantages of electronic trade into mass public use. The following points are extracts from a lengthier attempt to define such a system that genuinely delivers the promise of this formidable technology, while protecting its users' interests and respecting a wider responsibility to society. Containment of the potential service is crucial to these principles. It should be restricted by statute to its core role: provision of automated markets, whose management have sacrificed any power they might expect to accrue from their key position.

Such a system would benefit from a mature relationship with users. Human error and occasional machine failings would be near inevitable on such a complex project. They should be promptly admitted and remedial action detailed: a politicized culture of whitewash and misfocused recriminations would ultimately be self-defeating. Some principles that should guide a GEMs system are contradictory. On one hand it would want to give users a choice of regulatory regimes in any market, on the other it should prioritize simplicity of operation, for instance. Resolution will come down to editorial judgement based, as ever, on the balance deemed most likely to encourage market use. Ultimately faith in the system could depend on public perception of the consortium that runs it. If member companies see GEMs as a potential world-wide business opportunity, they would have every commercial incentive to see that their service adhered strictly to guidelines such as the following, where five key principles are outlined.

1. The system is programmed to automatically enforce fair trade

Each transaction is thoroughly enforced

■ Every deal in every market goes through a contract that can be amended by a seller; such amendments must be immediately obvious to a buyer. Except in the loans market, no user can be in debt to another user. Instead, payment is held in escrow by the system until such point as the contract has been clearly completed. In some cases (the decoration of a house for instance), this may entail release in tranches, as the buyer approves each stage of work according to steps laid out in the standard contract.

■ Sellers must provide proof of insurance cover to a level determined by the liabilities they could incur. These sums, held by GEMs so they are unquestioningly accessible, pay all earned interest to the company or individual who deposited them. Depositors should be able to stipulate how their bond is invested within the system's money markets, subject only to a requirement that the funds be automatically available at short notice by GEMs, in case of dispute. GEMs itself does not assess the cover required by any individual trader, that figure applies across all sellers in any given market: it is insurers who decide what it costs to find the requisite bonding. A hotel owner selling 100 rooms a night for a maximum $90 each, for instance, might have to deposit a bond of three times his room charge (the maximum likely payout to any disgruntled customer) multiplied by his number of rooms. If he has a credible trading record in related markets however this cover should be cheaply obtained from an insurer who judges him to be a worthwhile risk.

■ All GEMs are underpinned by immediately available adjudication, the steps of which are established in the contract between buyer and seller. In sensitive markets the first level of judgement if users can not agree reconciliation is the lower courts. For other sectors the system would establish panels of representatives from appropriate organizations. Judgement is funded by individual deposits and bonds. Some markets (childcare is one) require heavy regulation and verified entry requirements, others (fortune tellers for instance) will have to rely on 'best of ability' clauses in each contract.

■ GEMs tries to avoid allowing one organization to dominate adjudication in a particular marketplace, seeking instead to combine input from qualified groups who should be induced to agree on unified standards that will maximize turnover. Adjudication decisions are published openly on the system's information pages for users but identities of the parties involved might be removed.

■ The GEMs franchisee acts as a check on the power of adjudication authorities. He must see that they are acting within the broad aims of GEMs markets and building what amounts to predictable case law in judgements. If not, an alternative body has to be found: that process would be made public.

■ Franchisees must decide on the level of transparency appropriate to their market. Providers of medical services for instance might have to reveal not only their true identity but their full qualifications and professional history to prospective purchasers. Conversely neither sellers or buyers in a GEM for prostitution might be required to trade under their real names, the system alone knows who they are and would only release the information on receipt of a court order following criminal allegations.

■ The system can facilitate product recalls by allowing sellers to access their stored contracts with buyers and send a message to each. Before doing so they would have to sign a contract attesting to the genuineness of the recall. Abuse of the facility, by attempting to cross-sell under the guise of a recall for instance, would then incur sanctions.

■ The system is itself entitled to demand fair treatment from users. Any seller seeking to use GEMs simply as a means of listing their availability: displaying themselves in the electricians market for instance but then taking bookings by phone to avoid the strictures of a GEMs contract should be penalized. If they consistently list themselves but then withdraw from the market without a booking made over the system they could be warned automatically and eventually suspended. This should be explained as part of a contract with the system to be signed online by new users.

■ Provenly responsible buyers and sellers must be able to prove their status to each other.

Market conditions are structured around the needs of buyers, rather than favouring particular sellers

- The only deals enacted on the system are straightforward. There is no facility for instance to allow inertia selling where a purchase is made in a month's time if not stopped by the buyer within a fortnight.
- Customer-specific information, the extent of no-claims bonuses accumulated by a motorist for example, is owned by, and automatically verified for, the customer, who can use it to freely shop around.
- Full comparisons – cost per litre for various sizes of wine bottle for example – are always available. Where suppliers use contrasting classifications – measurement of audio amplifier power in RMS or MPC for instance – the system will convert between the two or, if that is not possible, invite sellers to input measurements in both and allow buyers to select which metric they wish to use. In a highly confusing marketplace, mobile phone tariffs perhaps, the relevant GEMs franchisee might construct a grid of options and invite sellers to input their rates in such a way that they can be fairly shown alongside competitors once a buyer has ranked her requirements. Sellers would not have to enter information for the grid but would risk losing sales by not doing so.
- The system trades in units of need, not sources of supply. Someone wanting to book a journey, for instance, could see different combinations of available rail, bus, taxi, rideshare and car hire options ranked according to their priorities.
- If a buyer's query turns up multiple sellers charging the same price all are listed but displayed according to randomizing software. Someone who wants a new copy of a widely available book delivered tomorrow, for instance, might find several hundred bookshops could meet that requirement with no price differential. In the absence of prioritizing from data in the buyer's user questionnaire (preference for local stores perhaps) all the shops will be displayed in jumbled order.
- Clear cataloguing is essential to each market. Sellers are responsible for categorizing their offering and not allowed unjustified listings for which they are penalized if reported. Someone selling places on a 'learn to fish' holiday, for instance, could justifiably offer them in markets for sports teaching, country breaks and angling holidays. Once all available places had been sold that offering would disappear from all three sectors. Conversely someone trying to list their

humorous wedding congratulations product in all sectors of the GEM for greetings cards would be stopped by the system.

- Big companies trading on the system would have to decide whether to accumulate a corporation-wide trading record or a spectrum of records on a division by division basis. They could not switch between the two to disguise a poorly performing division.
- Sellers are made to input a pricing formula in such a way that a straightforward price can then be calculated for each buyer's enquiry.
- Tougher conditions are imposed on probationary traders. A driver in his early weeks, due to pick up a vehicle at a specified truckstop might have to arrive, and sign in on the location-specific terminal there, 60 minutes early so there is ample time for the software to hire another driver if the probationer does not log in.

Everything possible is done to attract wide-ranging sellers into each marketplace

- Cumulative selling is enabled. So, for instance, a swimming pool manager could tell the system his facility would open late in the evening once a minimum of 12 buyers paid for an hour in the water. (He could also instruct it to roster one of his approved lifeguards before letting the sales go through.) Or a property developer could offer a building for conversion to flats, subject to a minimum number of apartments being pre-sold. The system will always tell prospective buyers what the required figure is, and the number of currently confirmed takers.
- GEMs can facilitate trade in digitized products and can if desired act as their delivery medium. A company selling digital streams of music on the system, for instance, could choose between having them delivered via GEMs or from their own web site. The music could only be sold directly via GEMs once the core computer had received it and confirmed its technical suitability for playout. If this was not possible, or not desired by the seller, buyers would be sent automatically to the seller's web site on completion of their contract. Failure to receive the song would then lead to a disputes procedure. An icon would tell potential purchasers which option applied to each song.
- The system is committed to full market information for all users. Where there is demand that is not being met in any market the extent of enquiries for the non-existent service would be freely available.

- Sellers can keep their offerings out of certain markets. Someone selling live rabbits for instance could stipulate in the contract they are only to be purchased as a pet and not be available to rabbit farmers. Similarly, potential buyers can be defined, down to one individual if desired. Someone who had successfully hired a neighbour's car in the past, for instance, might phone them and ask if the vehicle could be made available that evening. The owner could then put the car on the market with full GEMs back-up but only one buyer listed as acceptable.

2. The system is committed to maximum usefulness

Each market must deliver the full benefits that electronic trading technology has to offer that sector

- Guaranteed electronic markets operate no protectionism, seeking only to match each buyer with the best seller according to the purchaser's priorities at the time. They should not restrict their potential to preserve any existing or nascent structures of business or government.
- The system itself needs constant public scrutiny to see that it is not delaying low-value markets out of fear they will cannibalize higher-value sectors. For example, management focused on the short term might be reluctant to open up a local deliveries market for the benefit of teenagers with bikes because those trades would undercut delivering by adults in cars, who charge more and therefore earn the consortium more commission. The order in which sectors are unfurled must be publicly justified.
- Markets should cater for the smallest possible units of need so, for example, someone seeking a child's play house would be offered not only purchase options but a hire market in case they only required it for a week or less.
- The system can offer 'soft matches' between suppliers and buyers seeking a custom-made product. It will bring together each purchaser with an array of sellers who have expressed interest in a particular category of work, then facilitate messages about requirements before binding the messages, with potential for amendment, into a contract for the final work.

■ GEMs must have full indexing of products on offer and allow users a choice of ways of navigating the market categories.

■ Any user could use the system to pay his household bills if he and the recipient desired.

■ The system should offer users the opportunity to boycott certain sellers, or categories of sellers. However, it has a duty to see such boycotts can be 'turned off' at each user's discretion, and not remain in force through inertia long after the issue that prompted them has been resolved. A reminder of boycotts in force at perhaps three monthly intervals with buttons for ease of cancellation might be one solution.

The system is committed to simplicity of operation for users

■ As each user becomes familiar with GEMs displays the number of key strokes in each transaction can be reduced, by displaying a symbol for 'standard contract not amended' against purchasing options, for instance. Buyers do not then have to call up the contract before signing. Likewise, a trading record can be expressed as a percentage, based on a standard formula that factors number of assignments, number of customers and number of complaints: this would enable easy comparison between traders.

■ Ways of loading options for sale into the system must be constantly made easier. For example, the computer should be able to recognize every barcode on every product in the country of operation. Anyone wanting to sell food, books, records, clothes, toys, furnishings and so on need only find a barcode reader connected to the system to swipe in full details of their inventory, which will then be displayed on screen.

■ In many sectors GEMs would need to grade its sellers so buyers can instantly select the level of service for which they are willing to pay. Wherever possible these increments should mirror existing structures for professional grades.

■ All the formulae by which each market operates (grade levels, scales of fines and so on) are to be published openly.

The way options are displayed is to be constantly improved

- Information is always presented in the most visual way possible. Sellers should be offered opportunities to individualize interactive displays; for example, cinema managers would be able to create a seating plan of their auditorium that could be used by buyers to select unsold seats for each showing. (The system would allow movie goers to click on a film title to see a map of cinemas in their area showing it, then call up available seating for each performance.)

- Shoppers are given the widest range of criteria from which to prioritize a custom search. Someone selecting a holiday, for instance, could see available options listed in order of monthly average temperatures at destination, price, type of accommodation, precise depart and return dates, departure airports, availability of facilities selected by the buyer and so on. Once fully developed, GEMs should enable an individual to have exactly the best holiday for his personal requirements, constructed from a market of hundreds of thousands of offers.

- Refinements should be added to each market as lessons are learned. In the pet-walking market, for instance, the franchisee might offer pet owners a chance to add a 'prone to biting' clause in each contract. That would ensure sellers were forewarned (at the risk they might charge more for such engagements) and could lessen the dog owner's liability in case of any subsequent claim.

- Computer Aided Design software should be customized for GEMs. In the market for stairlifts, for instance, the interface would allow a buyer to construct a plan of their stairs by inputting measurements as requested. It then offers prices for that particular length and shape constructed from the pricing formulae of competing manufacturers coupled with similarly costed quotes from installers.

- Bargain hunters should be allowed to shop with full flexibility. For instance, it should be possible to tell GEMs to book a journey 'when cheapest' in a window defined by two dates.

The system is committed to low overheads

- Electronic markets must be cheap to be truly useful. GEMs should be fully featured but totally automated; no franchisee or member of system staff ever gets involved in an individual transaction. There must be external mechanisms to deal with trades that go awry, and provision for funding of those mechanisms within the terms of each user's acceptance into the market.
- The behaviour of traders is regulated by the market, not by staff, but the system is set up to heavily penalize those who are found misbehaving. This involves holding its own copy of contracts for perhaps a month after each transaction. A manufacturer can make unrealistic claims, for instance, but they will be enshrined in every contract with a buyer. If one of them sues for misrepresentation and wins, the system will offer all other buyers from the previous month the chance to form a class action with an online lawyer. As ever, this is an immediate software function, not something decided on a case-by-case basis by staff. This principle – that traders' promises are not checked but they can expect competitors and consumers to challenge any dubious claims – translates into voting. Users could pose any question they like but, once the poll is complete, the fairness of the question has to be verified by an appropriate body before the result is deemed to have any validity. By asking a biased question, organizers would know their efforts will be wasted.
- The system itself must be soundly financed with ample revenue-protection devices incorporated.
- GEMs do not offer any function that requires human judgement on a day-to-day basis. The system can operate (if permitted) a range of lotteries, for instance. It would take in funds from users and pay out winnings, after deducting its own flat rate commission, according to a random number generator. But the system itself can not operate as a bookmaker because the setting of odds requires daily judgement; it is up to users to provide a market-making facility.

3. The system's neutrality is to be aggressively asserted

GEMs stand alone, divorced from political ideology or vested interests

- All discussions between government and system management are on the record, posted on the system's own information pages.
- Any decision about market operation that can be made outside the GEMs organisation – by a relevant regulatory body or by government – is resolved in that way.
- Operating companies and staff must declare any business activity or affiliation that could give them an interest in a particular market sector; this information to be openly available to users.
- Because of the danger of an unrepresentative elite emerging to run the system, senior staff are only allowed to work in day-to-day management for eight years (excluding a launch period); after that they can become consultants, but relinquish hands-on control. There is nothing of course to stop an individual then working on another country's GEMs-style system.
- There are to be no favoured means of access to the system: it can be carried by any cable company, Internet provider or similar channel that can match required security standards. Nor can the system favour particular consumer technologies, including those of its consortium members. Because of its size, GEMs should accept input from all widely used types of smartcard readers for instance.
- No outside body that is regulating a market on the system is to be allowed to use their involvement to propagate a particular ideological view of that market. In particular, the system does not pursue regulation to the point where it bars innovative 'fringe' traders from GEMs. For example, if registration of therapists was in force in the country of operation, that GEM might still allow unregistered practitioners to trade while making the distinction clear.
- Offerings in a market can be ranked according to user choice by volume of sales, newest entries first, locality of traders and so on, but there are to be no 'GEMs recommends' selections. The system is neutral. It should, however, allow buyers to navigate its markets through templates constructed by outsiders. There might for instance be a 'Martha Stewart recommends' filter (created by an

outside company who sells it to users) through which options in the home furnishing markets can be viewed.

■ A clear route for complaints about the system itself needs to be established, perhaps to an independent ombudsman who publishes findings openly. He might additionally pass on complaints to the rotating international bodies paid to inspect the system. Attempts to skew the markets or otherwise interfere with system purity should be a criminal offence.

The system has no other purpose than provision of electronic markets and immediately related functions

■ The system provides only the minimum service needed for a fully featured electronic markets operation. Additional facilities must be the preserve of competing outside suppliers. For example, many users would want to tailor their interface with GEMs as an alternative to the system's standard design. The consortium does not market a range of value-added interface options but ensures that any outside designer who wants to market software that converts the image sent by GEMs into something more distinctive can do so.

■ The GEMs brand name is not be to be applied to any other service.

■ The system knows its limitations. It is a marketplace not an information service, or a message forwarder. Any encroachment into these areas is only where required to facilitate specific trades.

■ A market in peripheral services could grow up with GEMs: digitizing traders' photographs and sending them to the central computer, for instance. Beyond ensuring that access is available to any company wanting to provide this service, the consortium should not get involved.

No one is to be coerced into using the system or deepening their level of involvement with the system

■ Management must not permit any attempt to make the use of the system mandatory. They should, for instance, actively oppose any plans to compel a user to file tax returns though GEMs.

■ GEMs are not to be used as a social order device, requiring offenders to sign on at a certain time to prove they are abiding by a curfew, for example.

■ Any user can sign off the system at any time once all their contractual obligations have expired. If their parallel economy account matches the number of points they were awarded on joining then no record is kept of their membership. If they have spent their points, minimal details are kept to ensure they do not receive a fresh supply on rejoining.

■ There is no minimum level of service for users and no 'relationship-building' attempts to increase usage. The consortium can buy poster space to advertise new features on GEMs, they cannot send messages to individuals, identified by the central computer as low users, promoting its wider benefits.

■ The system does not set out to limit access to any other online service, by stipulating monopoly carriage to cable TV companies, for instance.

■ A user can choose between having copies of contracts they sign on GEMs filed in their personal folder on the central computer (in which case they would be destroyed if the user closes his account) or downloaded to his own computer.

All adult users are treated equally

■ All sellers must submit to GEMs' verification, bonding, escrow and contract procedures, regardless of their size or trading background. This is an automated market that makes no exceptions for big brands or companies pleading exceptional reputations.

■ No one earns preferential treatment in the GEMs marketplace through spending power, frequency of use, type of business or ideological viewpoint. The only exception is emergency services; a verified doctor requiring a defibrillator, for example, would be able to click on a 'rush' icon and go ahead of any other users in a queue for available deliverers at that time.

■ Junior users must be restricted in terms of the trading responsibilities they can take on (only being able to agree a contract with a parent's PIN as counter signature, for instance) and the sectors they can access.

4. The system has responsibilities to the society in which it operates

In recognition of the importance that a mature GEMs network could acquire within the national economy, management have a special duty to run the system responsibly

- Management should publish an online annual report focusing particularly on objectives for the following 12 months.
- The system's own accounts must be compiled openly on its 'information about GEMs' pages so any user can see which markets are most – or least – profitable and monitor those sectors with added vigilance.
- Despite the absolute commitment to user privacy, some sectors should track sensitive purchases: guns, pelts, rare animals or explosives for instance. These transactions will generate a data shadow enabling, say, a particular gun's ownership to be traced back for years if police gain a court order to open the records. Users must always be informed when these records are being compiled. Honest purchasers, of course, have nothing to fear from the process.
- GEMs' technology could eventually be applied to sensitive social work, matching foster children and approved parents for initial meetings, for example. This should be provided through closed markets, only available to foster parents and social workers.
- Provision must be made for checking traded items against a list of stolen goods, administered by the police.
- The system could acquire a pivotal role in the nation's money supply and must be subject to publicly issued edicts from the government. In particular, there is a danger that the efficiency of the GEMs loans markets could create an unprecedented multiplier effect in cash circulation. Parliament may want to dampen this with minimum periods of borrowing.

GEMs could, eventually, become part of the checks and balances of a democratic society

- Like a healthy press or broadcast industry, GEMs cannot afford to be cosy with government. Management must be relentless in their focus on rolling out unimpeded benefits of trading technology unless restrained by law. There are to be no backroom agreements with anyone.

■ The only exception to the foregoing is at times of national emergency. GEMs recognizes its potential usefulness in a crisis, helping orderly evacuation of a city, for instance, by allocating places on trains or pick-up points for coaches, while issuing codes to residents of a particular zone who are to be allowed through road-blocks. Like the broadcasting networks, government could take over the system in a crisis: the central computer would seal personal data, wiping it rather than revealing information beyond that legitimately required in an emergency. GEMs should not bear the costs of setting up this programming which should be met from civil defence funds.

■ Where the system's usefulness is restricted – by government limiting trade on GEMs that is legal in other forms, for instance – management must alert users that they are trading in a hobbled sector.

■ System management must make public any information they obtain by virtue of their unique position but need not do so with information they chose to gather from sources available to all. Averaged patterns of GEMs usage through the day, for example, must be published. But should management decide to hire a polling company to assess public reaction to the system they can keep the results private because there is nothing to stop any other body conducting the same exercise.

GEMs have responsibility to existing organizational structures

■ The system is not opposed to any form of doing business and will do everything – short of restricting its own potential – to accommodate existing organizations into its marketplaces.

■ Brands are to have their status preserved; they should be displayed in illustrative material supplied by the maker (but not allowed to mislead in any way). Additionally, a brand owner is entitled to have pirated versions of his product range removed from the system. This would need to be done through the courts.

■ GEMs would probably increase the sales of second-hand books, pre-owned movies on video and other items likely to deprive copyright holders of income. Policy makers might decide that a levy be made,

on each such sale, that is automatically transferred to the originator of the material and the system should facilitate this.
- Charities must be able to collect donations on the system.
- Without lowering its commitment to political neutrality, the system recognizes the desirability of according certain status to some government functions. When parliament launch a referendum on the system, for instance, it must be showcased on the voting page, not simply listed amid polls launched by ordinary users.

5. Maximum security is an overriding priority

The system has automatic protection built in for users

- Any user who fears their communication with the system is being monitored through a tap on the phone line can make use of a room at the GEMs building which allows direct access to the core by nervous users (who may be running a sensitive political group on the system for instance).
- Management should recognize that security is as much a human as a technical consideration. The consortium must encourage a culture of openness and recruit from all sections of society. In particular they should:

  - place no restrictions on staff talking to the press if they have concerns about the system's probity.
  - set up a 'whistleblowers' page where authenticated staff can leave indelible messages readable by any user browsing the page. This would leave the consortium open to embarrassing attack by disgruntled workers, but a vulnerable management is preferable to a potentially omnipotent system.

- Nobody is allowed remote access to the core programming. Franchisees who want to change the layout of their market front end compile the changes remotely but then have to send them to a secure control room to be assessed for security and uploaded.

As a natural monopoly, with so much potential for difficult-to-detect interference, the system is too sensitive to be regulated by any one body

- Tough, and increasingly ingenious, inspection is to be welcomed. The system must genuinely have nothing to hide and everything to gain from showing its willingness to be dissected by inspectors with a range of ideological viewpoints and technical experience. Money should be set aside to fund these inspections (by organizations across the political spectrum from around the world) via an independent body which publishes their findings immediately.
- The consistent points for inspection are always verification that any user can leave the system with all personal data irrevocably destroyed at any time and that the software has triggers which will warn users automatically of any attempt to tamper with data.
- Mechanisms that provide for independent inspectors at short notice must be set up. Management cannot alter the central code unchecked, by pleading special requirements in an emergency.
- A GEMs consortium that has been sanctioned for monopoly of government approval must accept it has forfeited rights to normal commercial secrecy; it has no comparable competitors, while demonstrable integrity has become its most important long-term asset. Nothing can be concealed from inspection teams.

Security of individual trades is an equal priority

- No one can use the system without an identifying password or PIN. These can be changed whenever a user believes her personal security might have been breached. Additionally users can opt for an array of passwords, insisting on an additional word for trades over a certain amount for example. Partial-access code-words can also be generated; a frequent motorist for instance might have a code-word that allowed a colleague to access his account, but only for a restricted one-off visit to book a mechanic in case of a breakdown.
- Apart from an automatically compiled trading record, the system does not hold any file on users that they cannot control fully.
- One party in a transaction cannot obtain any information about the other except what they have chosen to reveal.

■ Information entered by a seller to flesh out a details page is their copyright and must be protected from unauthorized downloading.

■ Any automatic transfer of information is flagged to the user. In the UK, for instance, anyone buying a television must by law have their details passed to the TV licensing authority. GEMs would tell buyers this was happening.

■ With company accounts the user is identified by their title within the organization (that is, senior purchasing manager, Acme Corp.) not in any way that links to their personal trading account. Any sanctions are applied to the company as a whole, to avoid shifting job titles as a technique for escaping punishment.

A business model for initiating GEMs

Overview

This model is an attempt to outline one possible route for companies who seek to make the GEMs vision a reality. It is not a detailed business plan. As with previous launches of public infrastructure there can be no numerical evidence of final demand, but omens abound. To take one example of desire for underpinned screen trading once provided: the French futures exchange, the MATIF, experimented with online markets in April 1997. The plan was to see after a year or so if they could establish a niche alongside long-established open outcry trading by traders. Within two weeks however electronic trading had won so conclusively that the trading floor was wound down.[1]

Although a fully integrated GEMs system could only be initiated by government there might be opportunity for interested companies to propagate the potential of public markets while positioning themselves as logical first port of call for any parliament wanting to offer such a system. This demands an unusual business model: part hearts and minds campaign, part international lobbying effort and part partnership-building exercise. Many computing success stories have been born out of previously unthinkable commercial strategies. The newborn Netscape gave away its sole product without charge, to establish quick critical mass; Digital developed the AltaVista search engine with no income line in sight, motivated only by an urge to grow the Internet. Despite the uncertainty and enormous investment required to construct a GEMs core computer, however, it is worth reiterating the scale of potential return: accumulated commissions (individually small but aggregated automatically) on what could be a significant proportion of domestic transactions in the countries of operation for the period of concession.

Awkwardly for a project likely to lead to the demise of so many corporations, GEMs could only be effectively promoted by large companies. A small start-up, however ambitious, would find it hard to open doors to senior politicians and be taken seriously by their electors. Nor could it pull together the heavyweight partners required to build such a demanding system while ensuring that the vision remained true. Only a sizeable organization could withstand the resourceful, high-level, hostility public markets will inevitably attract. The corporate mind-set required for GEMs is far from the short-term, technology-driven, opportunism that pervades Silicon Valley. An authentic commitment to inspection, transparency and preserving national identities might seem laughable in the early days of such a business but if it is to succeed the final consortium would be trusted unthinkingly by millions of people around the world, many of them having little faith in their own govern-ment's rectitude. Like an airline predicated on enhanced cabin service but dispensing with safety procedures, a GEMs builder viewing their task purely in technological terms could enjoy only short-term success. Because of the unique core competencies involved, the companies that bring fully fledged public markets to the world may come from far outside the computing establishment.

What a business model must deliver

- Decentralized control to make GEMs acceptable to diverse populations.
- Long-term perspective in an industry constantly restricted to short-termism by ever-changing technical foundations.
- Public trust, even affection. There are lessons to be learned from companies like Apple Computer and Hewlett Packard that, in their formative stages, reaped considerable benefits from a positive culture of humanity when compared to unimaginatively commercial behemoths like IBM. If the relationships within the organization are

right, GEMs, with its dedication to rolling out trading advantages for the benefits of all, could have the potential to become a very popular institution in the mind of potential users and prospective employees.

■ The system needs to be prepared for a swift growth phase when, perhaps, dozens of new market sectors are being launched every week with all the attendant advantages of momentum in roll out. However, the markets being launched need to be properly thought through, intuitive to use and competently edged towards critical mass.

■ The markets offered, and features within them, should be driven by a diverse array of entrepreneurs, each believing that they can make a particular sector work and not controlled by a core staff. However, all markets have to pass GEMs' rigorous requirements for guaranteeing transactions.

■ As market usage builds, GEMs would need to remain closely in touch with the needs of users in each of its thousands of sectors. The sophistication with which buyers and sellers are matched, and the enforcement mechanisms underlying the safety of each transaction, must be constantly evolving to increase the attractiveness of each sector.

■ Enduring 'reality antennae' would be crucial. Seismic shifts in technology and customer expectations have, in the past two decades, exposed the corporate complacency of once indomitable industry giants like IBM and Apple. As a semi-protected industry, GEMs could be particularly prone to a collective mind-set that calcified the *status quo* while the outside world moved on.

Structure of the core organization

This business model assumes a board representing a consortium of three companies or more, divided into three areas of expertise.

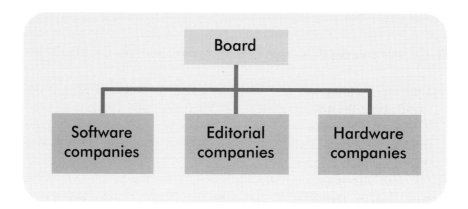

Of the three areas of expertise bought to the enterprise by these companies it is 'editorial' that would drive the business plan. Hardware requirements have past precedents to rely on: the enormous installations at the heart of long standing systems like SABRE, AMADEUS and WORLDSPAN for instance. Likewise, software provision has antecedents on which to draw (SQL databases, CGI interfaces and PDF document technology, for example). It is what can be loosely termed 'editorial' – the writing of market interfaces, liaison with outside verification bodies, political negotiation and dealing with opposition – that will break new ground and determine the system's success. Like media organizations, those who define GEMs' editorial stance will have to live with unending controversy about their decisions. This model focuses on the editorial process and assumes the technological side, although undoubtedly demanding, need not be elaborated at this point.

The editorial companies would need to be in a position to provide the following:

- Funding
- Willingness to allow GEMs to be a stand-alone brand with its own identity and values
- No ideological or self-preservation restrictions on GEMs' potential
- Understanding of concepts around governmental independence
- Clout for consortium building and political networking
- Willingness to engage with opposition.

A timetable for the operation

This model assumes three phases to the GEMs business. They are:

1. *Start up.* Building awareness and lobbying parliaments around the world about the advantages of a GEMs system underpinned by law.
2. *Tendering.* The point at which one or more governments is inviting tenders for a system to which they will grant the required benefits in return for their particular concessions.
3. *Officially underpinned growth.* Having won the tender in one particular country, the system must now move swiftly and smoothly to mass usage.

Each phase will now be examined in detail.

Phase 1: Start up

The key strategy for phase 1 is to position the consortium as clear market leader for phase 2. A small team is envisaged within an editorial company keen to initiate the project. They would have six distinct tasks:

1. *Launch at least one initial GEM market sector on the Web.* Big software schemes, launched from scratch, have a tendency to implode. Nine out of ten software projects overrun.[2] A small-scale web-based GEM, initially in just one sector in one country, would create a test case of how the enforcement mechanisms, even without governmental support, should ensure a free and open market. It would also give a head start in refining the core programming to drive this kind of service.

   Characteristics of trade sectors where a GEM could have maximum impact include:

   - Multiple buyers and sellers with high rates of Net connectivity
   - Requirements of both sides changing constantly
   - Potential users who can be cost-effectively targeted with advertising.

Possible sectors for a web-based market might be:

- Load space – a market allowing truck operators to trade space in empty and half-empty lorries already committed to a journey.
- Computer equipment
- Short-term professional services

2. *Begin building a pool of qualified people who understand the project.* Through public meetings, Internet discussion and presentations at conferences, the team aim to communicate the aims, and culture, of GEMs to qualified individuals who are encouraged to enlist on the project's web site (currently www.gems.org.uk) as potential candidates to work within the system at a later date. Ownership of this database, listing people who had engaged with the project, and understood how it needed to proceed within their particular area of expertise, could be a significant asset (compared to latecomers) once phase 2 was underway.

3. *Begin constructing the consortium.* Potential software, hardware and connectivity partners can be sounded out and given explanations of the project and its aspirations.

4. *Promote independent thinking about GEMs and their uses.* Academics, think tanks and journalists should be encouraged to explore the social applications of GEMs with any seed money offered, free of editorial control. The aim is to give any government contemplating phase 2 a range of voices and areas of knowledge that have been applied to the concept. Genuine scepticism about the project will also be useful: it emphasizes the undoubtedly real commercial risks being taken by the consortium who, perhaps, should also anticipate criticism of any financial success in later years.

5. *Spread awareness among carriage providers.* GEMs could be a killer application for digital TV. For Web users a browser button, similar to the one negotiated on British copies of Internet Explorer by BBC Online, would be an asset.

6. *Begin lobbying governments around the world.* Countries like Singapore, Sweden and Ireland who have demonstrated deep official commitment to IT projects would be logical places to start. Their small populations would limit the scale of potential return from one of these nations but technologically literate users would probably be more tolerant of the glitches that will inevitably blight a first GEMs launch. Some of the arguments that could be used in support of the project when approaching politicians or opinion formers at organiza-

tions like the International Monetary Fund are listed below. It would take only one government to fully appreciate the benefits GEMs have to offer for phase 2 to begin.

Selling GEMs to politicians

Some points to be made:

- GEMs is not about regulating or restricting electronic commerce. Instead it creates an additional track to the technology's development which companies and businesses can use if they wish. No one would ever be forced to trade on the system.
- GEMs would cost the taxpayer nothing.
- A mature GEMs system could mobilize much of the resources of a country's economy for inward investors at very short notice.
- The first country to go down this route would become a focus for international attention.
- Global 'free market' electronic commerce threatens to diminish nations' control over their own economies. GEMs gives that control back.
- GEMs can clean up an economy because each transaction is automated and contracted. A government might target tax decreases to encourage deals currently in the grey market onto the system.
- GEMs could be the 'killer application' that encourages a population to move online and further drive infrastructure and terminal development. This is particularly applicable to countries like the UK where the government has politically committed itself to digital TV.
- The notion of government awarding a protected monopoly to enable deep private investment is more common than many realize. It is, for instance, how the Channel Tunnel was built.
- Inviting GEMs into your country does not involve handing over to a foreign company: the markets would be run by franchisees, all of whom will be nationals.

Above all:

- Uniquely among commercial e-commerce schemes, the GEMs project has every incentive to extend sophisticated facilities to even the poorest in society. Public access terminals in depressed areas make business sense for the consortium because, having unlocked the economic potential of those residents, the consortium then takes a flow of commissions from their resulting activity.

Within a year of formation, the GEMs team could be nourishing a growing database of desirable potential employees who already share the culture and aspirations for the project. There should be a web of potential consortium members and governmental contacts around the world. Intellectually, the project would be underpinned by at least one operating market and a spectrum of expert thinking independent of the consortium. This would be accomplished against a backdrop of increasing public awareness of the potential of point-and-click purchasing and, if the team are competent evangelists, a growing realization of the limitations to come in an uncoordinated online marketplace versus the potential that guaranteed electronic markets have to offer.

Phase 2: Tendering

Phase 2 begins when a government announces they are committed to setting up officially underpinned, universally available, fully featured electronic markets and invites bids to construct and run the service. If phase 1 has been pursued with sufficient vigour, one consortium may be the only candidate to run such a service at this point. A focused early start to phase 1 could be a highly effective barrier to competitors. Other consortia who have not meticulously prepared the groundwork and developed the principled commitment to neutrality, national identity and ruthless inspection could find it hard to convince politicians that they are ready for an unembarrassing launch and smooth trajectory to critical mass in the new markets. Just as in the 1970s 'no-one got fired for buying IBM', in the first decades of the 21st century no politician should have any problem explaining why they entrusted their country's fledgling public electronic markets system to a well-prepared consortium.

It is important to differentiate between the character of a final GEMs service and the tone of any campaign to win a tender which would inevitably involve a high profile in the relevant country. The former should be impartial, unobtrusive and banal in its reliability. The latter could be much more spunky.

Phase 3: Officially underpinned growth

Phase 3 begins with the winning of an officially backed universal electronic markets concession anywhere in the world. The consortium should eventually confine itself to providing core functions of this system with independent franchisees running each market sector: one person franchised to launch the GEM for industrial clays, for instance, another licensed by the consortium to operate the house cleaning market. Franchisees would be responsible for drawing up the front-end screen designs for that market, while all the processing is carried out by the core computer. They earn a percentage of commission from their sector.

Why adopt this model rather than simply employing staff to oversee the markets?

■ Public trust in the system will be higher if the people running its markets are sole traders from a variety of backgrounds spread around the country with their own financial stake in the project rather than employees of one monolithic enterprise.

■ Each market must be run by someone who is constantly motivated to grow the number of buyers and sellers using that sector daily. They do this by progressively adding new sophistication to the buyer–seller matching process (in conjunction with the consortium software writers) and by promoting their particular GEM to relevant companies and individuals. There is every reason for someone who is running, say, the manufacturers' pigments GEM to remain with that sector, developing their relationships and knowledge, over many years. Employees would expect to be promoted, constantly destroying the system's knowledge base.

■ The consortium's requirement for start-up funding is lessened. Franchisees could bear the unique costs of establishing their particular market.

■ An employee-based operation would open a gap between high profile markets, which everyone wanted to run, and less desirable, low turnover, sectors. The right franchising formula, however, can financially motivate the less attractive markets on to an equal footing.

■ Franchisees act as a check on management that should keep the consortium constantly alert, avoiding complacency. Witness, for example, the recent determined response from McDonald's franchisees to the company's unpopular launch of a 55 cent burger in the USA. Employee managers would have been far more reticent.

■ A rogue franchisee is less likely than a rogue employee because of a financial stake in their particular market. They would however be harder to dismiss.

■ New markets can be added organically by entrepreneurial would-be franchisees who approach the consortium with an idea for a market that centrally directed development could not have imagined. A committed individual for instance might want to launch a GEM for 'home tea parties' allowing anyone who wished to sell places at a gathering in their home to neighbours to do so. Assuming that individual was judged sound enough to operate under the GEMs name and could find the cash to set up their market they could then attempt to establish a whole new area of trade.

How the franchising might work

GEMs' requirements of its franchisees would not be unique. The individuals must become part of a strong corporate culture, remain motivated for long-term growth in an otherwise short-term industry and use individual flair to drive their small part of a highly standardized operation. Other organizations have mastered this formula already. In his book *Behind the Arches*, author John F Love says of the company that pushed its fast food operations around the world: 'McDonald's is run neither by one man nor by executive committee. Indeed, it is not even a single company. It is a federation of hundreds of independent entrepreneurs – franchisees, suppliers and managers – united by a complex web of partnerships and creativity... a contemporary franchise system flourishing on an unparalleled scale.'[3] Eighty-five per cent of McDonald's front ends (high street outlets) worldwide are franchisee operated. Individuals running their particular sector within a government backed electronic market system would probably require greater powers of diplomacy and lateral thinking on a day-to-day basis than the manager of a fast food operation but there is much the GEMs franchising operation could learn from McDonald's. In particular:

■ franchisees are required to commit themselves for lengthy periods; 20-year contracts are the norm at McDonald's

- the company will only franchise to hands-on individuals, not companies, groups, families or absent investors
- prospective franchisees must become thoroughly immersed in the company's culture and values, starting with a period working menially in an existing outlet before graduating to one of their 'hamburger universities'.

Like McDonald's, GEMs would aim to present a very simple and uniform face to the world, one that masks a complex and evolving structure behind the scenes. The burger giant, for instance, famously imported new cattle breeds and potato varieties into Russia before opening their Moscow branches rather than endanger customers' expectations of consistency. GEMs need to be this invisibly resourceful to a mass of unattached customers who take the service completely for granted. The project should build a pool of potential franchisees who have imbibed – and contributed to – its philosophy. The roll out plan is based on these individuals each becoming completely immersed in their eventual sector, using their developing knowledge to grow that particular market. If they are properly trained, and supported, the system should be capable of unveiling, perhaps, a hundred or more new sectors a week during phase 3.

Franchisees would be overseen by a 'markets executive' who is in charge of a group of related sectors, ensuring the markets blend into each other seamlessly and consistent standards are imposed across that area as a whole. The franchisee for curtain making and fitting for instance would be supervised by the markets executive for home furnishings. Franchisees would pay no up-front fee to the consortium but might have to put a sum in bond to cover any professional negligence. Additionally they would be responsible for financing support services for their particular launch. These would include lawyers to write the contracts (within a house style), archivists to collect photographic material and data such as manufacturer's model numbers, and screen designers who translate the franchisee's vision into a GEMs-compatible display to users. The consortium should not restrict the market for these suppliers with a licensing system but encourage competing provision by setting up a GEM for those who wish to enter the market, enabling new franchisees to hire traders at the price and experience level with which they are personally comfortable.

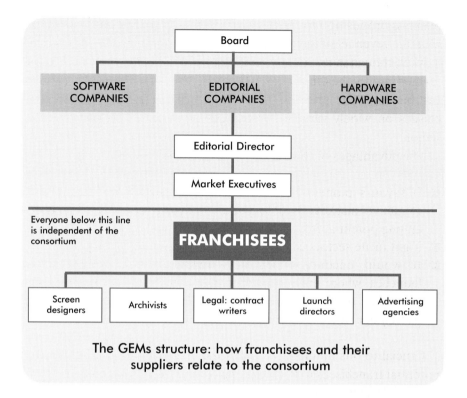

The GEMs structure: how franchisees and their
suppliers relate to the consortium

The franchisee funding formula

In pursuit of simplicity and universal value, GEMs should charge its
users a single flat rate percentage of each deal across all markets. How
are franchisees rewards calculated? They can not receive a fixed
percentage of turnover in their sector otherwise everyone would want to
run commission-rich markets like office rentals while no-one could
make a living from a low value sector such as surgical appliances.
Instead, franchisees bid for the percentage of commission they would
require to run a particular market. In a high-turnover, easy-growth,
sector like overnight accommodation the franchisee might agree that 98
per cent of commission received goes to the consortium, the remaining
2 per cent could still amount to a significant income for the individual.
On a less attractive sector, say the market for hearing aids, the
successful franchisee might have stipulated the consortium keep only
four per cent of the commission earned. The latter is still a valuable

business proposition for the core companies: 4 per cent of something is a better revenue stream than 0 per cent of nothing. The hearing aids market, though in itself not a money spinner, would help to drive GEMs further into the health service, where other sectors can reap more lucrative benefits. The price of universal, flat rate, service to users is franchisees on widely varying percentages of revenue generated by their sector.

The advantages of this funding formula are:

- It favours pioneering, risk-bearing franchisees who can bid for attractive markets at a high percentage rate before competition among potential franchisees is fully developed
- Tight niche sectors can still be profitable for franchisees
- It would encourage organic growth through entrepreneurial launches, where only one person was convinced they could make a particular sector work. They would be able to negotiate a high percentage in return for the risk they undertook.

Crucial to this funding formula is the maintenance of a large pool of potential franchisees to keep bidding competitive. This should enforce a humane tendering system: if a franchisee is outbid for one sector it is worth encouraging them to go for others rather than simply rejecting them. Like McDonald's, the GEMs consortium should seek out sympathetic financial institutions who understand the business plan and will construct loans specifically for successful franchisees who do not have their own funds to invest.

The stages in rolling out a new market

Consortium management would have a sector-by-sector roll out timetable which would be published openly. Anyone could bid to run a market on that timetable or come up with a sector of their own that is not on the list of obvious GEMs markets. Potential franchisees would then be assessed by a panel of consortium staff. They would be expected to have absorbed the project's values, in the early days through attendance at public meetings or Internet discussions and as the system develops, by spending time with working franchisees.

Candidates would be assessed on:

- the percentage of commission that they wish to retain if awarded the contract
- their understanding of, and commitment to, GEMs values
- coherence of plans for harnessing core GEMs software functions for that particular market and plans for further functions they may require
- their knowledge of, and contacts in, the proposed sector
- marketing plans to target potential users of the new sector
- relevant experience running some sort of service.

Once a franchisee was selected they would be expected to hire an experienced GEMs launch director to provide assistance and, from their own funds, have to complete the following within a fixed timescale of perhaps three months:

- 'Storyboard' potential screen designs to be demonstrated in rough to potential users whose input is then used to further refine the way options are presented.
- Assess whether there is a need to offer additional regulatory options to ensure confidence in the new market. This process would not be unique to GEMs. In Britain in the 1980s for instance aerobics instructors were hampered by lack of any recognizable qualification for their skills. A group of them initiated a new certificate in teaching of exercise to music. Occasionally a GEMs franchisee might need to encourage something similar in sectors without any existing structure for sellers who wished for external assessment of their abilities.
- Hire a lawyer to draw up the standard contracts and their permissible variations for that sector within the guidelines laid down by the consortium's legal department.
- Find insurance to cover their personal liability within GEMs' terms of operation.
- Set up verification and adjudication panels that can grow organically as their market expands. By far the easiest way of doing this would be to induce an existing organisation to take on the responsibility and ensure that they are sufficiently rewarded through the price charged to potential traders for assessment. For example, the franchisee for the locksmiths sector on a UK GEMs system might ensure the Master Guild of Locksmiths set the standards for market entry

and acted as arbiter in any disputes. The principles of guaranteed electronic markets lay down ground rules for these relationships.

- Ensure government are advised of any likely regulatory issues inherent in the new market. If planning to launch a GEM for raw meat, for instance, it would be wise to see if officials planned to restrict sales to licensed butchers on public health grounds.
- Define the range of parameters for market overview screens covering their sector.
- Hire an advertising agency to work on promotional materials; like the screen displays these would be within a GEMs' house style.
- When ready, launch their market on the system. During this initial period the interface appears with a white border around the screen containing the words 'not guaranteed'. Users are warned they should take all the precautions they would in an ordinary trading environment: dealing only with sellers they will trust, not relying entirely on the GEMs contract, confirming a deal by phone if it is complex and so on. No commission is extracted from transactions at this point, the aim is to get a market going and take feedback.
- Over following weeks the border progressively fades as turnover increases, potential loopholes are closed, user navigation is tightened and transactions become more solid. Eventually the border is removed, signifying GEMs and the franchisee now take full responsibility for the service, and the market starts to take commission.

What do franchisees do after their launch?

Once a particular market is running the launch director withdraws and the franchisee settles down to life managing that marketplace: continually looking at ways to constantly attract new buyers and sellers. Franchisees could work from home or in local office accommodation of their choice, not in a consortium building. Their consistent priorities would be to publicise their service while monitoring reaction from users and to look for new functions and categories to add to their sector. Additional software facilities, however, should be coordinated at consortium level so the core programming is not fragmented and new functions can be shared around. The franchisee for fresh vegetables, for instance, might want to give growers the option of inputting a batch of carrots for sale at a certain price while telling GEMs to automatically drop the price if they remain unsold a day later. This time-related pricing mechanism could be equally useful in, say, the periodicals sector, where sellers may want to charge a high price on the day of issue and drop it progressively in the days that follow. Once demanded by one franchisee, a new software function must then be available across the system. When considering in which order to develop functions, the core software team could prioritize the needs of markets in which the consortium retains a high commission percentage: the needs of the overnight accommodation franchisee taking precedence over those of the hearing aids market operator.

A GEMs-style market would probably encourage a far wider range of offers than the uncoordinated world where shoppers are so restricted in the range they can access. Franchisees would be responsible for encouraging new offerings, many of which could scarcely exist outside the system. They do this by providing new contract clauses to sellers who want them and displaying icons that allow higher level sellers to identify themselves from the start of a buyer's search. To take an example: some computer owners who need repairs to their machine are deterred by the way technicians unnecessarily peruse the contents of hard drives in order to establish the level of data corruption. A hardware repairer selling in GEMs who wanted to offer a 'guaranteed confidential' service, in which customer drives were assessed by another computer, and not human eyes, might start to write such a clause into contracts himself and list that facility on his details page. Others might follow his lead. The franchisee should then see that his lawyers fashion a defining paragraph for that level of service, which is made available to all sellers when they enter the market, while a 'click here if you are willing to pay extra for confidential service' facility is offered to buyers.

Another part of a GEMs' franchisee's job would be monitoring the cataloguing of their sector. The system's need to provide order for shoppers must not drive out innovative sellers who defy any existing category. Each GEM should include a 'miscellaneous' section where offers far from the mainstream could be browsed and purchased in safety. Someone who wanted to offer a horse whispering service, for instance, would probably find no GEMs section existed for their chosen profession but they would be welcome at the veterinary services/equine/miscellaneous marketplace. Here they would be asked to type in a name for their uncategorized offering, their qualifications to offer it and a pricing formula. With no intelligent questions available for people who heal sickly steeds by murmuring in their ears, GEMs would have to fall back on a standard formula for unclassified suppliers to assess the bonding required for buyer protection. It might for instance insist the seller provide a minimum five times the highest fee they planned to charge for any particular assignment and accepted judgement by the country's leading animal charity in case of dispute. Anyone who repeatedly mis-filed their offerings, trying to pointlessly input details of their horse whispering into the optical supplies marketplace perhaps would be treated in the same way as a driver who behaves badly on the roads. If they persist they are warned and finally banned: in the case of GEMs this process would be automatic and inescapable. Each franchisee would monitor their miscellaneous section in search of new market trends. If horse whisperers were proliferating, the individual running the veterinary services/equine sector would have every incentive to discuss their priorities then build them a specific marketplace.

Kickstarting the markets

It is sometimes argued that a GEMs system would be hamstrung by 'the telephone trap': once everyone is using the new system it becomes invaluable, but until that point is reached there is little incentive to join. This 'Catch 22' kept telephone usage low for several decades. Like the phone network, GEMs relies on critical mass for much of its appeal. However, GEMs would be free of many of the drags on usage experienced by pioneering telephone companies:

■ GEMs would not require users to invest in specialized hardware.
■ Much of the cultural conditioning required to appreciate the value of GEMs will be carried out by other service providers. Potential telephone users had to be educated into the notion of having a number that related to each friend or business contact and speaking to them down a wire. By the time GEMs launches, populations will have access to point and click shopping through the Internet and interactive television. The cultural leap from online purchasing to an open electronic marketplace is far less than that from meeting friends to phoning them.
■ Entering the GEMs marketplace as a buyer or seller would be free, you can see what the system has to offer for your particular needs without cost. Public kiosks would make this facility available to even the least connected household.
■ GEMs could facilitate impulse registration. Browse the system as a non-user, see something you want to buy or a niche in which you want to sell, take your passport to the Post Office (or other registration centre) and return ready to buy or sell. It costs nothing and there is no delay for installation.

■ GEMs would function as a non-trading terminal for anyone reluctant to take a first step to selling online. A hairdresser, for instance, could type appointments taken over the phone into a GEMs diary and have all their records and accounts intelligently compiled by software that understood the mechanics of their business. This would cost them nothing, but would make it a very short step to entering a pricing formula and accepting bookings on the system.

Even without critical mass, a GEMs system offers significant benefits when compared to other forms of trade:

■ Neutral, watertight contracts. If hiring a plumber through the Yellow Pages for instance it could be worth a householder telling him she wished to sign a contract in the GEMs household services market just to put the relationship on a solid footing.
■ Verification of traders. It is very much in the interests of say, temporary secretaries to offer themselves on the system because a reliable automatically compiled bookings record would validate future claims about levels of experience.
■ Market overview facilities allow sellers an instant pricing guide that will be less precise, but only marginally less useful, in a system that has not attained critical mass.
■ The parallel economy within GEMs effectively gives users money for nothing, but it can only be spent on the system.

GEMs would offer its users not novelty or short-term promotional benefits but deep and sustainable trading and shopping advantages. The fledgling system should not be reticent about spreading this message:

■ GEMs' publicity budget is probably most effectively spent at franchisee level rather than on a national message. The franchisee for gym sessions for instance should have the funds, and the growing web of contacts, that enable her to have 'make your next booking through GEMs' posters put up in changing rooms across the country. Likewise the market operator for quarrying equipment could be advertising in the relevant trade press, maybe with running weekly totals of the kinds of equipment available within his sector. These targeted messages, within a house style, could be funded in a partnership between franchisee and consortium. The aim is to bombard a population with messages about GEMs' particular relevance to sectors in which they personally might trade.
■ Carriage providers could have much to gain from cross promoting the service on their existing output.
■ Inevitably the system will have a news profile as for instance the UK National Lottery did.
■ Each franchisee is responsible for evangelizing their particular sector, constantly selling the service's advantages to substantial buyers and sellers in the relevant industries.

■ System management could adopt an aggressive policy of 'First Aid' – aid for the first big player in any given sector to move into GEMs selling. For instance the car hire companies might hold out against the system because they feared competition from ordinary motorists now empowered to rent out their vehicle on their own terms with total security. Management might in effect say to the biggest five companies 'the first one of you to commit to selling on GEMs alongside your existing routes to market will have the interfacing with your computer systems, that will allow you to rent out cars automatically in GEMs, paid for by us. Later entrants will have to fund their own interface or rely on staff manually updating vehicle availability in GEMs.'

How the franchisee system might develop as GEMs grew

As usage increased, two further refinements would be needed to keep franchisees motivated with clear areas of responsibility.

Half markets

If A runs the market for dental appointments and B is the franchisee for cosmetic surgery who handles the market for cosmetic dentistry appointments? This borderline sector is a 'half market', it could be established and run by either individual but the other is encouraged to increase its usage through a share in the proceeds, where a user has clicked through from that franchisee's market. Similarly, templates spanning several markets would be run by franchisees who negotiate a percentage with their counterparts running the markets covered. Someone setting up a 'wedding arrangements' page for instance would need agreements with the franchisees for bridal wear, photographers, ceremonial cars and so on, which the system would then automatically apply to income.

Market splits

As GEMs usage increased, sectors in which one person could initially oversee day-to-day operation would start requiring much more work if they are to continue growing. The overnight accommodation market, for instance, could start by providing just the basics of matching on price and location with facilities for sellers to add some rudimentary details. As usage increased it might need to become the work of three people, each supervising a higher level of technical sophistication, user liaison and publicity for the budget, mid-range or luxury sectors respectively. As growth continued there would be demand for additional segmenting, splitting budget accommodation between someone charged with group bookings and a colleague in charge of individual overnights for instance, in turn the group bookings market might then fragment between adult groups and youth and school parties, and so on. In a fully fledged system operating in a country with significant population there could be perhaps fifty people running the overnight accommodation market with responsibilities along a spectrum from luxury hotels and homes to tent pitches.

The initial franchisee who launches an overnight accommodation GEM should not be allowed to turn this predictable growth into an empire employing increasing numbers of staff who are neither motivated nor committed to their sector's long-term strengths while he enjoys an ever increasing revenue stream. Nor should one entity be allowed such influence over the country's hoteliers and accommodation providers. Once a GEMs market reaches a level in demand where it requires more than one full-time person to realize its further potential it should have to split: the original franchisee decides which part he wants to continue to run himself and offers the remainder to a pool of approved GEMs potential franchisees who bid to buy that sector. The successful bidder's whole payment goes to the initial market operator, the new one takes on the percentage of commission of the original market. This formula would encourage franchisees to grow all areas of their market: a healthy mass of buyers and sellers will earn them a higher fee than a neglected, low-turnover market when they come to sell the split franchise.

Users, needless to say, would remain unaware of this segmenting franchise structure; their interface must remain seamless. A buyer seeking overnight accommodation would simply input her desired dates, area, price range and number in the party to see her options displayed in a standardized way. However, she would realize that as the market grows the range of options increases. If booking accommodation for a school trip for instance she probably wouldn't spare a thought for what amounts to a family tree of franchisees who have split the market into ever narrower areas of responsibility over preceding months but she would notice how the software allowed her to be increasingly precise about her requirements and perhaps how new sellers had been coaxed into the market. A franchisee concentrating on this tight sector might, for example, launch an initiative through the agricultural press to attract farmers with unused, but comfortably habitable, barns for camping to rent them overnight in GEMs. Like the McDonald's model, there is a motivated individual, focused on long-term expansion, invisibly behind each part of the uniform interface.

If the system needed to contract, the split markets process would be reversed. One franchisee could buy out the sector of another and personally run both. The key principle is that each franchise is the full-time work of only one person. This structure would offer all the cultural advantages of distributed computing – individuals spread around the country thinking independently from each other, dissipation of power and so on – with all the cost savings of a centralized hardware and software operation.

The ethos of a growing organization

Ray Krok, the former salesman who built McDonald's, instilled the 'Q.V.S.' dogma into the heart of his budding empire. Just as relentless commitment to Quality, Value and Service enabled a high-standard, world-wide roll out for the burger giant, so GEMs should have a consistent ethos that pervades all levels of the organization. It too has three points:

Integrity: A franchisee running the GEMs for portable music players must not be in any financial relationship with Sony, Aiwa, Grundig or anyone else who may be selling in that sector. Nor can they themselves ever sell in the marketplace they run. Certainly there should be ongoing conversations about new products and additional software facilities to make the GEM more useful to both sides of its transactions but they are conducted openly and without favour.

Simplicity: As new functions are added to each market they must not be just bolted on to the existing interface, becoming an added complexity for users. The basic design needs to evolve so the new function is incorporated as an intuitive question. A vegetable grower putting his produce up for sale is asked 'Do you wish to drop your price automatically if these carrots are unsold within 24 hours?' and not told 'Click here to activate time related pricing mechanism'.

Growing markets: It would take considerable initiative but GEMs offer the chance to bring previously unrealized resources to market. Inducing their owners to trade would be a key task. A themed party company in Australia for instance already offers the opportunity for demolition companies to sell the chance to push the plunger on their latest job as the highlight for a birthday celebration. A GEMs franchisee running the parties market might seek to raise awareness of this possibility among building clearance companies and, if they started selling, look for some press coverage of the latest sensation in his marketplace. Despite the system's desire to be an unremarkable essential, widely taken for granted, some of its franchisees could become national figures, particularly those running sensitive areas such as the hospital beds market.

The mature organization

Collectively the GEMs consortium would not be selling hardware or software, nor would it have any stake in specific channels of distribution. Companies involved in the consortium could market their expertise gained from the project of course, but the agreement with government should forbid brand extension of whatever name the final service is given. Otherwise the consortium could leverage their officially awarded position into new areas of dominance. The consortium business plan is driven only by the need to bring ever-increasing numbers of buyers and sellers into regular usage, accessing the system through whatever technology they wish.

Sources of income

The mature system would have four revenue streams:

■ Commission on transactions: the main income line.

■ Float management: substantial amounts of money would be held in escrow by the system on behalf of users for known periods. This could be invested in the system's own loan markets. Float exploitation would only be available on funds held pending completion of a deal, not on insurance bonds held on behalf of sellers. The latter must pay out interest in full to the provider otherwise the system's demand for a bond would constitute a market entry cost, anathema to the GEMs vision. Purchase costs only are acceptable.

■ Flat fee services: offering legal contracts and agreements for business partnerships, for instance, or for individuals wishing to join a club in the appropriate GEM.

■ Value-added services: a user who wishes his details sheet to show a photograph of himself or something he is selling could get it scanned at a copyshop or on their own equipment and then sent down the line to the core computer. The user would be given a receipt number against which it could be retrieved later and added to a details page, but could be expected to pay for the facility. A photograph is not essential to start trading so these fees would not detract from GEMs' commitment to no-cost market entry.

A potential structure for the mature organization

(See chart overleaf)

Some notes on this structure

■ The loans market would be too crucial to the system, and too extensive in its potential liabilities, to be handled by an individual franchisee. At least one established financial institution would need to be in charge. They would agree a percentage of flat rate commission to be retained like any other franchisee.

■ The core program team would constantly look at the most basic cornerstone programming in the system. In a mature GEMs service in just one country this could be matching buyers and sellers many millions of times a day. If just one instruction set can be tightened further that soon amounts to a significant saving in processing power.

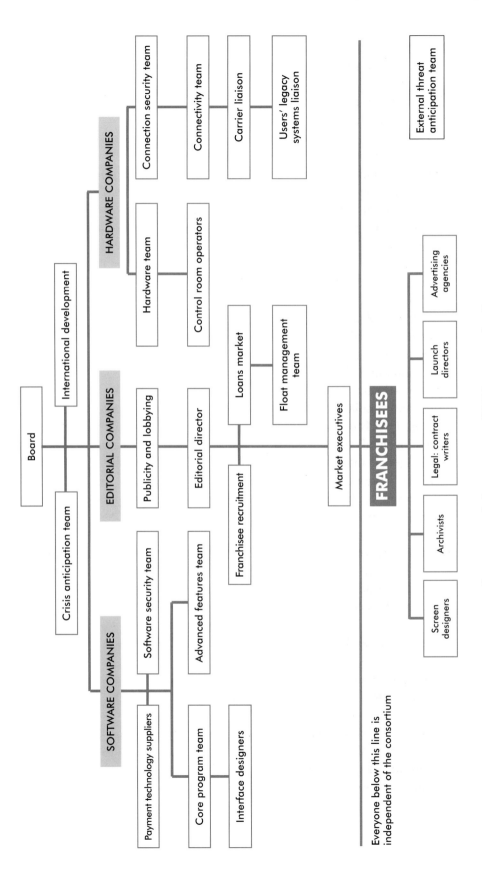

Board

International development

Crisis anticipation team

SOFTWARE COMPANIES

Payment technology suppliers

Software security team

Core program team

Advanced features team

Interface designers

EDITORIAL COMPANIES

Publicity and lobbying

Editorial director

Franchisee recruitment

Loans market

Float management team

Market executives

HARDWARE COMPANIES

Hardware team

Control room operators

Connection security team

Connectivity team

Carrier liaison

Users' legacy systems liaison

External threat anticipation team

FRANCHISEES

Screen designers

Archivists

Legal: contract writers

Launch directors

Advertising agencies

Everyone below this line is independent of the consortium

Structure of the mature GEMs organization

Big computer projects rarely go as planned. The organizational structure is designed to recognize this.

- The prominence of a crisis anticipation team is intended to recognize the inevitability of unplanned incidents, particularly during the early days when any evidence of disarray could be most effectively exploited by opponents. The team would consider all potential sources of disaster and plot a series of responses based on core principles of immediately telling the truth publicly, compensating any users who have directly suffered a loss, swift external investigation and knowledge-gathering internal response. More importantly, they would look at how hardware, software, corruption-induced or financial disasters can be avoided and should have sufficient clout in the organization to pursue an escalating programme of preventative measures.

- The external threat anticipation team is an attempt to avoid the fate of companies like IBM and Apple Computer who each, during a period of enormous success, lost track of changes in the market and became complacent in their own culture. This team would be funded by the GEMs organization but based well outside any of the companies involved, their only contact being a one-way flow of ideas and intelligence into the consortium. This group constantly asks how GEMs' opponents might attack the project, either politically (by spreading doubts about its honesty, or over-publicizing small problems, for instance) or competitively (could the GEMs markets in expensive goods be undercut by a start-up operation charging a lower rate of commission for example?) Analysis is fed into a rebuttal unit within the publicity team, in preparation for prompt counter-attack to possible charges from opponents, or into the board, when competitive position might be under threat.

  This team is emphatically not envisioned as a remote outpost for out-of-sight and out-of-mind executives but an established route into the top layers of management. It is worth remembering that GEMs' principles mandate that no-one remain in management of the system longer than 8 years to avoid any accusations it was being run by a privileged clique. Newcomers who had spent a year thoroughly looking at GEMs from the point of view of a predator could be useful elements in this evolving view at the top, arguably more informed about the project's strengths and weaknesses than someone who had spent years soaking up the culture at headquarters.

Expanding beyond the first country

Once a GEMs system was working in one country with confident franchisees driving its further development, consortium focus could shift to
rolling out similar systems elsewhere around the world. This is when the
project's commitment to political neutrality becomes crucial. The
system must keep government in a first country of operation at arm's
length and not become associated with any one set of political values.

Despite using loosely-standardized core software, a consortium
driving GEMs forward should not seek to impose one uniform name for
the service across the world. Attempting to bulldoze a global brand
name into the heart of national economies would probably be counterproductive. Instead Russia might have its *Sistema Obshchestvennykh
Rynkov* (Public Markets System) while perhaps Brazil offers its citizens
the *Serviço Eletrônico de Comércio* (Electronic Trading Service.) Like De
La Rue, banknote printer to the world, the consortium should be
content that key opinion formers would know about the depth of their
operation while allowing national identity to take precedence over any
desire to force that message on ordinary users. The consortium would,
however, have every reason to help individual users distinguish between
a GEMs system that was being allowed to operate free from any
prospect of political interference and its counterparts in less democratic
nations. As one small part of the checks and balances around the system,
users need to know if the consortium is happy that they are operating
with all the independence they require. Otherwise the companies propagating GEMs could be seen as malleable by governments, a damaging
perception likely to arouse significant resistance to use elsewhere. The
consortium could adopt a purist stance, of course, refusing to launch a
system except where they were assured of a place among the institutions
in a democratic society, but that would cut them off from many emerging
economies. Instead, member companies could adopt a phrase such as
Guaranteed Electronic Markets as a master brand, akin to Visa or
Mastercard on credit cards issued by multiple banks, bestowed as a seal
of approval on systems operating in a healthy society. The logo might for
instance show up fleetingly in a screen corner each time a user logged on
to the system, but not in countries that insisted on government supervision extending beyond legitimate law making or where authorities
demanded access to information not available to all users.

Even in countries which would appear to be grateful for any kind of reliable markets service the consortium should actively seek to factor-in full democratic protection. A disintegrated economy in an immature democracy such as Russia might look like a chance for easy pickings by offering electronic markets without the more costly protection and inspection protocols citizens in a first world country would demand. But GEMs would be aiming to lift Russians out of their parlous conditions. Once they were more prosperous they would be likely to place the system under much greater scrutiny. A half-hearted approach to their rights at any point could then become a problem.

Would public electronic markets in different countries communicate with each other? Might a resident of Mombassa displaying his paintings on a Kenyan system find he had a purchaser in Sydney who had been browsing the artwork for sale in an Australian GEM? Could the levels of protection that define these new markets extend to cross-border trade? That will be decided by parliaments: would the Kenyan courts uphold the rights of a New South Wales art lover in an automated referral if the deal went to dispute and could not be resolved any other way? It is likely a patchwork of agreements on a sector-by-sector basis would arise over time but the countries that had a seal of approval from one of the consortia building public electronic markets would be logical partners in upholding each other's citizens' trades.

Once the core software was fully developed and easily transferable around the world smaller countries would have to decide whether they wanted to share a GEMs system with a larger neighbour or offer a diminished level of service in an exclusively national system. For instance a mature GEMs in Andorra (population 55 000) might only be cost effective with a full complement of 100 franchisees, each of them covering a huge swathe of categories. Neighbouring Spain (population 40 million) conversely could have several thousand franchisees after fragmenting areas of responsibility as the system grew. Andorrans would not necessarily be limited in the range of goods available to them in GEMs, anyone could import and sell anything on the system, but they would find marketplace management far less precise than that on the lower slopes of the Pyrenees. They may prefer to trade on the Spanish system if courts would uphold their rights and those of their contractual partners. Alternately they could lobby for a European Union-wide GEMs system which should be able to offer all member nations a phenomenal degree of sophistication and initiative in each sector.

After a number of countries had a public electronics markets system running with competing consortia demonstrating viable business models, remaining governments could be in the awkward position of justifying a decision to stay out of GEMs and deprive their populations of its benefits. Once that point was reached it could be the consortium that had been rigorous in asserting its probity and maintaining the highest standards for its master brand which became the most sought after by populations. Thus, sound business logic encourages the spread both of democracy and of atomized capitalism.

Notes

1. The twenty-first-century stock market, *Business Week,* 10 August 1998, p. 52.
2. BBC Television, *Disaster: the Millennium Time Bomb,* transmitted 9 June 1998.
3. John F. Love, *McDonald's Behind the Arches*, Bantam Books, revised edition, 1995. Quoted in McDonald's brochure *Thinking about a Franchise?* 1998.

index